Praise for THE CONVICT LOVER

"A tour de force. Simonds's prose is alluring, her historical detective work is flawless . . . what makes *The Convict Lover* soar off the page, though, is Simonds's ability to probe into the psyches of real people, and to find there imaginative truth." —*Globe and Mail*

"A remarkable book . . . A seamless weave of fact and fiction that evokes one of the strangest illicit relationships ever made public in Canada." —*Maclean's*

"Exquisitely written and finely detailed." —*Toronto Star*

"In Simonds's capable hands the story both touches and seduces the reader . . . Through exquisite, precise prose, she transports us back 75 years."
—*Quill & Quire*

"Simonds has that lucky combination of the journalist's eye for detail and the novelist's gift for story and character . . . if Merilyn Simonds doesn't win some major award for this book, I think we should all go on strike."
—*Montreal Gazette*

"This is a beautifully controlled story that makes speculative use of intriguing materials. Simonds provocatively pushes the genre to its limits." —Jury citation, 1996 Governor General Literary Awards

"Extraordinary and luminous . . . The writing in *The Convict Lover* is consistently fine, and at times inspired . . . the book's themes are grand ones: the enduring power of words on a page, and how communication with another human being can make the unbearable bearable. For all the pain and darkness it describes, *The Convict Lover* is less a book about a dungeon than about letter as lifeline, which makes it a book about hope."
—*Ottawa Citizen*

"Constantly compelling . . . *The Convict Lover* is a virtuoso performance that combines the factualness of a 'true story' with the techniques of fiction. It conveys historical truth with unfailing accuracy because it is told with the vitality of imagination." —*Financial Post*

"*The Convict Lover* is a riveting story that reclaims an obscure segment of Canadian history. Pushing the boundaries between fiction and nonfiction, the author illuminates the experience of imprisonment . . . She also tells secrets—a private one, about a forbidden relationship, and a larger and darker one, about Canada's penitentiaries." —*Queen's Quarterly*

Praise for GUTENBERG'S FINGERPRINT

"*Gutenberg's Fingerprint* is well-timed and does for our books what Margaret Visser's *Much Depends on Dinner* did for the food on our plates: Each ingredient is revealed in all its complicated glory, with sections on paper, type, ink, presses and finished books . . . *Gutenberg's Fingerprint* is a love letter to an ancient craft—but it is also, and more importantly, a reminder that the briefest way to get your story out there might not be the truest." —*Globe and Mail*

"In a mix of historical inquiry and technological experiment, Simonds (*The Convict Lover*) creatively grapples with the meaning of the paradigm shift that has transformed words pressed onto paper into digital pixels on screens . . . Simplicity of narration, curious facts, and the personal angle of the story will fascinate book lovers from beginning to end, no matter whether they are devoted to print or to digital, or move between the mediums." —*Publishers Weekly*

"Simonds wraps an on-the-scene report on choosing type, ink, paper, endpapers, and bindings around an entertaining history of book production and reading . . . a surprisingly fun read." —*Booklist*

"Merilyn Simonds's seventeenth and latest book, *Gutenberg's Fingerprint*, fits firmly and delightfully in the genre of bibliomemoir . . . A nimble work—part history, part memoir, part technical manual, part tribute—that makes important connections between our reading past and present that we can and should carry into the future." —*Hamilton Review of Books*

"Merilyn Simonds has an essayist's mind, swooping and dipping here and there as fancy (and especially an attractive word, or a revealing phrase or story) lures her." —*Literary Review of Canada*

"My copy of *Gutenberg's Fingerprint* bristles with post-it notes, reminders of passages that I wish to remember far down the road . . . *Gutenberg's Fingerprint* is a gift for all readers including those of us who love books." —*Owen Sound Sun Times*

"A gorgeous meditation on the past, present, and future of books . . . The challenges and contrasts are striking, but Simonds reconciles them in ways that make claims of the death of books seem entirely premature." —*Ottawa Magazine*

"*Gutenberg's Fingerprint* gives book lovers food for thought as to what it is we love about physical books and what digital books have to offer us. Simonds leaves no doubt that print books will likely endure, but does leave room to ponder—what may come next?" —FallingLetters.ca

"A magnificent hybrid of memoir and non-fiction . . . Learning about the ins and outs of the processes, print and digital, the ways in which they are similar and different, complementary and wholly foreign, was so illuminating." —Kerry Clare, PickleMeThis.com

"Avoiding all reference to a foretold apocalypse, and firmly this side of idolatry, *Gutenberg's Fingerprint* is a wise love letter to the printed page, as trustworthy as paper and as true as ink." —Alberto Manguel, author of *A History of Reading* and *The Library at Night*

The
CONVICT
LOVER

A True Story

Merilyn Simonds

Published by ECW Press
665 Gerrard Street East
Toronto, Ontario, Canada M4M 1Y2
416-694-3348 / info@ecwpress.com

Cover artwork: Lori Richards/loririchards.ca

LIBRARY AND ARCHIVES CANADA
CATALOGUING IN PUBLICATION

Simonds, Merilyn, 1949–, author
The convict lover : a true story /
Merilyn Simonds. — New edition.

Previously published: Toronto: Macfarlane
Walter & Ross, 1996.
Includes bibliographical references.
Issued in print and electronic formats.
ISBN 978-1-77041-447-1 (softcover)

1. Cleroux, Joseph David, 1892 or 1895–. 2.
Halliday, Phyllis, –1986. 3. Kingston Penitentiary.
4. Prisoners—Ontario—Kingston—Biography.
I. TITLE.

HV9505.C54S53 2018   365'.44092
C2017-906190-9   C2017-906191-7

The publication of *The Convict Lover* has been generously supported by the Canada Council for the Arts,
which last year invested $153 million to bring the arts to Canadians throughout the country, and by the
Government of Canada through the Canada Book Fund. *Nous remercions le Conseil des arts du Canada
de son soutien. L'an dernier, le Conseil a investi 153 millions de dollars pour mettre de l'art dans la vie des
Canadiennes et des Canadiens de tout le pays. Ce livre est financé en partie par le gouvernement du Canada.*
We also acknowledge *the support of the Ontario Arts Council (OAC), an agency of the Government of Ontario,
which last year funded 1,737 individual artists and 1,095 organizations in 223 communities across Ontario for
a total of $52.1 million*, and the contribution of the Government of Ontario through the Ontario Book
Publishing Tax Credit and the Ontario Media Development Corporation.

PRINTED AND BOUND IN CANADA   Printing: MARQUIS   5   4   3   2   1

For Wayne

A letter always seemed to me like immortality.

———————

EMILY DICKINSON

Letters

The past is never dead, never over and done with.

———————

JACK HENRY ABBOTT

In the Belly of the Beast

INTRODUCTION I

PROLOGUE 5

Fall, 1919

October 13

November 50

December 88

Winter, 1920

January 133

February 168

March 217

Spring, 1920

April 257

May 301

June 332

Summer, 1920

July 365

EPILOGUE 389

AUTHOR'S NOTE 397

ACKNOWLEDGEMENTS 401

Introduction

Thirty years ago I climbed into my attic and found a cache of letters, evidence of an illicit relationship between a convict in Kingston Penitentiary and a girl living in the village outside its walls. Thus began an eight-year odyssey to discover the identity of these people and the truth about the penitentiary that brought them together and kept them apart.

I spent a year gathering the scattered pages into letters by matching the scraps of paper—toilet paper, filched letterhead from the Warden's office—and the pencils, inks and crayons the convict used. Only three of the seventy-nine letters were dated: Christmas, 1919 and St. Patrick's Day and Easter, 1920. To order the others, I searched for internal story threads and studied newspapers of the day, pouncing on references such as the sighting of the first spring robin, the day the new Warden arrived. Through those daily readings I met the third protagonist of this story, William St. Pierre Hughes, the first superintendent of Canada's prisons.

The convict's letters—and four from the girl on which he wrote his replies—were the breadcrumbs that led me deep into the caves of history and into the bowels of an institution I had never thought much about. My research, like history itself, was shaped by a winsome mix of serendipity and selection. The cells and walls that had held prisoners since the prison opened in 1835 were still in existence. In the 1970s, when the penitentiary was renovated, only a few representative volumes survived from the hoard of Punishment Books, Visitor Registries and Duty Rosters in the prison basement—none of them from the years of my story. But prison staff had salvaged records as mementoes, and by the time I came along, those documents were making their way back to the Penitentiary Museum.

The attic where I found the letters was strewn with diaries, pamphlets, news clippings and clothing that had belonged to the girl, who had grown into old age in that house. I arranged the beaded flowers and photographs of her dog on my desk, dressed up in her 1920s clothes, which fit me exactly. Eventually, I met the niece who had looked after the old woman in her final years, and when she opened her photograph albums, although I had already written a description of the girl, I did not have to change a word.

The Convict Lover marked my debut as a literary writer. I struggled to devise a form that could accommodate both truth and imagination. Unwilling to abandon these people to the shadows of history, I decided to use their real names and reproduce their illicit correspondence in its entirety. In order to bring their story to life, I allowed myself an artistic recreation of that forbidden place and that long-ago time.

There was a purity to the project, a simple contract between me and the story. I thought, as I wrote, that maybe a dozen people would be interested in reading this old-fashioned tale. I never imagined that the book would become a bestseller, a winner of prizes. That this timeless story would continue to touch readers more than twenty years after its publication.

I did hope, as I dipped my straight pen in my inkwell to write these pages, that *The Convict Lover* would stand among the handful of books that bear witness to life on the inside. That it might, by casting light in the dark corners of socially sanctioned punishment, nudge open public attitudes towards those who break our laws.

MERILYN SIMONDS

KINGSTON, ONTARIO

May, 2018

Prologue

On a summer afternoon in 1987, I set a ladder beneath the attic hatch of my bungalow in Kingston, Ontario. I suppose my intention was simply to close the trap door: the gap had stared down at me for two months, and now it was stifling under the eaves of the low cottage roof.

My hand, fumbling at the edges of the opening, fell on papers everywhere I touched. I balanced on top of the ladder, waiting for my eyes to adjust to the half-light. Between the hatch and the tiny window were rows of bulging sugar sacks, their tops tied with rags; dozens of tins and boxes spilled papers across the floor. I grabbed a small green tin with a handle like a tackle box and carried it downstairs. The stamps on the envelopes first caught my eye: two-cent portraits of George V, the British king during the Great War. But most of the pages were loose, crammed in the tin, some rolled in bundles, tied with ribbon or string.

For the rest of the day, and the days thereafter, I sat on my kitchen floor, absorbed in the bits and pieces of an unknown woman's life. Among the pamphlets, bills and greeting cards was one complete, brief correspondence. Reading it was like overhearing one side of a telephone conversation. Who had sent these letters? Why were there no dates or postmarks? What had she written in reply? From the careless jumble of papers, remarkable characters and events emerged. A convict, a penitentiary, a village girl. The end of the Great War.

Someone else ferreting about in these words and phrases might have discovered another story. This is what I found.

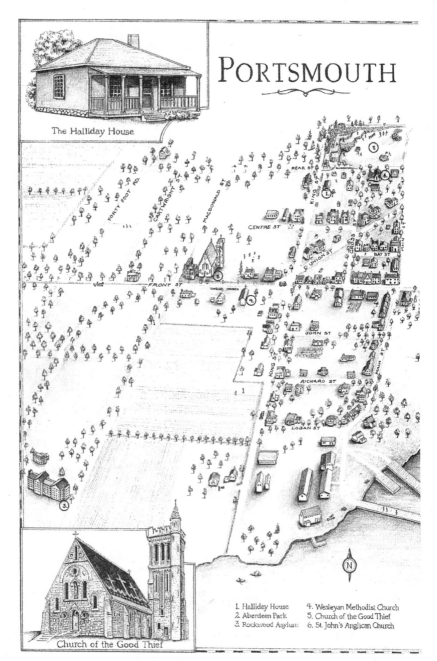

PORTSMOUTH

The Halliday House

Church of the Good Thief

FORTY FOOT RD

CARTWRIGHT ST

MACDONALD ST

CENTRE ST

REAR ST

KING ST

UNION ST

BAY ST

MAIN ST

FRONT ST

JOHN ST

KING ST

RICHARD ST

MAIN ST

LOGAN ST

N

1. Halliday House   4. Wesleyan Methodist Church
2. Aberdeen Park   5. Church of the Good Thief
3. Rockwood Asylum   6. St. John's Anglican Church

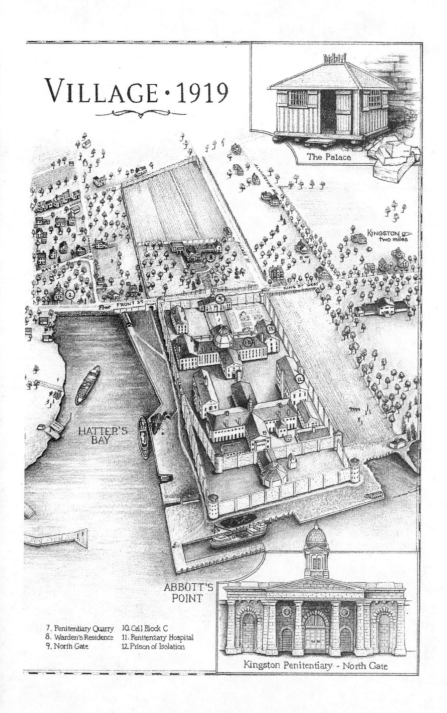

VILLAGE · 1919

The Palace

Kingston
two miles

HATTER'S
BAY

ABBOTT'S
POINT

7. Penitentiary Quarry
8. Warden's Residence
9. North Gate

10. Cell Block C
11. Penitentiary Hospital
12. Prison of Isolation

Kingston Penitentiary - North Gate

FALL, 1919

Even a crook may cast a straight shadow.

DAILY BRITISH WHIG
September 5, 1919

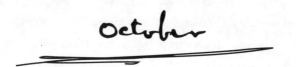

October

I'm out, thought the prisoner. Blessed Mary, I'm out.

Not all the way out: guards still walked ahead and behind. But the North Gate was closed, and he was on the village side.

The prisoner's feet, accustomed to the flat surfaces of well-worn stone, stumbled on the slope; the macadam shifted treacherously under his boots. The flowers and the birds distracted him. How could he have forgotten such colours? Pink and purple asters, hollyhocks and morning glories. Cedar waxwings squabbling over berries in a mountain ash. From his cell, he'd often watched gulls wheel darkly in their caged rectangle of sky, but these, these were as brightly painted as fall-fair figurines.

G852! Look smart!

When passing through the village, convicts shall keep their eyes front. Convicts shall not look at their surroundings, nor hold communion with anyone, nor give anything to anyone, nor receive anything from anyone. A convict must understand that the remission authorized by the statute is entirely dependent on his good behaviour, diligence, and industry.

He mustn't forget himself now.

By the chill in the air he knew he had served close to a year, but being sent outside to work was proof: almost half his time was up. All he had to do was stay out of trouble for another twelve months and he could put those stone walls behind him forever. He'd walk down this road and keep right on going, up the hill, past the church, never once look back.

Not that the village was so bad, from what he could see. In fact, on this early autumn morning, he loved it. Every blade and stone of it. Every house, with its sweet patch of grass, lace curtains at the windows. He imagined families behind the lighted panes: children eating hot, buttered toast with crab-apple jelly; men hoisting suspenders over ironed white shirts, looping Alice-blue ties around upturned collars; girls plaiting their hair into smooth braids; women tying the ribbons of their camisoles.

Nothing could suppress the prisoner's happiness that day. Not even his first sight of the quarry, a gash in the hillside on the north edge of the village that opened before him like a rougher, makeshift prison: jagged limestone walls that rose thirty feet on three sides, the floor littered with monolithic stone blocks. It hardly mattered that he would have to break rock for hours and hours. There were trees swaying at the quarry's edge and a fresh wind in his lungs.

By the time the convicts were marched back to the penitentiary at midday, there were people in the street. Their forms delighted him. He had not seen a dog, nor a cat, nor a child for a year. He'd seen a woman up close only twice, when his sister visited, and he'd glimpsed vaguely hourglass shapes across the prison yard when the door to the women's compound opened. But nothing like this. A young woman, a girl really, not six feet away, walking along the boardwalk as the prison gang left the quarry. One step and he could touch her, if he dared. The weather was warm and she wore no coat, just a long, white blouse belted over her skirt. Such a narrow waist. The curve of hip. He could see her ankles, thin, delicate as a bird's, tightly laced in brown leather.

He took those ankles back inside the prison and that night, in the dim light of his cell, he undid the leather lacings and stroked the fair skin until feet emerged, small shapely toes with painted nails, and above the ankles, slender legs and thighs. He kneaded those few inches of flesh into a full female form, then, pleased with himself, he slept.

•••

On his second day outside the walls, the prisoner pondered his new surroundings.

As he swung his sledgehammer against the shelf of limestone, he noticed that the officers seemed less attentive in the quarry than they did on the inside. Here, convicts ignored the rule of silence, easing surreptitious conversations between strokes of their pounding mauls. Twenty-five convicts; three guards. One observed them from the crow s nest, a watchtower that rose on stilts from the quarry's upper edge where penitentiary land abutted the village street. Another guard stood at the centre of the pit, by the crusher that ground boulders into gravel for village roads. A third supervised the convicts who hoisted rough blocks of stone onto wagons, then rode with the load out the east end of the quarry, rattling the stained glass windows of the Anglican church on their way to the stone shed inside the prison, where another gang of convicts hammered the rock into sills, lintels and monument stones. The quarry instructor, Peter Beaupré, circulated among them, directing convicts where to drill the stone, setting dynamite charges on the face marked next to fall. The Scout, on horseback, stood sentry on the grassed-over mound of rubble that softened the northeast wall. Still, the hole in the ground was vast enough to cradle the village of Portsmouth itself: a convict could work all day and never stand within spitting distance of a penitentiary officer.

The prisoner noticed something else. When the convicts left the quarry, no one stayed behind. Tall cement pillars circled the excavation, but the wire fencing strung between them was about as stout a barrier as a line toed in the sand. There were two gates: a wide one at the bottom of the quarry where the carts and some of the gang entered from Cross Street; and a narrow one at the top of the pit, on the southwest side, where the convicts who worked the uppermost ledges entered. The gates had no padlocks, just lengths of chain looped from post to post. After dark, someone on the outside could easily make his way into the quarry and hide a flask or a pouch of tobacco in a crevice of rock. The next day it was a simple matter for a convict to retrieve the hidden treasure unnoticed by the guards, or so he'd heard.

But who would do that, the prisoner wondered, who would do that for him? He knew no one in this village. And even if he did, there was no way to lay such a plan. One letter a month, a visit every two, family members only: that was a convict's allotment, every word, written or spoken, passed before a guard.

The prisoner paused to straighten his back and flex the skin of his palms, seared from the weight of the maul. He'd been assigned to work the topmost shelf of stone, close under the crow's nest. Through the trees that rimmed the pit he could see a house on the other side of the dirt road that separated the quarry from Portsmouth village. Twice a day, a convict carried water buckets along a path that wound out of the quarry across the road to the pump in the middle of that yard.

As the prisoner watched, a young woman, a girl really, ran across the grass, fell on her knees by the shed at the back of the yard and threw her arms around a black spaniel that leapt and strained at its chain. The girl's schoolbag lay on the grass, an arm's length from the path that led from the quarry to the pump.

Sweat evaporated on the prisoner's brow, chilling his skin.

Suppose this girl had a generous heart. Suppose she took pity on a man without freedom, family or friends. Suppose when his turn came as water-boy, he tossed a note from the path. Suppose she answered. And brought him tobacco. And money to pay off the guards. Suppose Beaupré found the note instead. Suppose the guard in the crow's nest saw him drop it. Suppose the girl told her father, and her father told the Warden, and the Warden sent him to the paddle, to the Hole.

The prisoner heaved the sledge over his head and brought it down sharply on the iron wedge in the stone. Suppose she didn't. Suppose she tucked his note in her dress and never, not so long as she lived, ever told a soul.

• • •

Inside the prison walls, the autumn air was rank with the smell of onions. To the left of the cement walk that led from the North Gate to the Keeper's Hall lay a neat square of black earth streaked with rows of reddish brown, fist-sized bulbs, their straw-coloured stalks streaming over the damp soil.

William St. Pierre Hughes flared his nostrils at the earthy odour released by the rain. It was only the second time he had visited Kingston Penitentiary since becoming Superintendent of Penitentiaries six months before, but he was no stranger to the place. For twenty years he'd worked in the massive cruciform building that loomed ahead, first as Clerk of Industries, then Chief Keeper, Accountant and, finally, Inspector. Daniel O'Leary, the man who walked beside him, had been Deputy Warden for most of that time, a consistent bass note to the rising tenor of Hughes's career.

The two men walked side by side in silence, O'Leary keeping stubbornly outside the shelter of the Superintendent's large black umbrella. Apart from the prison, O'Leary and Hughes shared only one thing: a deep and abiding hatred of one another.

Behind the two officials walked four men, newspaper reporters on their first visit to a federal penitentiary. This wasn't just any federal prison: the penitentiary at Portsmouth was the oldest and most notorious in the Dominion, the subject of rumour and investigation since it had received its first convicts eighty years before. All summer, stories had circulated about conditions inside Kingston Penitentiary. Exaggerated tales from former inmates, Hughes had explained to the Minister of Justice. Publicly, he'd declined to comment. Instead, he had issued an invitation: perhaps reporters would care to accompany him on an unscheduled inspection?

The answer, of course, was yes.

A spare, lean man, Hughes was military in bearing but with a bookish bent. His angular face was broken by a brush moustache and blue eyes set in sockets so deeply gouged that his brow formed a precipice over his countenance. He bore little resemblance to his infamous older brother, Sir Sam Hughes, the man who, as Minister of Militia, had muscled Canada into readiness for the Great War. Strong as a bull, fearless as a lion, ferocious as a tiger, that was Sam. He had a wrestler's body, an athlete's stance. He'd been a terror on the lacrosse field—he always said he wasn't at his best until he felt warm blood running down his face—and he'd brought the same reckless, bullying bluster to the floor of the House of Commons.

William was not as inexorable as his brother—there was more fairness to the set of his mouth, more generosity in his gaze—but he shared the family penchant for striking to the heart of a matter. If his penitentiaries were under fire in the press, well, let the reporters come see for themselves. He was not afraid of their pens. *Water on a duck's back is creosote compared to the effect of criticism on Sir Sam Hughes.* The same would soon be said of brother William.

The reporters, keen to the barred windows, the armed sentries and grey stone walls made ominous in the gloom, were unmindful of the conversation that passed between the two officials they trailed.

How many inmates at present? asked Hughes.

Five hundred and ninety-two, sir. Two more expected today.

How many a year ago this date?

Three hundred and forty-nine, sir.

More than fifty percent increase in one year. Extraordinary. To what do you credit the rise?

I'm sure I don't know, sir.

There was nothing untoward in the words themselves. It was the peculiar shapes they took: the clipped edges of Hughes's queries, O'Leary's costive replies, the words pulpy, as if held too long in the throat.

Six years before, O'Leary had answered to a Royal Commission, their questions phrased to test the truth of Hughes's allegations: that the Deputy Warden persecuted guards, that he consorted with ex-convicts, testified falsely in prison investigations, was cruel and inhumane in his handling of convicted men.

You know something of this practice of shackling men up to cell doors?
Yes.

Have you recommended that?

I think I have.

How long would you say was the longest time you recommended such punishment as that?

I could not tell you.

Well, how long a time would you recommend a man be tied up?

Until he would consent to go to work.

Is it only imposed for refusing to go to work?

That is one offence.

And what terminates it?

When he would say, "I will go to work."

One witness testified to twenty-eight days.

I do not think it is true.

Is it not a fact that every man in the Punishment Cell is shackled to the door in that way?

Yes.

So if a man has been in there twenty-eight days, his hands have been shackled to the door in that way?

Yes.

Hughes had underestimated the Deputy Warden, a miscalculation that almost cost him his career. He'd spent months documenting the evidence, sounding out, ever so cautiously, the officers and convicts who would testify, taking his carefully prepared case to the Member of Parliament for Kingston. How well he recalled his jubilation at the naming of a Royal Commission when the most he had hoped for was an investigation by the Minister of Justice. Those first exhilarating days of testimony, convicts for the first time telling what it was like to live inside this wretched place. Through it all, his pride, his delight at making a difference, his arrogance blinding him to O'Leary's real power.

His efforts had come to nothing. *Major Hughes seems to have been misled by the gossip of the guards.* His judgement, declared the Commissioners, was clouded by his unfriendly relations with the Deputy Warden, a man they deemed neither cruel nor inhumane as charged. Their meagre recommendations—let the convicts grow their hair, read newspapers, smoke tobacco and exercise on Sundays—were soon scuttled by the wardens. *Kid glove penology, like some kinds of military boots,* warned the wardens, *is too light for active service.*

Thank God there had been a war to go to and a powerful brother in Ottawa to ease his way up the ranks. He'd left Kingston in 1915 a Major at the head of the 21st Battalion and returned three years later a Brigadier-General who'd earned the right to name his own reward. Long before the Royal Commission, Sam had tried to get William named Warden of Kingston Penitentiary, and at the time William would have settled for that. But war had widened his vision. Why stop at one prison, if he could have them all?

Superintendent of Penitentiaries for Canada, that's what I want, he told Sam. And that's what he got.

Hughes paused on the steps to the Keeper's Hall, waiting for the reporters to catch up. He was in no hurry. He wasn't a cruel man—although the shock on O'Leary's face when he appeared unannounced at the North Gate this morning with his entourage of reporters had brought him an unexpected rush of pleasure. No, he wasn't in a hurry to right the wrongs of the Royal Commission. He had plans for his penitentiaries, ambitious plans, and when O'Leary and his cronies were finally sent packing, he wanted the press and the public as well as the politicians firmly on his side.

The reporters and the two officials moved from the Keeper's Hall, where convicts were registered when they arrived at the penitentiary, through the ranges where they spent their nights in solitary cells, to a second cross-shaped building that housed the convicts' bath-house and the shops where rows of men worked in eerie silence sewing uniforms, stitching leather boots and forging the iron locks that held fast their cells.

At last they came to the stone shed, where a hundred men or more sat knee to knee on facing benches, leaning over boulders of limestone, filling the air with dust from the blows of their hammers.

Hughes raised his voice against the din. According to prison regulations, every inmate must pass his sentence in hard labour, he explained. There is rarely enough work to keep all the men busy. When the weather, like today, is too foul to work in the quarry or at the farm, there is no choice but to put these gangs on the stone pile, too. Only the sick may be idle.

May we speak to the convicts?

Certainly.

The reporter from the *Ottawa Citizen* approached a young man. His face, observed the newspaperman in his notebook, was not a strongly limned one but neither was it criminal. One can tell criminals by birth and breeding, he wrote. They have a shifty look, a sinister glance and a distinct physiognomy. This youth showed none of these.

How old are you?

Twenty-four.

What are you in for, and how long?

Two years, for escape.

Escape?

From Burwash, up north, the industrial farm.

And why were you there?

Joy riding.

Joy riding?

I stole a motorcar and went joy riding and the judge sent me away for two years.

And how do they treat you here?

Oh, I ain't kicking. But I'd give the world just to get out in God's open country again.

As they moved from shop to shop, Hughes chatted casually with the inmates. Some had been in Kingston Penitentiary since he'd been Chief Keeper. Both he and the lifers had been young men then. Several asked him to hear their complaints, and he promised to return soon for private interviews.

Outside the North Gate, the newspapermen were grateful; they smiled warmly as they shook Hughes's hand. O'Leary kept his eyes on them as he pulled the bars to and locked the gate from the inside. He was more than glad to see all of them gone.

• • •

Of all public institutions, none is such a closed book to the
people at large as the penitentiary. To the average citizen it is
either a grim, grey pile of masonry, barred and impregnable,
the inside of which is a mystery, or it is a place spoken of in
jest as "the pen." One hears of offenders against the law being
sentenced for a term in the penitentiary and there interest in
the law-breaker ends. That is where interest should begin . . .

OTTAWA CITIZEN
October 18, 1919

• • •

The prisoner kneaded first one hand, then the other, liberating his fingers from the stiffness of the cold and the calluses on his palms. From his shirt pocket, he took the stub of indelible pencil he'd found on the road. He gnawed at the wooden casing until the purple lead showed through. It was dark outside; the ten-watt bulb screwed into the ceiling lightened the cell to a perpetual pale dusk. The prisoner waited until the guard passed on his rounds, then got up from his bunk, took a step to the toilet in the back corner and pissed. The rush of his stream ricocheted tinnily through the range. More than five hundred men and hardly a sound, just furtive rustlings, like animals restless in their stalls.

Perhaps it was the oncoming cold that made him desperate. Perhaps it was the sight of the Superintendent and his conversation with the reporter that made him bold. Or perhaps it was simply that six days of breaking stone had not beaten the thought from his brain.

He pulled a handful of papers from the wad suspended beside the toilet and stuffed them in his shirt. He sat on his bunk, facing the bars to catch the first footsteps approaching down the range, then he smoothed one thin, brown rectangle on his knee. He licked the exposed tip of purple lead, careful not to stain his lips.

Little friend, he began.

•••

The burning barrel stood halfway between the house and the shed at the back corner of the yard. On Saturdays, it was Phyllis's job to burn the week's rubbish—newspapers, red butcher's paper, letters already answered, occasionally scribblers filled with last year's lessons.

This morning the air was honed with the edge of winter. Grey clouds bore down from the north, so low they threatened to snag in the bared branches of the trees. Phyllis could see her breath, white and wispy, as if a fire smouldered inside her. She pressed a shoebox into the mess in the barrel, then picked up a newspaper from the pile on the ground, twisted it into a tight taper and lit one end with a match. She held it at an angle until the flame crept halfway up the shaft. Then she touched the burning tip against an envelope, the corner of a tooth-powder box, the blue and yellow rim of a soap wrapper.

She liked this chore. She liked being outside. More than that, she liked being away from the crush of family, alone and out of sight, nestled by the lilac hedge, the cedars and the elm trees that shielded her from the wagons and motorcars that clattered down King Street towards the centre of Portsmouth village. On the other side, the property sloped steeply through three vacant lots to Cross Street. In theory, Rear Street connected King to Cross, but in fact, the dirt road extended only along the back of her father's land, a thin boundary between the last house in the village and the prison quarry. The house itself with its large windows and broad veranda faced King Street; no windows looked onto the back yard.

Phyllis reached into the pocket of her coat and closed her fingers around the roll of paper, thin as a cigarette. Lying in her palm, backlit by the flames, it did not seem remarkable at all. Thin brown paper, striped with faint purple markings.

For a week, the paper had lain first in one pocket, then another, coat to schooldress to apron to nightdress. She had picked it up in curiosity, boldly hidden it for days, but she could not bear the burden of her secret any longer. Whoever he was, this convict who dropped notes by the road, she would have no part of him.

When the letter touched the flame, the pages parted in the heat, opening like blossoms on a hot summer day. Words, illuminated briefly, pleaded ... *never fear* ... *little friend* ... *trust me* ... , then withered and blackened. The embers spiralled skyward with the smoke, but the words remained.

Convicts were a fixture of Portsmouth life. Clusters of uniformed, silent men shovelling the sidewalks, cutting deadfall behind the town hall, moving in lockstep two abreast through the streets to the quarries, to the penitentiary farm. Unmistakable in their red and grey checkered prison clothes; indistinguishable, despite the numbers stamped on their backs. A single, solemn face, shaped in the imagination. Phyllis had never dared look one in the eyes. When she was younger, boys would come to school breathless, bragging about the gangs they'd followed, the criminals they'd teased to talk. And she'd often passed recesses with her friends, speculating on the convicts' crimes, which one had murdered his mother, drowned his children, set fire to his neighbour's house.

You mind now, other mothers would say, or you'll end up in the pen with the rest of the scoundrels. But at her house, the prison was too familiar to be a threat. Her grandfather and her great-grandfather had worked there all their lives. Her uncle Alex had been Chief Keeper until the summer past; both his sons were still guards. Convicts, her father often said, were men more to be pitied than scorned.

For almost as long as Phyllis could remember, the convicts of the quarry gang had passed her house on their way from the penitentiary to the limestone pit and back again. When she left for school in the morning, they were already at work, pounding and blasting rock, deepening the cavity that lay like an open wound on the other side of the road. At the end of the day, she sometimes met them as they marched back to the prison. Every morning she awoke to the sound of the prison bell, and every evening, as the family gathered around the supper table, the bell sounded again and they paused, as did all the families in Portsmouth village, to glance at the clock, sometimes moving the minute hand a little forward, a little back, adjusting their timepieces to the signal that all in the prison was well.

Phyllis fed more rubbish to the flames. Nothing like this had ever happened to her or to anyone she knew. It was the stuff of books, novels like *Daddy Long Legs*. Jerusha Abbott had been seventeen, too, when a mysterious man had rescued her from the orphanage and paid her way to college, asking for nothing but letters in return.

Jerusha had an imagination—an imagination that would get her into trouble if she didn't take care.

At the moving-picture matinee the previous Saturday, Phyllis had marvelled at how perfectly Mary Pickford portrayed Jerusha Abbott. She was exactly as Phyllis had imagined her. Courageous. Good-hearted. A spunky girl with a conscience, unwilling to bend to the matron's rules. She was small, like Phyllis, but prettier, with light golden hair plaited in long braids, and blue eyes that snapped and danced. Phyllis's own eyes were dark, her hair unruly, her forehead too broad, her features plain.

On her way home from the theatre, Phyllis had seen the quarry gang in the distance, rounding the corner by the blacksmith's shop. Without thinking, she'd grabbed the cord, ringing the streetcar to a stop. She kept her eyes on the boardwalk—step on a crack, break your mother's back—until the front guard had passed and she could safely look at the men.

Their caps were slouched with dirt and sweat, their skin grey with stone dust. Some looked at her sideways, without shifting their faces from the numbered patches sewn on the backs of the convicts in front. Their eyes were sullen, sneering, empty, tired. Some looked at her in a way that made her feel ashamed. Which of them, she wondered, hoped to be her friend?

Just as the Scout reined his horse alongside, Phyllis averted her gaze. She could smell the horse's flank steaming in the late afternoon chill, glimpse the sheen of a rifle butt rising from the saddle beside the outrider's leg. She heard the reins snap against the animal's neck. Horseshoes clattered down the street, towards the middle of the gang. And the men were gone.

Kicking along the roadside between the back shed and the path, Phyllis had watched for another note. There was none. Neither was there one the next day, of course: Sunday was a day of rest even for convicts. Every day after school she'd played with Watch at the back of the lot, searching in the grass for a roll of paper while the spaniel nuzzled her neck and licked her face. But there had only been one letter, and now it was gone.

The wind shifted; Phyllis stepped away from the smoke. At the bottom of the hill, a line of carts moved out of the quarry, past St. John's Anglican Church. She heard the shuffle of boots on gravel as the rest of the gang rounded the path from the top of the quarry onto Rear Street. When the convicts passed the shed, one hand might drop a roll of paper. She would burn it too, of course. Still, she was curious to know from whose hand it fell.

What with the snapping of the fire, the grinding of the cart wheels and the background snare of horses' hooves, Phyllis missed the first drone of the aeroplane. By the time she heard it, the flying machine was practically upon her, so close the flames bent flat across the barrel's mouth. She could see the lamb's-wool collar on the pilot's leather coat. He tipped his wings, bruising the treetops, then arced suddenly upward, releasing a blizzard of papers that spun lackadaisically to earth.

Phyllis reached up and caught one mid-air. The men broke ranks and grabbed at them, too, silently lunging, darting.

A sweetly innocent face stared out from the leaflet, and beside it, a bottle with an oversized X drawn through it.

THE BEER OR THE BOY?

"Booze" has starved little children and clad them in rags.

"Booze" has made fiends out of men and rewarded the tender affection of women with abuse.

"I have never known of a single case of wife murder that was not committed under the influence of drink," said the Chief Warden of the old Central Prison, Toronto.

ON OCTOBER 20, WIVES WILL VOTE "NO!"

The convicts found their voice: they hooted and whooped. They squashed the papers in their fists and pitched them at one another like snowballs. Someone started a cheer—Hip, hip—but the crack of a gunshot cut it short. The Scout shouted, his rifle pointing into the empty air. The men shifted back in line.

Phyllis looked away. The convicts moved out of sight. Prohibition propaganda skittered down the street.

She walked to the edge of the road and scooped up a handful of papers and with them, the note that poked out from the debris. The propaganda she dropped into the burning barrel, then slowly she unfurled the page, written margin to margin in a flowing purple hand.

Little friend, it began.

• • •

The Halliday house near the corner of King and Rear was so full it was a wonder the rough-cast plaster finish didn't crack and split. When Jack returned from France late in the winter of 1919, he'd spent a few months in Mowat Hospital recuperating from mustard gas, then although he was twenty-two, he'd moved back home, into his old room with Gordon, who had just turned fourteen. The three girls, Marion, nineteen, Phyllis, seventeen, and Betty, eight, shared one room. In the summer, when Jack, still unemployed and living at home, married the fourteen-year-old beauty Winnie Young, Gordon was shifted to the daybed in the summer kitchen so the newlyweds could have a room of their own. Only in the outhouse could a person be assured of privacy and even there, someone was usually shifting from foot to foot on the other side of the door.

It had been a summer of making do, of eating out of the garden and cutting down cast-off clothes. No one had steady work. Phyllis's father, a machinist at the Canadian Locomotive Works in Kingston, had been on strike since May when the metal workers' union had laid down their tools in sympathy with the Winnipeg General Strike. Even after the Manitoba strikers were locked in Stony Mountain Penitentiary, the metal workers in Kingston had continued to walk their picket line, waving hand-lettered placards: We aren't Bolshevists; It's a better life we want; Give us what you promised when we went to war. William Halliday, secretary of the Metal Trades Council, spent his days at the union hall. Jack walked the streets of Kingston looking for work. Phyllis's mother, Augusta, and both Marion and Winnie volunteered at Mowat Hospital where the wards were crowded with wounded veterans. Phyllis, Gordon and Betty took on what odd jobs they could, cleaning house, minding neighbours' children, running errands during the holidays and after school.

The random ebb and flow of bodies in the house was stilled for a few hours on Sundays when the family gathered after church in the parlour. Betty practised hymns on the piano; her mother knitted in the corner; Winnie and Marion gossiped in hushed voices on the chester-field. The men claimed the table, where they spread open their books and newspapers on the cutwork cloth.

It had been easier than usual for Phyllis to escape this Sunday. The family was absorbed with the provincial election: votes in Portsmouth would be cast next door, at Uncle Alex's house. Phyllis listened to the voices rising and falling below her. The escalating price of butter and sugar. The signing of the Peace. The strike at the Locomotive Works, finally settled after six months but with no raise in pay. The Farmers' Party. The social gospel. Prohibition. The women's first vote.

Politics. It meant nothing to her. Sitting cross-legged on the bed, Phyllis opened her scribbler to the middle, pried apart the staples and eased out the centre page.

She would simply ask him, straight out, who he was, why he was in the penitentiary, what he wanted from her.

Dear convict . . .

What on earth was she doing?

Communicating with a convict was strictly against the law. She knew that. She'd been just a little girl, barely in school, when the quarry first opened and her father agreed to let the penitentiary take drinking water from his pump. He had instructed his children sternly then: do not be unkind, but neither be friendly towards the men in the quarry gang. She had been tempted by the first letter; it was polite and enquiring, hardly the work of a hardened criminal. But she had been right to burn it. She should toss this one in the fire, too.

Music filtered up through the floorboards from the parlour below. *Stand up, stand up for Jesus, the trumpet call obey*. The convict had seen her by the burning barrel and had dropped another note. Clearly, his words were meant for her.

Your courage rise with danger, and strength to strength oppose. Perhaps he needed her help. A loved one, sick or in danger. The risk of learning more was small, surely, weighed against the good she might do.

Stand up, stand up for Jesus, stand in His strength alone. In her seventeen years, she had rarely acted on her own. What if she were caught?

Where duty calls, or danger, be never wanting there.

She would write the letter, and leave the rest to God.

But how to address the convict? Her greeting, when she read it again, sounded too familiar, too direct. She took another page from her scribbler.

Dear Adventurer, for that was how he had signed his notes. I *would like to correspond with you but I must know your crime before we can be friends.*

She crumpled this paper, too.

How queer, thought Phyllis, to write to someone you have never met. Jerusha Abbott had not known the name of the man she wrote to either, but she had seen his shadow cast against the orphanage wall. Everyone in the theatre had gasped. All crooked arms and legs, black as India ink, elongated by the light from the headlamps of the motorcar. *Daddy Long Legs.* Jerusha's name for her benefactor had suited him perfectly.

Phyllis had seen only a line of shuffling men, nothing from which she could fashion a nickname. Her greeting, of necessity, would be as anonymous as a stone tossed into the quarry. The notion was oddly comforting. There was safety, after all, in obscurity. She took courage from that.

To the convict who left the note by the path . . .

● ● ●

When Phyllis awoke early Monday morning, the sky was pale, washed clear by Sunday's rain. She heated some milk and poured it over the broken pieces of stale bread in the dog's bowl. While her mother stirred the oatmeal for the family's breakfast, Phyllis carried the bowl to the back of the yard and set it on the grass beside the shed where Watch had his own corner with a blanket spread over a mound of straw. She checked the house, then walked quickly to the road and looked in both directions.

No one was about.

She dropped the tightly folded square of paper onto the roadside, close behind the shed, near the path to the pump. Watch paused, eyeing her curiously. The yard was silent except for the dry rattle of the elms, dismantling leaf by leaf.

She kicked gravel over the note. Then she bent and raised one corner more distinctly into view. She was tempted to walk down the road, as he would, to determine if the paper could be seen, but she didn't dare. She knelt by Watch as he ate, and rubbed his ears, the warmth of his fur a balm to the confusion of emotions that constricted her chest.

That evening, as she returned from school, she walked slowly along Rear Street. The letter she had planted was gone.

Near the spot where she had left the note lay a small maple leaf, perfect in every respect. Against the dusty ochre and damask of the fallen leaves, it lay green and flat, fresh as spring. She took it for a sign. She picked up the leaf by its stem and, inside the house, pressed it between the pages of her Bible, where the Old and New Testaments divide.

●●●

A POLITICAL REVOLUTION!

Twas the women who did it. They carried the Temperance Act to victory, and yet they downed Premier Hearst who fathered the Act. Aren't they the funny lot?

Portsmouth, however, has the distinction of being one of the
very few villages in the province that voted for booze.

The Portsmouth Philosopher
DAILY BRITISH WHIG
October 22, 1919

• • •

Phyllis was home early from school. The bedroom was deserted, a
small miracle for which she thanked God. She closed the door, emptied her schoolbag on the bed and, listening for footsteps on the stairs,
carefully extracted the roll of brown paper from between the ledger
sheets of *High School Book-Keeping*. It had rained heavily all day,
but the note, hidden under sheltering leaves, was only slightly damp.
Phyllis sat on the floor, her back against the door. She opened the
page, pressing it flat along her thigh.

noon Tuesday

Little Friend:

Your most pleasing note duly met & contents carefully noted. I do
not think you in any way bold, especially when you ask me who I
am! It will not take many words to explain that originally I'm from
Detroit Mich U.S.A. but was working for a Canadian firm B/4 I
unfortunately fell into trouble at Hamilton, Ontario & the crime
I am in here for, is speculating with other people's money, was
sentenced to two years on the 8th of Sept, 1918 but I am young yet,
being 24 years of age, & it is my honest intention to accomplish
something good with the remainder of my life after leaving here.

As regards the contents of your notes, you can rest assured
I am the only one who reads them, & although you may not

see me tear them in your sight, nevertheless, they are destroyed
immediately & I only find one fault, that this one was so brief.
Don't worry concerning the officers in charge knowing what I am
doing. We have what is commonly known to us as a ½ way house
& sometimes I spend an hour in there, not a very pleasant spot,
but one is sure of not being bothered. Should anything happen
out of the ordinary, I will let you know some way, but I've all the
confidence in the world that nothing will ever happen.

> *In a Hurry,*
> *"Joe"*

(Trust me)

The convict did not address her by name. Phyllis noticed this first, with relief and some disappointment, since the signature at the end of her letter had given her more pause than the salutation. Although she had disguised her handwriting, as an extra measure of safety she had also given herself another name.

She hated her Christian names. Phyllis Gertrude. As old-fashioned as the handed-down shifts and camisoles she had to wear. Her family had shortened it to Phyll, but that didn't suit her either. Its sound was too tailored, a sensible percale shirt waist when what she longed for was sheer white lawn, tucked and trimmed in shades of heliotrope, garnet and plum.

For a moment, Phyllis had considered calling herself Jerusha, but the orphan-girl had despised her name, too. Isabella, Jessie, Dorothy, Anne. Phyllis discarded the names of grandmothers, aunts and cousins, all the girls and women she knew. She would have a name without a face, one she could make her own.

Peggy. The name leapt from nowhere. Peggy: carefree and modern, robust, bold.

As Phyllis read the convict's letter, it was Peggy who heard his words; Peggy who made a place beside her on the floor for this young man, this American, so far away from home; Peggy who reached out to pat his hand as he told her his troubles and confessed his mistakes. His concern for her safety touched her. And if the words *should anything happen* alarmed Phyllis at all, the warning was too muted to hear.

The convict signed his letter "Joe," but Peggy was no fool. She did not expect for a moment he had used his real name. Nevertheless, to be perfectly safe, she would christen him herself.

Daddy Long Legs.

She wondered that she had not thought of it before. First, she would explain about the movie. Perhaps someday she could lend him the book.

•••

The prisoner lay on his bunk, his arms cushioning his head. He gnawed on his bottom lip. He wanted a smoke badly, but he was no longer willing to do what was necessary to get one inside the prison. He would wait, and let desire hone the details of his plan.

The smoothness of the first step astonished him. It had been as simple as asking for a dance. A hand offered. That brief moment when a girl could refuse. Once she was in his arms, the odds were on his side. It was up to him to lead, and when the time was right, to press a little closer, move into the shadows, have his way. She could call a halt at any time, of course, but once the connection was made, there were arguments to consider, consequences to weigh. The time for blunt rejection was safely past.

The prisoner got up to stretch his legs: three paces to the back wall, one across, three to the bars, one back. The constrained pattern of his steps concentrated his mind. He shut his eyes and slipped out of the prison, past the stone walls. He often did this, but never before to such purpose. And never to imagine himself once again on penitentiary ground.

The quarry rose around him. He had come to think of it as just another, larger cell, but now it appeared to him as an intricate architecture, brilliantly conceived and custom-built for concealment. As if every rock face camouflaged a safe. The means was at his fingertips; he had only to choose.

But once he chose a hiding place, how to communicate its position to the girl? That was the question the prisoner pondered through the night. Every signal he devised—pebbles arranged in patterns in front of a gap in the stones, codes etched on a flat rock face—was a public announcement, as easily interpreted by convicts and officers as by the girl.

When it finally came to him, the answer was as simple and secret as a smile passed between friends. In the morning, she would wait at the back of her yard. As the convicts were marched through the upper gate, he would raise his cap. He would not even have to look at her, just remove his cap to wipe his brow. The action would say, a letter waits. In the afternoon, she would note where he was working and at night, when the quarry was empty, she would go to that part of the wall to find his note, his "kite," tucked discreetly between the rocks. And if she smiled in his direction the next morning, he would know to look for a letter in yesterday's place.

The coffee tasted sweet at breakfast; the dry, dark bread, as soft as a bakery roll. And the quarry when he entered it, smiling, was brilliant with morning light. He breathed in the air like a tonic. Although he had not slept, he had never been more alert in his life.

• • •

Phyllis dug the garden fork into the soil alongside the leeks, pushed the tines straight down with her foot and tilted the thick white fingers gently out of the earth. The air was crisp with the promise of frost.

Go down to the cellar and get another couple of baskets, would you, Betty? We still have the beets to lift.

Phyllis scooped up an armful of withered stems and leaves, walked to the compost heap, deposited the debris and with a quick backward glance, moved swiftly across the road, through the gap in the trees, her heavy wool skirt brushing against burdock, until the limestone cliff fell away at her feet.

The low evening sun slanting through amber leaves lent the rocks a peculiar hue. Phyllis wiped her hands on her apron and brought them to rest on the pocket where his note lay, an amulet against the trick of the light. She stared at the stone, struggling to fix the point where the convict had stood earlier in the day.

By the time Betty returned, Phyllis had resumed her work. The digging steadied her. The convict was right, of course. They could not rely forever on the roadside. Anyone might find their notes. And the guards would soon become suspicious of a convict who was so eager to be water-boy or one who stumbled each day at the same spot in the road.

The convict had another reason for the change. Would she, he asked, mail a letter for him? He'd heard a friend was ill. The penitentiary allowed convicts to correspond only with their families, and he couldn't bear to think of his friend dying without hearing from him again.

Unfinished business, he said.

• • •

A harvest moon, yellow as a ripened squash, sat on the lip of the quarry, casting ragged shadows deep into the pit. Phyllis pulled the collar of her coat closer. She walked quickly, her footsteps amplified in the still air. The moon illuminated the path that swept along the top of the pit, but she turned instead towards the first wooden ladder and climbed down into the shadows. The gap in the trees where she had stood earlier in the evening was directly above her now. She moved deeper into the darkness, her fingers scrabbling across the limestone. White dust lodged in her cuffs. Stones unseated by her fingers and by the toes of her shoes clattered to the quarry floor. She gasped as something winged whirred past her hair and scooped across the barren ground, disappearing into the blackness of the far wall.

Later, she wondered that she had persevered. Marvelled that she had not turned back. That she had found the smooth paper wedged between the cracks. She lay under her quilts, as cold as the moon that hung, now shrunken and pale, high in the night sky, her legs still weak, her heart thrilling, the letter to the convict's friend secure beneath her pillow, his note curled with the others in the Ovaltine tin under her bed.

● ● ●

Phyllis carried the flag up the stepladder and, taking care not to let it fall to the carpet, unfurled the Union Jack before the parlour window. Small, stiff paper flags lay scattered on the table: two to be crossed on each veranda post. The lintels of the front door and windows she would drape with red, white and blue bunting, but the flag was too fragile for outside. It was kept folded in tissue in her mother's blanket box, removed only for its annual airing on Dominion Day. Today was an exception: the Prince of Wales was coming to visit.

The old silk crackled as Phyllis shook out the folds. The Union Jack had travelled in her great-grandfather's valise when he emigrated from England to Upper Canada in the 1840s. No one knew exactly what had brought William Atkins—her father's mother's father—to Portsmouth. Perhaps, poring over a map of new settlements, he was struck by the name. The scattering of houses and shops on a rough grid of dirt roads couldn't properly be called a village—it hadn't even a post office then—but at least it had a promising name.

A dozen years before William Atkins arrived, the place was nothing but rock and bush around a dimple in the lakeshore called Hatter's Bay. Then the site, two miles west of Kingston, was chosen for the colony's first penitentiary, and the village sprang up in its wake. The sons of Loyalist settlers were hired to clear the scrub oak and hickory and to quarry the limestone that shrugged up through the soil. When the penitentiary was just a shell, the first convicts were delivered and put to work cutting stone and enclosing the cells. Forges, lime kilns and workshops edged along the road that snaked around the swampy headland, and on the other side of Hatter's Bay a rooming house and a tavern appeared, then one by one, small stone and stucco cottages for the overseers and convict guards, blacksmiths and carters, stonecutters and shopkeepers who came.

The penitentiary absorbed all of Abbott's Point, the knob of land on the east side of the bay; on the west, the land was divided and sold and divided again. By the time William Atkins secured a lot on the northwest edge of the village, the settlement no longer called itself Hatter's Bay, but rather, Portsmouth, in honour of the seven-hundred-foot pier built to close in the harbour. The place was christened after Portsmouth, England, with its thriving Royal Dockyards, as if the prosperity of the mother country could be transferred like a dowry with its name.

For a time, it seemed that Portsmouth might live up to that promise. The harbour was deep and snug; shipbuilders set up shop along the shore. The penitentiary was a reliable repository of diligent labour. In the huge vaulted workshops, convict carpenters and joiners, tailors, shoemakers and blacksmiths worked for entrepreneurs who set up their businesses inside the walls. When Kingston was named the capital of the united Canadas, the Governor General built his residence, Alwington House, within sight of the penitentiary towers. Wealthy merchants and professional men bought lake-front estates on both sides of the village and commissioned elegant stone villas to match the viceregal home. Land prices soared; the quarries worked dawn to dusk. The road from Kingston was extended straight across the swampy tip of Hatter's Bay on a causeway built by convicts with quarry debris.

But Kingston was too vulnerable for a nation's capital. The United States of America lay practically within sight on the other side of the lake. The politicians moved on, and Portsmouth settled back to what it had started out to be: a prison town. Its population was guaranteed. According to the Penitentiary Act, every keeper and guard had to live within sound of the prison bell. It rang morning and night at the end of each shift, a signal that the convicts were counted and locked in their cells. The sound of the bell at any other time of day caused village doors to be flung open and off-duty officers to rush into the street, pulling on their uniforms as they hurried up the hill to join the manhunt for the convicts who'd escaped.

Phyllis draped a swag of blue bunting above the door. If she leaned back just a little, she could see her great-grandfather's house. It had a sunroom now, and a closed-in back kitchen and the roof had been raised to make bedrooms upstairs, but when William Atkins was a guard, it had been a one-storey frame house, too small, surely, for a family of seven. And as if the house weren't full enough, he'd taken in a roomer: another guard, James Halliday, a Scot and a widower, with a family of four girls, almost grown. Great-grand-father had taken pity on him, living in barracks inside the prison walls; his daughter, Isabella Atkins, had fallen in love.

Phyllis's grandmother still lived across the street, in the grand stone house that James Halliday had bought as his fortunes at the penitentiary rose. Frail now, with little to do but sit and talk, Isabella loved to tell how happy she'd been to escape the crowded little house, though she'd only moved down the path to the back of her father's lot where James had torn down the cow barn and built another little frame house for her and James and his family of four girls. And she'd often said, over cream biscuits and tea, how wise she'd been to give herself to an older man. James had died before her sons were twenty, making them landowners when they were barely men. The stone house went to James, the eldest, still a bachelor and the Portsmouth Reeve. The house on the back lot, Isabella's dowry and matrimonial home, went to William, her second son. Isabella's brother, Alexander Atkins, took over the family homestead at the front of the lot. Phyllis, born in the house her grandfather had built, on land her great-grandfather had settled, was surrounded on all sides by kin.

Although most of a century had passed, the Halliday-Atkins property still marked Portsmouth's northwest edge. The growth of the village was stunted, hemmed in on the east by the penitentiary and on the west by the Rockwood estate, the grandest of the villas, converted to house the province's criminally insane. To the south was the lake, and to the north, the penitentiary quarry that inched a little closer every year. The village claimed fewer than a dozen streets in all, and even these weren't truly its own. According to the Act, wherever a convict set foot was penitentiary land, and so the boundaries of Portsmouth village flexed as the prison work gangs passed.

At its height, just after Confederation, when James Halliday arrived, Portsmouth was a village of fifteen hundred souls, three churches, two schools and fifteen shops. But when the wealthy moved away, construction stopped and steamship commerce on the lake faltered. Only the penitentiary remained secure, its jobs handed down within families—the Beauprés, the O'Learys, the Atkinses—like jealously hoarded heirlooms. When the factories inside the prison walls closed, the penitentiary found work in the village for the convicts. They filled in the swamp and made Aberdeen Park, carting stone for the little town hall. They raised the walls of the Roman Catholic church. They smoothed the roads and repaired the boardwalks, stitched leather satchels for the guards and dug wells in their back yards, securing the walls with expertly fitted stone.

By the time the Prince of Wales arrived in the fall of 1919, no one was surprised when Portsmouth was not among his stops, though it was scarcely two miles from Kingston and its villagers were loyal Brits and Scots. For Portsmouth had a certain air about it, not unpleasant exactly, but pervasive, like the faint odour in a room where the very young, the infirm or the aged have been. It wasn't only the grim stone walls and the armed tower sentries that stood guard over the entrance to the town. It was something in the sharp plane of stone in the walls of the town hall, in the wrought-iron railings the children rattled as they passed on their way to school, in the gravel under their boots. It was in the horsehair chain a widow wore. It was in the grooved iron frogs that shunted under the trains at night, in the grey breeches and scarlet tunics of the North West Mounted Police officers who delivered convicts to the North Gate. It was in the dust on the black hem of the chaplain's surplice as he walked up the hill to the Church of the Good Thief. It was in the horses' dung that steamed on village streets when the outriders passed, in the keening of the coal boat as it shunted from the prison pier. It was in the slow step of the women who rented rooms at the inn for a single night, twice a year. It was in the sound of the bell, and in the silence of the parlours when the clock struck six and the bell failed to ring. And it was in the din that rose from the quarry and wavered on the breeze that tugged at the bunting above the Halliday front door. There was nothing the convicts had not touched, and they had left their mark.

• • •

For the prisoner, working on the sidewalks was a mixed blessing. It was a relief to breathe air unburdened by stone, and after the monotony of breaking rock, spreading cinders seemed almost a holiday, one with unexpected rewards, for after just a few hours, the crisp grey band that edged Front Street had kindled in the prisoner the unfamiliar pleasure of accomplishment.

But he had not seen the girl. In his excitement at forging the connection with her, he had let slip one fundamental rule: a convict's life was in no way his own. It belonged to the penitentiary and it belonged to the guards. He could be moved here or there, without notice or explanation, made to do this or that, at their whim. However difficult, however meaningless, humiliating or frustrating the work, he had no choice but to comply, willingly, without complaint, with utter submission in his eyes.

The streets were beginning to fill with people. The entire population of Portsmouth, it seemed, was out. Every shop and house was draped with flags; every man, woman and child carried one too, crisscrossing stripes of red, white and blue snapping at the end of short, slender sticks. It was like the Fourth of July, he thought, without the Stars and Stripes. The street railway was crammed; young men hung off the sides of the car as it lumbered up the hill, past the penitentiary into Kingston. Cautiously, the prisoner stole glances at the passing faces, hoping to see the girl, but either she slipped by unnoticed or she had stayed at home.

The image of the girl standing at the quarry gate, staring into the empty pit, haunted him. What would she think? That he had lost his nerve? Or worse, that they had been found out?

He had to lay a new plan. Not only was he continually being moved from one work site to another, but the quarry, too, despite its solid weight of rock, was perpetually in flux. It was a landscape of disintegration, a reverse replay in accelerated motion of the slow accumulation of sea skeletons that had made the seams of stone the convicts blasted and sledged away. Even if he were free to return to the ledge he had worked the day before, there was no guarantee that the niche or even the wall where she had concealed her kite would still be there.

He needed a new hiding place, one that could be used again and again. A place secure from the guards and the curiosity of the other men. Especially that, for he was eager to push forward this enterprise.

There were two fixtures in the quarry: the crow's nest, which was out of the question, and the place that he had referred to, somewhat delicately in his late to her, as the halfway house. The convicts' outhouse was set amid rubble in the far corner of the quarry floor. The girl would have to cross open ground. But if he found the right sort of stone, one with a deep cleft in its underside, big enough to hold an envelope, he could set the stone in a particular spot by the door where it would be at once accessible to him and easily noticed by the girl, without seeming conspicuous among the other stones.

Take it easy, he reminded himself. Think it through, step by step. He would have to go gently with the girl if he was to have his way.

By the time the distant crack of twenty-one guns sounded, the streets of Portsmouth were deserted. Only the convicts remained, silently raking cinders in a straight grey band in front of the bolted shops.

•••

Monday noon

Hello Peggy:

Now I must say your nice long Kite of this AM certainly did please me & I am glad to know that our future meeting place is satisfactory, for I can reach it at any time.

Peggy, you were asking me if I spoke French. Will it surprise you when I say I am French? If you knew my name you would immediately see without any explaining. And if you think me not too bold, some time soon with your permission I will tell you. Yes, French American.

Your shorthand is very good. It would save so much time & space especially if we should continue to write thus. Let me know! Do you know the Morse Railway Code? If not, I can write it out for you. It is very simple & can be learned in an evening.

Referring to that picture, I believe it's opposite to what you say: & that instead of you spoiling same, you "topped" it off.

Say, that was funny concerning swallowing the kites. Ha, ha. Don't you ever worry! They will never have the pleasure of reading any of our kites. There are no deeks (Detectives) among us, but plenty of stool-pigeons, more commonly known to us as rats.

Rest assured no one but me reads the contents of your kites. The two boys that are working with me knew there was something in the wind. But now that we have our new meeting place, they will know nothing! & may I say so now, I am a little short of Tobacco so in my next letter if I ask for a few $ from my friend,

would it be asking you too much to drop your address in B/4
sealing it. The cash will come in a letter, no money order or any-
thing like that. Then I hope to be able to pay you for the money
you have been spending on stamps, etc. Please don't do it if for
any reason you are afraid. But I believe you when you say you
have all confidence in me.

I will make it my business to come on top of the Hill & I sure
will have my brightest smile. Did you notice me taking off my
cap this AM? That means "Good morning" & God bless you in
your studys.

So for now good bye, Peggy, I will be looking for that smile
of yours & will feel disappointed should you not be there as usual.

Dady L.L. "Joe"

• • •

Leaning against the halfway house, Phyllis heard the explosions. The
sound was near. She hoped it was Gordon and his friends. He had
shown her the red cartridges, their wicks braided, ready for a match
that would set the crackers firing.

Father catches you with that, you'll get a whipping, she'd whispered.

Well, he won't then, will he, Gordon winked. C'mon, Phyll. It's
Hallowe'en.

She'd been loath to come out tonight. There was mischief in the
air. It was the big boys she feared, tipping over outhouses and dragging hay bales into the street, building bonfires that they danced
around like demons, hooting and waving their arms. She'd calmed
herself with the thought that, although young children sometimes
played in the quarry, the older boys stayed away, already wary perhaps
of ground worked by those who had been found out for their crimes.

Another volley of explosions, this time farther away. Phyllis adjusted her coat to a more comfortable cushion against the outhouse door. The night was dark: she could barely make out the convict's words. She tilted the paper into the moonlight, her glance shifting between the page and the quarry walls, lest the old Scot adage proved true, that this being All Hallow's Eve, she might glimpse the ghost of her future lover among the stones.

...Oh, Peggy, but I am acquainted with this part of the country. I've been in Kingston B/4, when I was on the road. I've also been in Gananoque, Napanee, back in around Smiths Falls, Merrickville & all these small towns & villages, also crossed & recrossed from here to Watertown, U.S.A., 65 miles by water. But the longest I've ever stopped in any of these small towns was in Portsmouth, on the Viarrent shores of Lake Ontario. I expect to stay for some time yet, also to come back after I leave, ha ha. A sure sign there must be some attraction besides the Mother Penitentiary, eh?

My Sis was telling me when she was last here that she had bought a post card picture of this place & what a beautiful place it looked. Of course I've always told her that this was a swell place, just like home & naturally she believes so. There's no sense in more than one suffering, not any more than is absolutely neces-sary any way, eh?

Some of the head officials are very strong on showing their Authority, especially when there are strangers around. But, I don't mind them. When I first came in I was smiling, and one big fellow says to me, we will take that smile off your face B/4 you get out of here. But they will have to hurry, for I am still smiling & as yet cannot see any reason why I should not continue doing so.

I better shut up or I might be wearing out the novelty, but I
could & love to write to you's all the time. I will get your address
B/4 my time expires.

Good Bye Peggy & God Bless You all

D. I. legs

"Joe"

(Trust me)

• • •

The prisoner, sitting in his cell, heard gunfire. Not a single pistol shot. A series of explosions. He put the spoon down in his bowl and sat very still. The rustlings in the other cells hushed, too, like a candle quickly snuffed.

Gunshots. Run. Through the woods, branches snapping. Dry leaves smashed underfoot. Shots overhead. Run. Run. Down the hill. Through the stream, in case they have dogs. Shots again. Distant now. Keep running. Run.

Then, silence, and the night. Rocks. White heaving breath. A thin chalice moon. Endless black tangle of hemlock, balsam, fir.

The prisoner pushed his bowl away and wiped at the sweat that sprang up on his brow.

November

Viewed against the dressed limestone tower and buttresses of the Roman Catholic place of worship across the street, the church of the Wesleyan Methodists seemed squat and homely. No steeple, no bell, no ruby-coloured glass. In fact, except for the elongated windows that perforated its cobbled stone walls, the Methodist chapel was not unlike most of the houses of Portsmouth village. In dimension and decoration it was unprepossessing, a church that bent to embrace its parishioners rather than direct their eyes to God.

Sitting on a pew near the back of the chapel, Phyllis lifted one thigh and pulled at the bunched folds of skirt under her coat. Her father sat perfectly still beside her, one hand set firmly on each knee, his posture erect, his head slightly bowed, his face prepared.

He was, she was sure, one of the Chosen, preordained by God to live in His Kingdom forever. He lived an exemplary life. And what was more, he made it look easy, as if he had never been tempted to bend the truth or take more than his due. As far as she could tell, he complied with every requirement of his religion without complaint, showing no more discomfort with its rules than with his starched Sunday collar and tight black suit. Nothing, she knew, was too much to ask of him, provided it was right in the eyes of God. When Phyllis thought of her father, which was often, it was as a hard, bright light, a beacon that had shone steadily through the war and through the strike. A brilliance that illuminated. A glare that exposed.

Until recently, Phyllis had known nothing but the Calvinism that her father's father had brought from his village at the mouth of the Firth of Forth. He had left behind the grey rocks and cold sea of Scotland, but not its stern, exacting faith, and it was this, more than property or wealth, that he'd handed on to his son. Every Sunday morning for as long as Phyllis could remember, the family had walked to the Orange Hall at the foot of King Street where a handful of Portsmouth Presbyterians gathered on hard wooden chairs to hear God's word. The congregation adjourned for dinner, prepared the night before to avoid labour on the Lord's Day, then they returned to the Hall for an afternoon of Bible Study and Sunday School. For a Presbyterian, the seventh day was not a day of rest. It was a day of prayer, of reflection and relentless examination of the soul.

Phyllis believed with all her heart what she had been taught: that she was a sinner, hopeless and depraved. On Sundays she reviewed her shortcomings and renewed her pledge to uphold the laws of God, though inevitably, by nightfall, her purity of purpose would be tainted with some prevarication or unkind thought. By midweek, the small deceptions, the oversights and misdemeanours would accumulate like soft spots on a piece of fruit and by the time she sat again on the hard chairs of the Hall, she would be certain she was rotten to the core.

Phyllis rubbed her fingers. Her skin itched inside her woollen gloves. She distracted herself by looking past the sober profiles of the Presbyterians to the Methodists, nodding and smiling to each other in the front pews. When the elders of her congregation received the invitation of the Methodists to join together to worship in the stone church, her father had been reluctant. The governing bodies of both denominations had agreed in principle to create a new Canadian church, a United Church, but official union had been delayed. A merger of the Portsmouth congregations at this time, he said, was precipitous. But it's the same God, her mother had pointed out, the same Commandments, the same Creed.

Practical necessities had convinced him, but from the first Sunday together, it had been clear: the Methodists were a different breed. For one thing, they stood up to sing. And they let loose their songs with a gusto that the stone walls could barely contain. Sometimes, the hymn singing reached such a frenzy that Phyllis dropped back to her seat breathless and dizzy, as if she'd been lifted without warning to a very great height.

For the most part, the pastor of the newly united congregation struck a middle course, choosing anthems and psalms and readings from the gospels that were beloved by all. His sermons, sedate and circumspect, bore witness to the life of Christ, a model for Protestants of every sect. But the familiar words did not obscure what Phyllis saw in the pews. It came as a revelation: there was more than one path to God. A life without sin led to salvation, she knew, but according to the Methodists, so too did a life of good works. And although it was only hinted at in the presence of the Presbyterians, Phyllis caught an inkling that the God of these Christians would save anyone at all, blotting out the blight on a soul for no other reason than that He'd been asked.

To be suddenly, inexplicably free of sin was too bold an idea to contemplate, but earning salvation through good deeds was a concept Phyllis could grasp. And so she'd abandoned her habit of silently cataloguing her faults and instead passed the long pauses in the service by ordering the events of the week gone by, setting her failures and transgressions on one side, and on the other, the good she had done. If there was only one God, and if the Methodists were right, then her soul would not suffer in the balance.

Oh come, let us sing unto the Lord; let us make a joyful noise unto the rock of our salvation.

Phyllis waited until her father opened the hymnal and got to his feet, then she stood and took one corner of the book, though she knew the words by heart.

Rock of Ages, cleft for me,
Let me hide myself in Thee . . .

• • •

On the wharf near the penitentiary's West Gate, convicts waded across the top of a growing mountain of coal. The black cobbles rolled and shifted like ball-bearings under their boots. Their backs to one another, they shovelled towards the slopes, flattening the peak before the bucket swinging from the barge's jib crane disgorged its next load. An easterly blowing down the St. Lawrence and into Lake Ontario scooped up the black dust that billowed around the men and pitched it in gusts against the officers standing guard on the barge, sprayed it across Hatter's Bay and swirled it against the shops and houses on the other side, scouring it into the stones.

In the hold of the boat, a dozen convicts shovelled coal towards the dusky shaft of daylight that indicated the open hatch. The prisoner bent and scooped, bent and scooped again. Every so often, his rhythm was broken by the huge iron jaw that dropped through the black mist and bit into the mound of coal. In the pause that accompanied the whine of gears, the prisoner straightened his back and watched the loaded bucket jerk up the pillar of light and out of view.

Hey, nigger.

Hey nigger, yourself.

The two friends grinned at each other, their teeth marbled with coal dust and saliva. Dominick Waters, nicknamed OK for his enthusiastic, accommodating ways, occupied cell C-2-17, the one next to the prisoner's. For months they'd shared whispered late-night conversations between the passings of the guard: OK was a Stratford lad but he'd come to the penitentiary from Sarnia and like the prisoner, he'd made both the American and Canadian sides of the Detroit River his territory. The arrival of the last coal boat before freeze-up had drawn both their gangs from the stone shed and the quarry to the wharf. The youngest and the fittest were consigned to the hold. Finally, working side by side, they could talk without a wall between.

The prisoner jabbed his shovel into the coal. He was shorter than OK and not so broad: despite his shaved scalp and calloused hands, he retained something of the air of the dandy—an ease about the mouth, a softness to the cheek that gave him more youth than his years.

OK was not as handsome as the prisoner nor was he as clever, but his eyes were never still. He nodded towards two men working deeper in the hold. They stood very close together, their backs towards the convicts working nearer the hatch. The air was so smudged with dust that the prisoner could barely make out their forms. One man turned to face fully into the bow. The other sank to his knees.

The prisoner heard the guards pacing the deck above their heads. From time to time, an officer might lean over to shout an order into the hold, but penitentiary staff rarely ventured into the suffocating black fog.

It didn't take long. The kneeling man rose to his feet; for just a moment, he took the other's hand. Then he walked past the prisoner to the water bucket, lifted the ladle to his lips and drank. With his palm, he wiped his mouth. The man returned to his place, one cheek distended just above the line of his jaw. And when the man paused from his shovelling to spit, his sputum was such a deep, warm brown that the prisoner felt saliva seep from under his tongue and pool in the hollows of his cheeks.

In his cell, after supper, the prisoner's thoughts returned again to that rich, silky stream. A plug of tobacco now and then made the prison almost bearable. His own stash was gone. The money that he got through the girl did not stretch far. On the street he could get ten plugs for a dollar; in here, four, if he was lucky, the price set by the guards.

The prisoner moved to the front of his cell, unhinged his bunk from the wall and lowered it flat on its chains. He lifted his blankets from their pegs and spread them evenly over the hair-felt mattress. It was a small gesture of independence, this making of the bed. From the time he awoke, his every move was governed by a gong or a guard, but between supper and lights out, he chose his own moment to retire.

It was time, the prisoner decided, to make the next move. He was tired of procuring contraband from the guards, of paying their price and toeing their line even when he broke their rules. Since he'd grown hair on his chest, he'd been his own man, had survived by his wits and guile. The risks were greater, but then so too were the rewards.

The exchanges with the girl had gone without a hitch. The crevice in their special stone was too small, however, for anything but a kite.

Inside the halfway house, after he'd read her notes, chewed the pages and spat them into the hole, pissing them deeper into the filth, his gaze had wandered across the rough plank walls, the sodden bench, the stained floorboards. Like a painter, his eye sought texture and shadow, the play of light on a surface that signalled a hollow, a cavity, a gap. He had found none.

Then, as if a guardian angel divined his need, the warm-up shack was moved into the quarry. Although the officers and convicts called it a shack, the little red-painted building was oddly ornate, with mullioned windows and a cottage roof topped with decorative carving. The building was mounted on skids: it moved with the men from one stone face to the next, the little box stove inside kept stoked by one of the convicts. At night the shutters were closed and locked, but there were cracks in the siding, spaces under the sills and, nestled between the skids, a long dark hidey-hole big enough to hold more than words.

The prisoner sucked the saliva behind his teeth. He had only to coax the girl.

Friday P.M.

Hello Peggy:

Does sound a little too bold, however here goes! Ha. ha. Its now just noon hour, & my time is very brief.

Sometime soon, we will all be working in a position where it will be impossible for me to reach my present spot. But I could explain to you where we could make sure connections. I am sure it would be asking too much, but it could be worked beautifully as follows. You know our little Palace (as you call it), well, its placed on two planks, one on each side. At the bottom underneath, in between the two planks, there is a space of perhaps 3 feet or so, & the planks raise the Palace up off the ground about 4 inches. Now

*you know our present little stone, well I will put that near the spot
as above said, so you cannot make a mistake. I figure you come
only at night, then it will be a sure thing. Your tracks will never be
noticed for there will always be our tracks of the previous day.*

*Now if this is too far away for your convenience, perhaps you
can think of a more suitable place. Will write a nice long Kite
as soon as I know if it is satisfactory. I've so much to say, it will
take me a long time to tell it!*

*I am not going to thank you for that last favour for the word
thanks would be mocking, & no, do come in the garden, for I
could not see you in the doorway as it was dark. I should not
forget to mention that I seen you wave your hand, only wished I
could of ans you!*

Dady long legs

*PS. I mean at the back of the Palace, or rather at the rear only,
and underneath. However, you will see our little stone!*

*PS. Oh yes, concerning the little house. No doubt it would look
suspicious to you, but it is there for the officer in charge so he can
keep from the cold & on account of us working so near the road.
Rest assured when I say that he is "ok". He never bothers any of us.*

*As regards a pair of knitting needles, yes I could easily
enough make them, but it's so hard to get the bone.*

Friend "Joe"

• • •

A.K. Routley, Tobacconist, stood on the south side of Princess Street,
between Simmons Brothers hardware and the newspaper offices of

the *Daily Standard*. From Kingston Collegiate, Phyllis walked east on Earl, turned left on Clergy, and right onto Princess, approaching the cigar store from uptown, a route designed to avoid Halliday Electric and a chance meeting with Uncle Jim. There were other tobacconists, but Routley's was well suited to her purpose. If its advertisements could be believed, it not only had the largest selection of smoking products in Kingston, but it also sold sporting goods, which would provide an excuse of sorts should she be discovered there.

Despite her careful planning, Phyllis faltered by the plate glass windows. The consequence of what the convict proposed stayed her hand on the door. She had trespassed on penitentiary land, yes, but the exchange of letters cheered an imprisoned man and did no one any harm. That she was also a courier for his other correspondences, she considered more an act of Christian charity than a crime. But supplying tobacco to a man in penitentiary: the penalty for smuggling contraband, she knew from her cousin-guards, was three months' hard labour or a hundred-dollar fine.

Phyllis closed her eyes and tried to imagine what would become of her if she were caught, but beyond the planting of the tobacco beneath the Palace, there was nothing: not an image, not an inkling, not the flitting shadow of a thought. She took this blank tableau as a sign that nothing ominous lay ahead. The convict had assured her it was safe; he would not put her at risk. Besides, she told herself, she could change her mind whenever she wished.

The front room of A.K. Routley's bristled with snowshoes, hockey sticks and skates. Behind the counter stood a battery of rifles. In front, three young men lounged against the polished oak, drawing on cigarettes. The opening door set a bell in motion, and at the sound, their conversation stopped.

Can I help you? asked the clerk.

I'd like some chewing tobacco, please. It's for my older brother. He's just back from the war, she added, not quite managing the nonchalance she'd rehearsed.

The clerk jerked his thumb towards the rifles. Other side.

The room beyond the archway was empty. It smelled sweet and rich and vaguely damp, like the woods on a warm fall afternoon, like some of the men who visited Jack. She looked through the glass countertop at the thin metal boxes arranged on the shelf: Player's Navy Cut; Prince of Wales Plug Tobacco; Wilson's Bachelor, The National Smoke: Still the most for the money, 10¢. If it were true, as her Sunday School teacher said, that tobacco was an allurement to other naughtiness, then there was enough bait here to feed the fires of hell for all eternity.

She could hear the conversation of the men on the other side of the store.

Papers are saying the Series was made to order.

Sore losers, that's all.

Did you hear Comiskey changed the club's name? They're the Black Sox now.

Laughter rumbled through the wall. Where was the clerk? Phyllis could not walk past those men empty-handed, but she knew that if she stayed much longer, her courage would dissolve. At last, a slight, elderly man came through a door near the back, carrying an armload of boxes, which he set on the floor. She pointed to the blue tin with the red heart— Prince of Wales, why not?—and handed the man her dollar.

Outside the air had turned cold. An icy drizzle blew against the back of her neck, but it did nothing to dampen her mood. How easy it had been! She faced into the wind, towards the bay at the foot of Princess Street. The water was a solid, silvery grey, like the mercury that had seemed so liquid until the science teacher smashed it to smithereens. In the distance, a streetcar was making its way in fits and starts up the hill. She turned her back again to the wind, gripped the tin under her arm and pressed her eyelids shut against the rain, willing the streetcar to come quickly to her stop.

• • •

The prisoner spread his legs. The guard bent and held him first behind one knee, then the other, patting with his free hand up the opposite shin to the prisoner's crotch. He reamed his fingers around the top of each boot. The prisoner shimmied as if he'd been tickled: some tomfoolery was expected of him. The guard straightened. He prodded the hollows under the prisoner's arms, followed the ladder of ribs down to his waist.

The search was usually perfunctory. Twice a day, at midday and again at night, the North Gate guard ran his hands over the body of every convicted man returning from work in an outside gang. Only the most reliable were assigned to work outside the walls: married men serving short time for minor crimes, men for whom, according to those who set the rules, escape and smuggling contraband were not worth the risk. But the guards understood: a man had to try. For a price, they'd ignore the bulge under a convict's shirt, but the search served daily notice of who was in charge.

The officer patted the front of the prisoner's coat.

Still feeding you pretty good, eh?

Yes, sir.

The prisoner smiled. It was a dangerous game of charades he played. If the guard took exception to the lilt of his lip or the tone of his voice, he would be ordered out of line and stripped naked to stand spread-eagled in the cold. Officers were attuned to arrogance: a convict who resisted authority was attacked and ground down. Yet they despised weakness as much as strength. A convict who submitted holus-bolus deserved no respect and got less. But the prisoner had grown expert: subversion and submission were balanced in his features in equal parts.

As the convicts faced front, the prisoner winked at OK, who had joined the quarry gang that day and—a stroke of unimaginable good fortune—had been assigned to stoke the Palace fire. With each movement of his hips, the prisoner could feel the bulk of the second shirt that his last plug of tobacco had bought. Under the waistband of his trousers, its contours muffled in extra layers of wool, lay a thin blue tin. Its red heart pressed against his belly like a stitch in his side, like the pain that comes from too much dancing or from running, breathless and hard.

●●●

William St. Pierre Hughes believed in rules. He was not naive: he understood they'd be broken. But to his mind, those who lost faith because rules were not inviolate missed the point. It was in the articulation of a code of behaviour that its real value lay. The noblest intentions of the human spirit rendered as an enduring template. A model to hold to when the will weakened, when competing necessities overwhelmed and confused, when monotony bred despair. The Ten Commandments, Hammurabi's Code, the Twelve Tables of ancient Rome, the Magna Carta, the Code Napoleon: the urge to codify was as basic as hunger and thirst in men.

Hughes opened the front drawer of his desk and removed his best ebony penholder and a fresh nib, which he inserted with care. From the cupboard in the pedestal of his desk he withdrew a single sheet of legal-size bond paper imprinted with the insignia of the Department of Justice and the words *Office of Inspectors of Penitentiaries* in black Gothic script.

With one broad stroke, he crossed out *Inspectors* and wrote *Superintendent* above. It galled him that six months after his appointment to the newly created position overseeing Canadian prisons, he was still compelled to begin each correspondence with an error, one that cast him as an impostor, a charlatan whose authority the recipient of his message would be quite right to question.

But he did not let petty grievances distract him now. For the third time in as many months, William St. Pierre Hughes was about to take matters into his own hands.

Memorandum for the Wardens of the Penitentiaries:-

The first memorandum he'd issued from this office was addressed to the Minister of Justice and marked Urgent. The rules and regulations that governed penitentiaries, Hughes had advised, must immediately be reviewed. Except for a few minor amendments, the rules had not been changed in thirty years. They were still rooted in Procrustean law: all men convicted by the courts, whether for stealing a loaf of bread or violating a child, were locked together in the penitentiary and managed under one rule of thumb.

As Chief Keeper at Kingston Penitentiary, Hughes had applied the old rules without question, but the Great War had changed him. He'd watched hundreds of men face death, each in a singular way. And what was punishment, if not a certain kind of death? What he'd learned in the trenches was corroborated by the theories of the new psychology, which Hughes wholeheartedly embraced: a man in authority must study his charge and determine how he came to be that way if he was to effect change. The discipline of rules was essential, but the rules themselves had to be worked into a special sort of cloth that could be cut to fit the distinct character of each individual.

Hughes had written his urgent message to the Minister in May. Two months later, the Minister had replied, requesting a report on prison conditions and the Superintendent's proposals for reform. Hughes had set his plan on the Minister's desk before the week was out.

The Minister himself did not reply. Charles Doherty had been Minister of Justice for more than a decade, since before the Great War. It was Doherty who had appointed the Royal Commission in 1913, and Doherty who had ignored its report. *I am not going to make prison life easy,* he'd said then and he'd been true to his word. But the amendments to the Penitentiary Act that created the Superintendent's post had also shifted to the Superintendent the power to rewrite the rules. Doherty had left it to his Deputy to apply the damper to this eager Hughes so bent on reform. *The memorandum hardly met the Minister's request for a plan ... While many of the observations contained in your memorandum commend themselves, they are of an absolute general character ...*

Hughes had not been discouraged. By the end of September, he'd compiled a fourteen-page document that laid out his program in such detail that even the cynical and lackadaisical could not fail to be convinced.

He would completely revise the Penitentiary Act, down to the very words in which the rules were phrased. A man committed to penitentiary would no longer be a convict, a name that conjured crime; rather, he would be an inmate, a label a man could discard with his prison clothes when he returned to the outside. The rules would be directed at making the best of a man, at encouraging him to set aside his past and work for a better future when his time inside was at an end. An inmate's freedom would be restricted as little as possible, so long as society was safe; and he would be able to earn further liberties as he proved his worth.

Hughes limited himself to fifteen recommendations, but they were the keystones around which the penitentiaries would be completely restructured. He would build seven new prisons, one in each region of the country, so first offenders could be separated from the perpetrators of serious crimes. He would put a school in every prison, so inmates could learn to read, study art or agriculture as they pleased. He would hire as teachers men with pure and lofty ideals, models of what a manly, God-fearing person could be. He would give every inmate useful work to do, and pay him wages that would be held until discharge to help him make a fresh start. Guards and keepers would be chosen, not based on whom they knew, but on their strength of moral character. And they would be trained in the gentle art of reformation before taking charge of convicted men.

The old idea that discipline meant harshness, rough treatment and punishment has no place in our penitentiary system today. Officers must be taught that men coming under their control are human beings, their fellow-men, and that they, as their guardians, must treat them as such, and that those who are placed in their charge are there not so much for punishment as for reformation.

If a quarter of a century at Kingston Penitentiary had taught William St. Pierre Hughes anything, it was that conversion to virtue could not be forced. Punishment might temporarily restrain manifestations of evil but only at the cost of rendering them more permanent and intense. Persuasion, patience and true religious influence—these were the instruments that would transform men possessed of wicked dispositions. To rebuild a man's character, his heart must first be touched.

The penitentiary staff Hughes inherited was so far from his ideal that it would have discouraged a man of less dedication and will. Officers were no longer hired on the basis of patronage—the new Civil Service Commission had eliminated that—but the qualifications set out in the Act would better fit a rubbish collector or a street cleaner than a prison guard: to be employed in a Canadian penitentiary a man had only to be under thirty-five; able to read, write and do simple maths; and have neither brother, father nor son working within the same walls. And even these minimal rules were as often as not ignored. Many of the men now taking the posts were returned soldiers who knew how to fire a rifle and obey a command but who had no notion whatsoever of how to influence a convicted man for good.

Keeping a stable roster of staff had always been a problem in the penitentiaries, but in the years immediately after the war, a steady procession of officers passed through the gates, a quarter of them leaving, usually not of their own volition, every year. Kingston Penitentiary was the worst. Forty-three officers—almost half the staff—resigned or dismissed within the past two years. Of the core of long-time instructors and guards who remained, at least a dozen had been under suspicion during the Royal Commission, their mail and their bank transactions closely watched. Although no evidence had been found to prove they'd been dealing in contraband, Hughes did not doubt for a moment that many were guilty.

Surviving such scrutiny must surely have bolstered the confidence of the corrupt. Their systems may have faltered, but tremendous traffic was still going on. Only the mutts, the novices, were caught receiving letters and post office orders from inmates' families and friends. Experienced officers hired a third party to receive the contraband, which they relayed to the convicts, exacting in payment a large fraction of what was sent. And then there was the trucking. Bone toothpicks and knitting needles, horsehair chains, tools and materials stolen from the shops: all sold for a pittance to the guards who marketed the goods outside the walls for what they were worth. How else could a guard support his family and buy a house on a salary of twenty dollars a week?

For inmates, money was not the object, but tobacco, the *sub rosa* currency of the penitentiary. With tobacco an inmate could bribe an officer, procure liquor, food or drugs, or pay another convict for services, loathsome and unnatural to a man like Hughes but inevitable among the confined.

Hughes held no prejudice against tobacco. He used it himself, and he understood how difficult it must be for a man accustomed to a pipe now and then to do without. But he had been at Kingston Penitentiary when each inmate had received a weekly plug and he had been there when the tobacco ration was stopped, and he knew that the contraband trade had been untouched by the change. Distributing tobacco inside the prison had not suppressed illicit traffic; it merely provided the inmates, free of charge, with an article of commercial exchange.

Tobacco was not the issue. The weed had never been kept out of the penitentiary nor would it ever be so long as human sympathy, human ingenuity and human cussedness endured. But trafficking, he believed, could be held to a minimum if the penitentiary were staffed by law-abiding, God-fearing officers who could not be bought.

Another two months had passed since Hughes sent his detailed plan to Doherty. There had been no response. Revising the Act was going to be a long, slow process. He was impatient to begin. In the aftermath of the war, the prisons were filling at an alarming rate. Whatever changes he could make while waiting for the parliamentary wheels to turn would benefit hundreds of incarcerated men.

Hughes bent again to the Memorandum before him.

Re: The medical examination of officers.

According to the existing Act, officers were required to be fit for service. An ill-defined rule, thought Hughes, one he could turn to his own ends.

• • •

It is reported that a medical examination is being made of all the officials at the penitentiary at Portsmouth in order to determine their fitness for the positions they hold. Such an examination has not taken place for many years and the older members found suffering from defects are likely to be retired with a gratuity, as there is no system of pension in force for prison officials. The examination was ordered by Superintendent of Prisons, Brigadier-General Hughes.

DAILY BRITISH WHIG
November 11, 1919

• • •

At precisely eleven o'clock on November 11, 1919, the whistle at the Canadian Locomotive Works blew. William Halliday stood, head bowed, beside his machine, thanking God once again for seeing fit to return his son to him. Not since the strike had there been such silence in the plant. The generator let out a steamy, long-winded sigh. At exactly eleven-o-two, the foreman flipped the power switch, reached up and pulled the whistle. William Halliday picked up his tools, and bent to his lathe.

• • •

Standing at attention near the middle of the auditorium, Phyllis flinched at the sound of the Locomotive Works whistle. The speeches had been long.

The first anniversary of the Armistice ... of the 900 who went from Kingston, only a hundred returned ... a shell-shocked world ... industrial and social unrest ... many have lost their

bearings and in all classes there is a tendency to regard the funda-
mentals of law and government as things meet for destruction . . .
Give us peace in our time, O Lord . . . Let us pray.

Thoughts of God failed to surface through the weight of memory. That crisp, still February night, not yet a year ago. Her sisters and brother gathered around the parlour table with their books. Her father in his big armchair reading the newspaper; she on the chesterfield, a makeshift sickbed; her mother beside her, sewing; Watch curled by her feet. It must have been nearing ten o'clock when the thumping and hammering began. Her mother's needle stopped in mid-air. The news-paper lowered to her father's lap. Again the thumping, louder than before. The door bursting open; Jack, thinner but still so handsome, clasping Mother in his arms. The rough wool of his bugler's uniform on her own cheek as he lifted her off the floor. The long night of laughing, crying, telling tales, all of it suffused with the fragrance of the eau de cologne Jack had brought her from Paris, France. But what she remembered best was the pure joy that flickered in her mother's eyes. She had rarely seen it before, and never again since.

• • •

The factory's whistle was carried on the wind out of Kingston, into Portsmouth and over the penitentiary quarry. The men looked up, their picks and shovels paused. They stood still as statues, as if lifting their faces to the thin piercing wail had turned their bodies into the stone they cut from the ground. Woollen pant legs flapped. One man, at the top of the rock wall, lost his cap in a gust.

The prisoner listened to the silence and wondered for a moment why the world seemed to hold its breath.

Then he remembered: streets filled with people, as if the shop doors had suddenly closed, pushing clerks and customers onto the sidewalks. Hundreds of people, thousands, shouting, crying, kissing, dancing, parting like the sea as the motorcar passed, grinning faces pressed against the window glass. The prisoner had leaned forward to hide the iron cuffs on his wrists.

What's going on? he'd asked the officer escorting him from the North.

Armistice. War's over. They signed the Peace this morning.

And that's what he'd whispered to the man who'd shaved his head later that day. Armistice. The prisoner had said little more, though he knew how keen the convict-barber was for news from outside. The prisoner had been happy to show his back to the street, to hear each of the four prison gates grind closed behind him. The inexorable stone walls had been a relief after the hope, the fear, the entreaties and farewells. He'd looked forward to his solitude, to serving his time and moving on.

As he'd been marched across the yard towards the cell blocks, the familiar mood of the place had settled over him. The massive grey buildings with their meticulously fitted stones and tall, arched windows that reminded him of church: righteous and unyielding, infused with a stern piety that in the cathedrals of his youth had been tempered with the play of light through coloured glass, here exaggerated with iron bars.

To the penitentiary officials, he'd been as insignificant as a stone kicked ahead of them down the path. But the convicts working in the yard had looked up as he passed. One had flashed a quick grin. A welcome: conspiratorial, tinged with pity and something harder. Shared knowledge of what was to come.

Whatever the prisoner had brought to the penitentiary, it had been stripped away within the first hour. He'd been photographed with a number at his neck, arms folded in front of his chest, eyes staring at the middle distance. Quarter turn to the right. Hold it. He'd stripped off his clothes and stood naked while a guard picked through his hair. He lifted one leg, then the other, exposed the soles of his feet. With a stick, they knocked his legs apart. He bent over as far as he could. He climbed into the tin bath, into brown water, sharp with disinfectant. They shaved off his hair. They ran their fingers over his skin, pausing at each mole and scar. They took his weight. They measured his height. They pressed his fingers, one at a time, on a black ink pad. They made jokes as he pulled on the coarse prison underclothes, the red and grey checkered trousers and shirt, several sizes too large, each piece of clothing from his socks to his cap stamped in black block letters: KP. It was not until they'd addressed him by the number on the white patch sewn to his coat that he'd remembered: it would be years before he heard his name again. And although he'd tried, he could not for the life of him remember who'd spoken it last, or when.

Chief Keeper Atkins had asked him questions—his habits, occupation, place of birth—as if it weren't already noted a few pages back in the great ledger, a book so enormous that a man with outstretched arms could barely span its width, so weighty it might have been St. Peter's at the heavenly gates. The prisoner had answered as he'd learned to, in monosyllables, without embellishment, except for "sir."

You have been admitted to this institution. It is my duty to tell you that having been convicted of a criminal offence, you have no rights. We will provide you with three meals a day, a place to sleep and work. We give these to you, not as a right, but because they are part of the rules of this institution. The rules I am about to read to you arc rules by which you must live, rules you must obey.

Chief Keeper Atkins's voice, slow and sonorous at first, had gradually gained speed and lost volume as he pronounced the twenty-five rules.

Every convict shall observe strict silence, and shall not hold communication with another convict.

He shall hold communication with the officer in charge of him on matters connected with his work, only; with the Surgeon on matters connected with his health, only; and with the Chaplain on spiritual matters, only.

When approaching an officer he shall do so in a respectful manner; and if desiring to speak, he shall address the officer as "Sir," and stand at "attention" while speaking to him.

He shall rise promptly on the ringing of the first bell, make up his bed, clean his cell and put it in order. He shall retire to bed promptly on the signal for that purpose.

He shall not be at any time in any place where he has not received permission to go.

The last rule had been barely audible, a slurred mutter:

The Statutory penalty for an attempt to escape, or for an assault upon an officer, is loss of all remission, a further term of imprisonment not exceeding two years and such further penalty as the Warden may impose.

Do you understand the rules?

The prisoner had nodded. Yes. Sir. And he'd been especially alert to what came next, for he understood that it was the unwritten rules that counted most.

Accept whatever happens to you. You deserve it. Mind your own business. Do your own time. Everything you get is a privilege. You are entitled to nothing. Understand? Nothing. In this place, you are nothing.

Live according to these rules, and you will get along very well. If you don't obey, we have ways and means of teaching you that it doesn't pay.

What an exception that first night had been, the end of the Great War softening every heart so that even in the penitentiary, the rule of silence had been lifted. Between supper and lights out, the convicts told stories and sang, liberated by their promise to be quiet the rest of the night.

The prisoner knew all the words to all the songs. When one had finished, he'd been among the first to strike up another: *K-K-K-Katy*, *Over There*, *Mademoiselle from Armentières*, *Oh What a Lovely War*. He hadn't thought of soldiers dead in their trenches or reunions with loved ones at home. He'd roared the words blindly, relieved to join a chorus, staving off the silence and the memories it would bring.

When the gong for lights out had sounded, the men kept their word. The cells went dark. Silence fell. Then out of the blackness, a final melody had risen from the ranges and resonated in perfect harmony through the vaulted chamber of the Dome. *God save our gracious King* . . . Somehow in the sweetness of the anthem and the sadness of the convicts' voices, the end of the Great War and the beginning of his time inside had become fused. He would never again think of one, or the other, without a tumult of jubilation, hope and despair.

The whistle blew a second time. One of the quarry guards yelled an order. The convicts picked up their hammers and shovels. The prisoner turned to face the stone. It had been exactly one year.

• • •

Phyllis sat on the horsehair sofa in the kitchen, a cup of rose-hip tea balanced on the cushion beside her. Her throat hurt. Her chest hurt. Each breath was a spasm in her lungs. She had felt ill all week, and this morning when her mother insisted she stay home from school, she had finally succumbed.

It was a significant defeat. Each winter, it seemed, she spent more time in bed than out, and so, in the fall, she delayed as long as possible the first admission that she was sick. From that moment on, her parents would be alert to her, watching for a glaze in her eye or high colour in her cheeks, forcing on her vile medicines that promised to induce robust health. She hated being the centre of attention, although she knew what they feared was true. The family had not lost anyone in last winter's epidemic, but the newspapers predicted another outbreak of influenza this year. If any Halliday were to succumb, it would certainly be Phyllis. She had always been the sickly one, weaker even than Betty, whom she coerced into leading the way to school as a windbreak for her lungs on the coldest days.

A rime of cod liver oil lay slick and bitter on her lips. It would be more difficult than ever to escape to the quarry from a sickbed.

She got up and poked a piece of wood into the cookstove. The house was chilly. Coal was scarce. Her father refused to buy it, not because of the price but out of solidarity with the coal miners and their strike. Phyllis paused by the kitchen window. With every breath, the sharp, warm scent of Keene's mustard rose from the plaster on her chest and mingled with the fumes from the wood. Outside, rain beat a haphazard chain of overlapping rings in the puddles on the street. The blackened branches of the elms, splayed against the dull November sky, seemed to her like roots; heaps of sodden leaves clung to the base of each trunk, as if the trees had buried their heads in the earth. She felt in her pocket for the convict's kite.

Friday, noon

Kind, Kind little Peggy —
Yours of this A.M. at hand! Now I have a very very sad story to
tell. My job at the little house is at an end. It was only tempo-
rary. The regular fellow, OK, was driving a horse & cart & I
was taking his place until they caught up in taking the stone to

*the crusher. But I can still get up there sometimes my-self. Here
is what we will do. We will make our connections on* <u>*Monday—
Thursday—&—Saturday*</u> *at noon and in the morning. In a few
more weeks I will be working back up there as B/4. We have only
a couple of more weeks work down below, then they will* <u>*have*</u> *to
put us same three back up* <u>*there*</u>, *for there is no place else to work.
But I will miss my morning smile, & that is the most of all.*

*I am sending you Sis's photo & if you notice the name on the
envelope, that is my name. I am in no hurry for you to give me
this picture back, any time will do.*

*This is noon, & as you know my time is brief, so you will
have to excuse such a short note.*

*Yours as B/4, Josie
DaDy long legs.*

*I'll write this P.M.
(Trust me)*

The photograph was creased deeply from corner to corner, distorting the woman's smile into a grimace. Phyllis squinted at the image, shortening the hair, exchanging the frill at the neck for collar and tie, hardening the line of the woman's cheek.

Joseph David Claro. Joseph. Josie. Joe. So he had signed his real name after all.

Phyllis went upstairs to her room, leaned over the edge of her bed and reached underneath, behind the boxes and shoes to the tall orange Ovaltine can. She pried off the lid and dropped in the letter and the photograph, then wrapped both her hands around the tin and shook it gently. The folded squares and cylinders of paper swirled like a monochrome kaleidoscope inside.

A coal barge groaned loudly as it made its way down the lake.

Another week and the boats would be silent. Eventually, the quarry would be silent, too. The hammers stilled. The men withdrawn. Winter was closing in. There was nothing she could do to stop it.

•••

In the absence of calendars and clocks, the prisoner devised his own measure of time. The setting of the sun and the tolling of the bell marked another day. The fullness of the moon, a month. The slick of morning dampness on the walls of his cell meant autumn had returned. And when the water in his basin froze, he would know that winter had come. The changing of the night guard signalled the passing of two weeks; the long lock-up in his cell, the end of seven days.

For six days the prisoner worked, each day an echo of the one before except for the food ladled onto his tray. Monday, pea soup. Tuesday, boiled beans and beef. Wednesday, mutton stew. Thursday, boiled beans and beef. Herring stew on Friday and on Saturday, barley soup. On the sixth day, work stopped early; the prisoner took his soup before the sun set. Then the bars were locked, the bell tolled and the seventh day began.

From four o'clock on Saturday until Monday morning at eight, the prisoner was confined to his cell. Forty hours in a room three paces long and one across. He slept. He ate, slowly kneading his bread into shapes that he nibbled bit by bit, a doughy head, a little fist, rolling the parts around in his mouth to pass the time. He paced, counting out his steps, enumerating his breaths, taking inventory of his thoughts, fortifying the walls that kept his memories caged. And he sat on his bunk, watching the fingers of sunlight on stone, keeping track of imaginary hours by the creeping shadows of the bars, the solitude and the silence stretching time until the prisoner could hear each second snap.

Sometimes he read. In his cell, the prisoner had a Catholic hymnal, one library book and the Bible. His literary taste ran to romances and dramatic tales of the courage of presidents, kings and soldiers, the fictional doings of real men. But by Sunday he'd usually read his one allotted novel several times, and so he turned to the Good Book. He read the story of the flood, when it rained for forty days. The story of Elijah, fed by ravens for forty days. Nineveh, given forty days to repent. Moses on the Mount, awaiting God's word for forty days, and Christ in the wilderness, without food for forty days. From God's own Word, he learned that the forty-hour lock-up was no accident of prison routine. It was the divinely designated number for the torture of the soul.

Sunday was the dark fundament of the prisoner's week; Friday, its crowning glory. On Fridays, the gang left the quarry early in the afternoon. Inside the walls, they marched single file past the ranges, crossed the yard and climbed to the second floor of the southernmost penitentiary block After the dust and the wind, the resonant tumble and blast of the quarry, the bathing room was intimate with clatter. The rap of boots on wooden floors. The churning of the laundry machines next door. The hiss and swish of the shower baths. The short scrape of razors; the clippers' brisk click-click-click. The rustle of clothing pulled off and on. Orders shouted. Bodies hustling from barber chairs to change stalls to shower baths to the long wooden bench that ran the length of one wall. Through it all the buzz and crackle of a dozen conversations, slyly boisterous, skittish with haste. Guards, easily distracted in the hubbub, turned away from bodies bent over each other like nestling spoons.

The prisoner yelled his number at the wicket and caught the bundle of fresh clothes thrown at his head. Incarcerated for barely a year, he was near the end of the line arranged according to prison hierarchy, from long-timers to new fish. The barber chairs and shower baths were already full. The prisoner sat on the bench to wait, his bundle on his lap.

The air was sharp with the smell of soap. He slumped against the wall, muscles relaxed, his body anticipating the steaming water, the luxury of being warm and clean. It wouldn't last long. By Saturday, the tang of lye would fade under the assault of his glands. But naked in the water, his face lifted to the spray, with neither prison issue nor iron bars to remind him where he was, he would feel almost human again.

The bathing room recalled languid afternoons passed in small-town barbershops. The barber's hands, soft and obsequious, gently tugging the skin taut as he scraped at the hairs buried in fragrant foam. The steaming towels, the jocular teasing of the older men, the sweet sting of Florida water on his cheeks, the swish of the soft little whisk across the nape of his neck.

There were no such niceties here. When the prisoner's number was called, he bent over the basin and lathered his own face and throat. He barely had time to work the soap into the week's stubble before the Shiv raised his razor to begin.

The Shiv was Russian, a professional barber convicted of theft. He could be counted on for a close shave, a generous hair clip and a steady supply of information from every corner of the penitentiary. Barbers were the news dispatchers of the prison, whispering gossip in a convict's ear—who'd just come in and for what, who had tobacco to sell, who O'Leary's target was this week, who was going over the wall—as they bared his cheeks and scalp.

Big shakedown with the screws, whispered the Shiv, wiping his razor on the grey towel that hung off the chair. Clippers buzzed and crackled around them like twilight insects aroused. The barbers stood ankle deep in hair. From morning to night they ran their shears swiftly over skull after skull, cutting close to the scalp, as the law required, catching skin and moles and scabs in their haste, sending convicts from the chairs with bright ribbons of blood trickling down their foreheads and necks.

Traffic to the chairs never paused long enough for a barber to sterilize his tin tools, and the prisoner once again thanked the guardian angel who placed him before the man whose skin erupted with syphilitic sores.

They're parading all the screws before the Surgeon. Some stiffs'll lose their connection, sure.

From time to time, the prisoner gave the Shiv a plug so he'd go lightly with the clippers or pass a package to a friend. The barber assumed, like everyone else, that the prisoner dealt through a guard. The Shiv's news was of no consequence to the prisoner, but it served his purpose to let the convict-barber think it was.

Thanks. I'll bring you a little something next week.

It's getting cold out there. How be I leave a little extra on?

• • •

Friday P.M.

Hello Peggy —

Once again I have the pleasure of scribing you a few lines. As regards to that photo, I know it must be ruined. I never put that there, for as you see it was Friday & we always go in so much earlier than usual, on account of it being our Shaving & Bathing day. So I gave it to the other fellow (the one whom I was referring to in my last Kite as OK) & he never knew what was in it, so he squeezed it up into a small parcel. He told me what he had unknowingly done & you can imagine how I felt. However, I never told him the damage he no doubt has done. I am anxious to know, so in your next tell me what it looks like. If it is very bad, tear it up, or do anything you like with it. Keep it if you wish to do so. With the help of God I hope I may myself be with her soon!

• • •

The prisoner crouched low and pressed his ear to the grate in the back wall of his cell. He thought he'd heard muted footsteps in the narrow passage between the backs of the cells. Officers of the penitentiary sometimes squeezed through the gap in their stockinged feet, listening for whispered messages, sniffing for smoke, spying through the Judas slits. The prisoner held his breath. For the first time since his correspondence with the girl began, he was losing his nerve.

The rumours in the bathing house had been confirmed by an odd rotation of the guards. Something was up.

Convicts afraid of losing their contacts were curious, suddenly, about how the prisoner came by his smoke. He felt the guards' and instructors' eyes on him, too. In the quarry. In the yard. In the line-up. In his cell. Their backs had stiffened in the past week. He knew what they were thinking. If worse came to worst, reporting a convict with a private connection might save a man his job without incriminating a fellow officer or jeopardizing his own source of extra cash.

Lock-up!

The call rolled down each range, the voices of the night guards spiralling into the Dome, tenor, baritone, bass, mingling in extended, discordant harmony like the chant of untutored monks. The convicts stood at attention in front of the bars of their cells. When his turn came, the prisoner wound his hands around the metal bars and pulled his own door to. The guard threw the bolt, rattled the door and moved to the next cell. Bang. Grate. Rattle. Cell secure. Bang. Grate. Rattle.

The moon was full, perfectly framed in the windows beyond the bars. The prisoner could hear OK shuffling about in his cell, lowering his table, putting his supper tray through the bars, making ready for bed. In the cell on the other side, soft guttural moans and a rhythmic swishing sound.

The guards had brought the new man in at suppertime, his hands jammed into a leather muff that constrained his arms close to his body. He did not look to be much more than a boy, but he was strong. It had taken two guards to lay him on the bunk and fasten the truss to the bars.

Poor bastard, thought the prisoner. In the next hours, the boy would learn how deep human misery can be. Before first light, remorse would flood his soul. He'd fear for his life, pray for death like a man being drowned.

The nights will get better, thought the prisoner. Monotony will drug you into nonchalance. You'll find interests in the prison to help ward off remembrance, then the thought of the day of your release will keep you going till the end. But tonight, the first night, that will be the worst.

The syncopated rhythm of lock-up beat in decrescendo through the range. The officers would be busy for several minutes. The prisoner took a paper, pencil and envelope from between the pages of his Bible.

Thursday P.M.

Hello Peggy:

I got Tob ok this A.M. Many thanks: It pleases me to know you are writing a letter to Sis. If you have not sent it yet, give her my best regards.

Please excuse short Tab. I'm getting more writing material in the morning. Oh, many thanks for them envlopes.

True Friend,

DaDy Long Legs

(Trust me)

The convict folded the letter and slipped it inside the envelope. He picked a piece of mortar out of the wall beside his bed and fingered a twenty-five-cent coin out of the crack. He pushed the mortar back in place and slipped the coin into the envelope, licking the flap to seal it. As an afterthought, he wrote on the outside

PS. Also get cigarette paper. Inside, note contents. DaDy

The prisoner tucked the kite in the waistband of his drawers. He took off his shirt and trousers, damp with perspiration and heavy with stone dust, and hung them on the pegs above his bed. He pulled on his nightshirt and climbed into bed, tugging the wool blankets up over his chest. He was tempted to pull them right up over his shorn scalp but he didn't dare, in case he fell asleep and missed the footsteps of the night guard who made a circuit of the range every forty minutes. A convict's head had to be near to the bars and exposed through the night, so a guard could see it every time he passed. In the mood the officers were in, they would report a man just for snuggling a blanket too closely about his ears.

• • •

Saturday A.M.

Dear little friend Peggy:
I got yours Monday AM at noon & as usual, was pleased to get same. This is Friday but I always put Sat A.M. knowing you will not get this untill then.

First of all, I must say that I was—well it would be mocking to try & express, how pleased I was to receive that box of choco-late. I tell you Peggy, they were <u>lovely</u>. <u>Grand</u>. I haven't eaten any of the meals to-day (except breakfast). And why should I eat. One can't after such luxuries.

*Me angry, at <u>any thing</u> you should say. ME ANGRY—
NEVER! In reading yours, I could never see any-thing but
kindness, pleasure & humour. Tell me where, & why, & how, &
when could I ever commence to thank you for all you have done
& are doing for one placed as I am. Not in miles would one find
people who would <u>look at us, let alone</u> do a favour. I've had the
opportunity of meeting all classes of people, & in all walks of
life, not only on some few occasions, but every day that I worked
in what I call my line of business as Salesman. And, as I believe
I mentioned once B/4 in one of my Kites, I am somewhat of a
physiognmonist & flatter myself with saying, I am a very good
judge of Character. Peggy, <u>believe me</u> when I say true friends are
scarce & we should always be ready to please & accomdate them,
any time the opportunity avails one the pleasure. You know the
true & familiar saying, that if one should throw his old friend up
for the new, he deserves well if he should lose both.*

*Peggy my little friend, I would not be writing like this, as
if I knew you for years instead of weeks, if I was not so sure <u>that
you are not</u> in the least narrow-minded. I am almost sure of my
ground, & know that you understand me thoroughly. Say, Peggy
I will write a letter to my Sis Ruth, as soon as I hear from you, &
perhaps I may leave same behind as usual Sat P.M.*

*OK, the fellow who is in charge of the Palace, was saying that
our instructor, Knowledge Box, was going to bank the Palace with
snow as soon as the snow comes, so I may have to explain some-
place else to hide our Kites. The Palace has two little doors. One
door is cut across the center so the bottom part can be pulled open
very easily. I will leave my messages right near, where they can
be easily seen & got. Also, you can leave yours in the same place.
The opening is large enough to crawl in, so don't have any worry*

of not being able to get any-thing in. That is, in the line of books,
Tob etc. As you know, me or OK are always in the Palace first,
for either one of us are always sure to have the key. But then, this
is only in case it should snow, & we would have to bank the little
Palace. I don't think we are going to (not if I have much to do with
it anyway) ha. ha. But its best to be sure, eh.

   With this $2.00 kindly get me smoking, the usual kind.
These little "picks" I am sending are not what I would really like
to send, but I know Peggy will understand. Its a foretaste of what
I hope to be able to give you for a remembrance of DaDy long
legs. So for now By. Bye.

Josie

DaDy, long, legs.

(Trust me) Excuse scribling, Hurry.

● ● ●

By the time her mother came into the kitchen, Phyllis was already measuring oats into the water steaming on the stove. Her mother lifted the yoke of her apron over her head and tied the strings loosely at her back. One hand strayed around her hip and massaged the side of her belly with gentle, deliberate strokes. The sky had momentarily reddened when Phyllis crept into the quarry at dawn, but it darkened now as the moon crossed paths with the sun. Through the twilight of the eclipse, Phyllis could see the pain that tightened the line of her mother's mouth.

   The woman looked thin and worn. Phyllis stared at her with a clarity of vision often experienced by travellers but which comes sometimes, too, in homely settings when a familiar object is cast suddenly in extraordinary light.

   Phyllis went to her mother and kissed her on the cheek.

Good morning, she said.

Her mother put her arm around her daughter's shoulder and bent the girl's forehead to her lips.

What's this? She fingered the curve of bone that held her daughter's hair in place.

Phyllis pulled back from her mother's embrace. She put her hand to the convict's pick and pressed it deeper into her curls. One of my school friends gave it to me.

Phyllis turned to the stove, her back a shield against her mother's voice.

I got the mail yesterday.

Her mother's tone was light, conversational. Phyllis concentrated on stirring the porridge. She had stopped for the mail after school. It was her job, after all. The mail slot had been empty. The postmaster had not told her that someone else had been there first.

This came for you.

Her mother pulled something from the pocket of her dress and laid it on the kitchen table.

Phyllis turned just enough to read the postmark on the letter. Detroit, Michigan. There was no return address.

Who is writing to you from the United States?

The question hung between them, heavy and distinct.

Phyllis had always thought of herself as a little slow-witted. It took her longer than most to figure sums or to catch on to themes. And she was always the last to get the point of a joke. But at this moment, her brain was spinning stories at a dizzying rate. A girlfriend had moved to Detroit. A chum was visiting a sick aunt in Michigan. The letter came from an evangelist she'd heard about in church. Frantically she followed the thread of each lie, but those that didn't end in hopeless tangles dissolved in her grasp.

And where did you get this?

Phyllis could avoid it no longer. She turned to face her mother. To look at what she held.

Bits of stone dust clung to the spine of *The Reckoning* by R.W. Chambers, the book Augusta Halliday held in her hand. Inside the red cloth cover was stamped *Property of the Penitentiary at Portsmouth*. Phyllis did not have to ask if her mother had seen the imprint. The casual questions had flattened to a demand.

Phyllis had slipped the convict's book among her other school texts, thinking that in the usual morning confusion, no one would notice it there. His letter was still inside.

This book is fiction but it's backed on Historical Facts. President Lincoln is my favourite character. I think he is grand. I know you will enjoy this book & after reading same, let me know if you want any more.

The floorboards creaked as the rest of the family moved about in the house. The oatmeal scorched on the stove.

Ain't this an ideal meeting place for our Kites? Suits me perfectly, no trouble for me (all for Peggy) but, who can tell, some one may help your Bro or Sisters in some sickness or accident, or in one of the many ways of helping one another in the world. Who can tell? Only God.

Phyllis could hardly bear to hear his words read aloud.

How is your dear Ma? You & her seem to be quite great chums. I notice her in the morning watching you until you are out of sight. Nothing like a good ma & we only get the one! & when she is gone, my God, I think I would go Bugs if I heard my ma Died while I was incarnased in this Hole.

Outside, day turned to night as the moon stood squarely in front of the sun. Watch whimpered softly in the yard. Augusta moved closer to the lamp to read the last lines.

As a keepsake & remembrance of Dady Long Legs after I leave here, if I should send you a nice little ring with Peggy on it, would that be alright?

Phyllis stood gripping the turned knob of the kitchen chair. When Marion came into the room, her mother spoke to her. Phyllis did not hear what was said. Her mother's hand closed on her elbow, guided her into the front room. The door clicked shut behind them. Phyllis sat on the chesterfield, her mother at her side.

Telling her mother about Daddy Long Legs was easier than Phyllis would have thought, had she been able to give shape to this circumstance at all. She confessed to mailing his letters, to passing on the letters that arrived at the post office for him. She told her about the kites she and the convict exchanged. The chocolates she had given him and the hair pick he had made for her from bone. And the book he'd lent her. She told her about going into the quarry late at night and, sometimes, early in the morning while the rest of the family slept. She did not tell her about the money the convict had given her or about the tobacco she had bought. And she did not show her the Ovaltine tin, half-filled with folded squares and rolls of paper, hidden under her bed.

Her mother refrained from asking questions. She sat still and let her daughter speak.

Do you think what you are doing is right? her mother asked gently when Phyllis was finished. The woman's fear was barely discernible in the smooth texture of her voice.

I don't know. It doesn't seem wrong to help him. Sometimes I'm frightened. I wonder what would happen if he was caught.

And what about you? What if you are caught?

Oh, but I've been careful, Phyllis said quickly. No one knows. Really. Her mother lilted her eyebrows. Except you, now.

What you are doing is dangerous. And you lied: that was wrong. But, she added slowly, it is not often wrong to help someone in need.

She should have known that her mother would not be angry. Hers was always the calm voice of compassion in the house.

When I am in doubt as to whether my actions are right, I kneel down and ask God's blessing, her mother said. If I can't do that, then I know that what I am doing is a sin.

Her mother went to the bookshelf and took out a small book, barely larger than her palm. On the inside cover was written, *Keep this for the Givers sake and read it for thine own, Portsmouth, 1884.* It was her grandmother's Bible. Her mother opened it near the back of the book and, with her eyes uplifted, let her finger fall on the page.

Romans 3:10, she read. *For all have sinned, and come short of the glory of God.*

She looked at Phyllis.

Christ is our model. He did not despise the convict who hung beside him on Calvary. We cannot abandon this man either. We are here to serve God in whatever way He presents to us. We have asked for God's guidance and He has spoken.

The morning sky began to lighten. Phyllis had broken her vow of silence, she had confessed to her mother; her father would know the details soon. She would have to tell Daddy Long Legs what she had done. She only hoped that he would forgive her and guide her in what to do.

December

Phyllis was barred from the quarry. No one had forbidden her, however, to stand at the edge of the yard and wait for the convict to pass.

The morning was brittle with frost. Blades of grass crackled under her footsteps as she crossed the yard. The house, the trees, the rocks were ashen, as if the cold had bled the landscape of its colour in the night. Only in the east was there some life to the sky, a ruddy flush behind the Dome that rose like a beacon above the penitentiary walls.

Phyllis still received the convict's kites. For that, she was grateful. Of all the words that passed her way in a day, only these few mattered. Conversations with her family seemed false by comparison, though she had known these people her entire life. The convict was all but a stranger, she had never looked in his eyes, never sat close enough to wonder if his hand might brush hers, yet she knew him and he knew her, better than anyone else on earth. She could tell him anything. And that was a pleasure as intense as any she had ever known.

The letters shaped her days. The writing and the reading of them, of course, but also the waiting, storing up the news she would share with him, the sweet, sharp anticipation of opening the envelope he had folded closed. It was impossible, she knew, but often, standing by the Palace, she'd been certain she could feel his touch still warm upon the page.

Her brother was the messenger now. A fourteen-year-old boy, her parents reasoned, would be less suspect among the rocks. Phyllis had known enough not to put up an argument, but her fears had proved true. The passage through her brother's hands altered the convict's words, undermined somehow the certainty of their connection.

As much as anything, Phyllis missed her moments alone among the rocks. The quarry had become her sanctuary, an unlikely secret garden of stones. Even after it was declared off limits to her, the place rarely left her thoughts. Its sounds haunted her. The heavy rhythm of the crusher grinding boulders into macadam. The sharp, metallic drip of hammers driving wedges deep into the stone. The explosions that made the window panes shiver and clattered the painted plates against the wall. The crunch of wooden wheels on gravel, the sound shifting, like a temperamental violin, with the weight of each load.

The din was a siren's call, drawing her back to the rocks. She could not resist for long. It would be so easy to arrange: one plant for the messenger, another for her. She would have to do it eventually, when the convict needed more from her than words.

Snow began to fall, flakes as big as flowers, weighty and luxuriant, crocheted into a gauzy fabric that draped between Phyllis and the gang disappearing through the quarry gate. She had not seen him look her way.

● ● ●

Wensday P.M.

Hello Peggy:

Say, Peggy! I was angry this AM. when I never noticed you untill I was almost past the corner. I am as a rule the last one on the left side of the line coming out & the 2nd from the front going in on the right side. I was busy talking with the fellow walking with me & unfortunately was not looking in that direction. I will not be fooled again.

Perhaps you are getting tired of my Kites but I would not like to disappoint your messenger, for its bad enough for the poor Kid to go through all this trouble, & then when he gets there to be disappointed. What could I give him for a present? Say, a jack-knife? A pair of woolen mittens? Darned if I know!

My little friend whom I was referring to in my last Kite is not crying to-night, but this A.M. I noticed his <u>very red eyes</u> where one could easily see that he put in a sleep-less night. Poor kid! I do really feel sorry for him! & believe he thinks I am someone of impor-tance, for he is at a loss to know how in the world I can get tobacco etc. But he will not be here very long untill he is all wised up! I see he is working in the Tailor Shop; he will be ok for the winter.

You see my manovers on the Hill of late, running, jumping & the hands <u>always continually</u> going. That's in order to keep warm, for all the clothes we have given us would not be enough to dust a fiddle. But you leave it to Dady L.L., <u>he will not freeze</u>. Two suits of underclothes, two pairs of socks, two pair of mittens. Of course, we are only allowed one pair of each, but I happen to know where they keep their issue & you know what the Good

*Book says, Ask & you shall receive, & the Lord helps those that
helps them selfs. Well, I am strong on the latter, ha ha.*

 *I had a beautiful dream some time ago. I dreamed I was
having a fine feast & was about to have a drink of something
good, was about to take it when I changed my mind & says, no,
I will have mine hot. While he was gone for the hot water, I woke
up. So I'll have mine cold in the future.*

 *Say Peggy, when I hear from you, I'll assure you, I will
write a nice <u>long, long</u> Kite, so hoping you will be pleased with
this literaly garabbiolo, I am as B/4*

Dady. L.L.

Joe

•••

William St. Pierre Hughes stood dwarfed by the North Gate of
Kingston Penitentiary. He had always found it odd that the prison was
so rarely called by its proper name. "The Penitentiary at Portsmouth"
was a trick of the tongue that distanced the namesake from its city,
which preferred to be known, it seemed, by its university, its military
college, and its cemetery, Sir John A. Macdonald's final resting place.
The prison that stood on the outskirts had been disowned, a mangy,
monstrous cat consigned to the doorstep. Hughes stretched his hand
through the bars and grabbed the iron ring, knocking it three times
against the wooden door. As the Superintendent waited for the guard's
key to grind in the lock, he made a mental note. Henceforth, this place
would be referred to exclusively as Kingston Penitentiary. When his
reforms were made, the city would beg to claim the prison as its own.

 O'Leary was waiting for him just inside the first gate. Good morning, Deputy Warden. I trust you received my telegram. I am here to inspect the penitentiary.

The cell blocks, the tailor shop, the kitchen, the hospital, the Prison of Isolation, the quarry, the farm: Hughes saw them all. At the dinner hour, he declined to eat. Instead, he passed the time alone in the Warden's Office. For almost three months, the penitentiary had been without a Warden. That in itself was not unusual. The position of Warden was not an easy one to fill: in the past eight years, six men had run the institution. But never had the top post been vacant for so long. And never before with a man like O'Leary left in charge.

O'Leary had an unhappy manner of dealing with his men. That was how he had put it to the Royal Commission. He had been too civil. The truth was, O'Leary treated both convicts and officers like some low-class kind of cattle.

In a penitentiary, the Deputy Warden was like a chief of police, responsible for discipline of every sort. He supervised the officers, assigning them their duties, visiting them at uncertain hours to make sure they were alert, reporting any man who was absent, drunk, slovenly dressed or conducting himself in a manner unbecoming to a penitentiary guard. It was the Deputy who investigated reports against convicts; it was the Deputy who presented each case to the Warden. In fact, most of what a Warden knew about his penitentiary was filtered through his second-in-command. Under a weak or absent Warden, the Deputy's power over convicts and guards alike was absolute.

Hughes looked around the Warden's Office. O'Leary kept the room with the casual nonchalance of one who expects to stay. Papers spilled off the desk; stacks of record books toppled in the corners. The glass fronts of the bookcases gaped, bound copies of reports and regulations leaning this way and that, none of them, as far as he could judge, shelved in order. It was a disgrace.

More than two months had passed since Hughes's first inspection. Hardly a hair was disturbed from the previous disarray. O'Leary had had time enough to come around. He should have known, Hughes chided himself, that the man never would.

When the course dictated by good sense was also that of self-interest, a man would be a fool not to turn in that direction. It might go against his character, but when the alternative was self-destruction, Hughes expected—not unreasonably, he thought—a man would be motivated to change.

But O'Leary had not changed. The officers were still slovenly, buttons missing from their coats, boots unbuffed, not a single hand raised in salute as he passed. The convicts looked cowed. The record books were haphazardly kept, if at all. He'd found maggots in the oatmeal, piles of horse manure not six feet from the well, the hospital ward a moaning, stinking mire. The Surgeon would have to kick aside manuals and soiled bandages to reach his patients strapped to the wooden examining table. And though he'd pointed out these things to O'Leary once again today, the Deputy had made no excuse. There was no deference in his attitude, no humility in his voice.

O'Leary's manner unsettled Hughes. The Deputy Warden's failure to make even a pretence of trying to impress the Superintendent caused Hughes to doubt his own judgement, to suspect the presence of some factor that he'd neglected to figure into his calculations, one that might make a mockery of his careful strategies.

O'Leary must know that Hughes was privy to all his petty scams. How he sold the top-grade pork raised on the penitentiary farms, bought the cheapest pork bellies to serve to the inmates and pocketed the difference; his trick of giving the hardest shift—thirteen hours of tower duty with meals hauled up on a rope and a honey bucket to relieve himself—to the officer who refused to play his games; the sexual favours he turned a blind eye to; the beatings and months in shackles that fell to inmates he chose to despise. The Deputy Warden ran the penitentiary like a private fiefdom, with the most corrupt officers as his right-hand men. Yet O'Leary showed no shame, not the least anxiety about his job. In fact, Hughes had the impression that his inspection was barely tolerated, as if O'Leary answered to some higher power.

Perhaps Hughes was wrong, too, about the politicians. He'd still had no response from the Minister of Justice to his outline for a new Penitentiary Act. Perhaps, despite his sound arguments, the politicians were not convinced, would never come around. Waves of apprehension and panic washed through him, leaving him clammy and weak, as if from a fever. He saw O'Leary's face, smug, impassive, across the courtroom as he was interrogated by the Royal Commission. He had planned to harness the past to goad his present work but now he felt his memories slipping out of control, threatening to engulf him, impel him to ends he did not intend.

Hughes put his hands on the scarred oak top of the Warden's desk and pushed himself to his feet. The medical examiner would find O'Leary unfit. As Superintendent, he would have no choice but to relieve the Deputy Warden of his duties.

The decision refreshed him. He would not humiliate the man. But he would see him out of this office. Today. For the sake of his penitentiary. For the sake of the men who lived on both sides of the wall.

• • •

MAY APPOINT OUTSIDER

Penitentiary officials who have served the institution and the Government faithfully for the greater part of their lives, and who entertained hopes of promotion to higher positions for which their training and attention to discipline fitted them are apparently doomed to disappointment. At the present time, Inspector Fatt is endeavouring to get things in order so that when the new Warden is appointed everything will be in good shape. Daniel O'Leary, the Deputy Warden, has gone to Florida on a three-months' vacation.

DAILY BRITISH WHIG
December 11, 1919

• • •

Sunday P.M.

Dear little friend Peggy —
Once again I have the pleasure of scribing you a few lines.

Ruth, my Sis, will be down to see me one day this week. I got a letter from her yesterday. My Bro is coming home for Xmas & perhaps he will come also, but I hope he don't. I don't want him to see me in this outfit. He would laugh, yes he would, & kid the life out of me, that's his ways, but he would do any-thing in the world to help me. To show you the difference, my other Bro in Detroit, the one who I was telling you about me ruining his car, etc, well if he seen me, at once he would start & give me the devil & end up with good advice.

I see the snow is here at last, but there will be plenty of tracks by noon. I don't know yet whether or not I will leave a few $ or not. If I do, you need not be in a hurry about getting same. Say, Peggy, am I not pushing this too far? Tell me if you see me imposing on your good nature, for honestly, since I've been in here & mixed up with so many different classes of people, I am forgetting how I should act towards friends.

I might leave a Kite in the evening, so if the messenger or

you should be playing around there, please have a look. This,
Peggy, is all the paper I have, & if you knew how my head is
bothering me I'm positive you would excuse Joe this time. So for
now, Good-bye.

DaDy, long, legs
Faithful friend,
Josie

(Trust me)

• • •

According to the official record, each cell in the penitentiary at Portsmouth measured five feet across, nine feet long, ten feet high. But the prisoner gauged the limits of his confinement in other ways.

The prisoner's cell was as wide as his outstretched arms. Standing in the middle, he pressed his palms flat against opposing walls, his body a conduit to the cold that hunkered in the bricks on either side. It crept into the flat of his fingers, snaked through the maze of metacarpals to his wrist, up his forearm, through his biceps, into his shoulder, insinuated itself between his ribs. It came at him from both sides, pressing towards his centre, the acid cold of the walls a thrilling antidote to the insistent, inescapable chill of the air. If he could hold the position long enough, he thought, he could freeze himself to death.

His cell was three strides long. In the time it took to count one, two, three, he could saunter leisurely from one end of his living quarters to the other. The slate floor was worn to a trough by almost a century of such strolls, more frequent in summer than at this time of year, when it was best to keep one's feet up off the ground.

Walking to the back of the cell, the prisoner faced a brick wall inset with two grates, each as big as his splayed hand—one, at shin height; the other above his head. Behind that wall lay the corridor where the guards patrolled, peering through the Judas slits. Across the darkness, the back of another man's cell. He knew these things as a blind man knows his neighbour's secrets: by muffled footsteps and whispered words.

Walking towards the front of his cell, the prisoner faced the bars welded inside a steel door frame set into stone. Seven cross-pieces made a grid of the gate, slicing each bar into uniform sections no more than a hand-span high. The bars were set far enough apart that the prisoner's whole palm slid through: he could wave his free hand in the air. The bars closest to the lock were doubled up, the space between them reduced to a finger's width. The prisoner caressed the groove at the top of a bar just under the crosspiece. A memento from one of his predecessors who had given up in despair or, he preferred to imagine, continued his patient filing elsewhere.

The cell was higher than the prisoner could leap. Arm extended, he jumped from a low crouch, straining to graze his fingers against the plaster. Again and again he leapt. His fingers swiped the spider webs in the corner, a splatter of fly specks, the light bulb's edge. Now and then, he would get up from his bunk and leap again, for the truth was that in the twilight of a sleepless night, if he stared at the ceiling long enough, it would drift away from him, and unless he reached out quickly, he feared, it would slip like the face of a half-remembered lover forever beyond his grasp.

The ceiling of the prisoner's cell was white. So were the tops of the walls. From the level of his shoulders down, the brick was painted green, thick layers of enamel that shattered against the toe of his boot, the chips fanning like a single-minded rainbow from the yellowed green of mucus to the grey-green of overcooked peas. Successive applications of paint had failed to obliterate the marks that previous tenants had made, the accumulated graffiti of dozens of petty thieves or, perhaps, just a handful of sophisticated felons. Numbers and dates were etched into every surface within reach, some only faint impressions, others gouged so deeply they would never be erased. The year one man came in. The date another was released. The length of sentence after sentence, spelled out in year's and months but mostly days. There were few initials: J.C., after all, could be anyone. Those who devised the penitentiary system assumed a man lost his sense of self when he was stripped of his name, but in a number, a convict's immortality was assured. At Kingston Penitentiary, there had only ever been one B16, one F327; as long as the building stood (and it had been built to last), there would never be another G852.

G852. The prisoner's personal identity code was etched, printed or stamped on every thing in the cell. Each item, prison issue. His clothes: one pair of trousers, one of underpants, one shirt, one undershirt, one pair of socks, also one pair of cell slippers, one pair of boots, one coat, one cap. A clean set each week. The bedding: one sheet, one pillowslip, changed every two weeks; one pillow; one mattress; one sleeping suit; one towel, changed each week; three blankets in summer, four in winter, changed every six months.

The hair-felt mattress and pillow stayed on the bunk, an iron frame with woven wire springs and fold-up legs that was hinged to the wall and hooked flat against it during the day. The pillow rested on a horizontal metal contrivance that could be raised or lowered as the prisoner preferred, but remained resolutely horizontal. Above the bunk, a length of painted pine with four large pegs held his bedding by day, his clothes by night. Hinged to the opposite wall, at the front of the cell, was a tabletop, three hand-spans across, supported underneath by folding brackets attached to the wall. With the bunk down and the table up, the prisoner could not walk between the two. On a shelf above the table stood his books and the signal stick, one end red for emergency, the other black for illness, the wordless code by which a convict caught the attention of a guard.

Between the table and the shelf, fixed permanently to the wall, were two boards as big as police posters. On one hung his eating utensils, fashioned in white nickelplate: a fork, a spoon and a runcible spoon, its oversized bowl clipped at one end into truncated, triangular tines. On the other, Kingston Penitentiary's Rules for Convicts, the canon of confinement, always within view.

Beside the table, a folding chair leaned against the wall. The only other furnishings were a lidless toilet bowl, set one foot from the side wall and one foot from the back, positioned so that when the prisoner sat to vacate his bowels, he was presented in profile to passersby. Beside the toilet, a packet of tissues, eighty-five per week, hung on a string from the wall. In the left-hand back corner, a sink, a quarter-hemisphere of brass, tarnished black and crusted with dirt. On the edge of the sink, a toothbrush, a dish of salt and an enamel-ware mug, dented and rusting. No drain plug. One tap. By the middle of January, the water in the toilet stiffened to a solid. The tap on most winter mornings ran dry.

Twenty cells, each identical to the prisoner's, were strung in a row to form one tier. Four tiers of cells rose one above the other. A narrow catwalk in front of each tier overlooked a common corridor. The only source of light for the bank of eighty cells: the narrow arched windows on the other side of the corridor. The only source of heat: the radiator pipes beneath the windows that carried warmth under the earth from the boiler room across the yard.

Four tiers of cells made up one range. Two ranges, back to back, joined by the spy corridors behind the Judas slits, filled one cell block. Four cell blocks radiated like the arms of a Greek cross from the vaulted tower at the centre—the Dome.

Each double range of cells was free-standing within its block. No cell abutted an outside wall. A prisoner at Kingston Penitentiary who tunnelled through the walls ended up in the spy corridor or in another man's cell. There was only one way out: through the cell door, along the catwalk to the balcony that circled the Dome's interior, down the spiral of iron stairs, past the guards. And no one entered a cell block, a range, a tier, a cell, except through the clearinghouse of the Dome.

For two years and a day, cell number 16, range 2, cell block C was the prisoner's home. Cell. From the Latin, *cella*, a storage closet. From *celare*, to hide. The root, also, according to the dictionary on his shelf, of the words cellar and conceal. Cell. A hollow receptacle. A cavity that contains. A monk's quarters. The basic structural unit of living matter.

• • •

Wensday P.M.

Kind, Kind Peggy —

Here I am again & only an hour or so since I seen you. You must of come home early to-night. Was you up there very long B/4 I appeared? I believe you are a wee bit bashful, are you? Its a very good point, I wish I was so.

I have not noticed Watch around lately. What has become of him? I seen him on several different occasions hiding his Bones. I called him by his name once, & you should of seen the look he gave me. If he looks at me like that again, why, I am going to steal his bones & bring them in & put them in some of the soup we get in here (some soup). Every time we have soup, I notice Lake Ontario goes down about twelve or fourteen inches. They should have a sign up—Pea Soup: Find a Pea, Get a Pardon.

Perhaps you have in your experience around the quarry noted how a hole is drilled in a stone in order to blast it out. Well, this A.M. I was striking the drill with an 8lb. hammer & the Boy who was holding the Drill was fooling & was putting his finger on top of the Drill & kept on saying, "Hit it Joe" "Hit it Joe". OK was kidding me for an hour, & by accident I did hit the poor kid's finger, smashed it. Oh, I almost fainted, turned me sick. But he only laughed, & would not go & tell the Boss & have something done for it. I told him I would go if he didn't, so he did & the Boss has been trying ever since to find out how it happened, but as yet he has learned nothing. Of course, he knows the hammer hit it, but that hand is not used when turning the Drill. Poor kid, I gave him some tobacco & here is what he said, "Joe, I'm going to have me other hand hit, as soon as this Tob is done." He's a little Irishman, a fine fellow, in here for stealing an Auto, always smiling, first thing in the morning & last thing at night.

Well, Peggy little girl, it seems a very long time since I've heard from you! I've been short of writing paper, but now I have plenty, bought a big pile when the clerk was out. I am as B/4

Your Affectionate Friend

DaDy L.L. "Joe"

I forgot to mention the letter I left, many thanks & (Trust me)

• • •

Ten cents each. The Inspector's request on behalf of the men in Kingston Penitentiary sounded modest enough until the number was multiplied by the eighteen hundred men in the federal penitentiaries. One hundred and eighty dollars, on top of the four hundred and fifty already allotted to bring Christmas to the nation's convicted men.

It is but once a year, even with a convict, the Inspector had said.

Christmas fell on Thursday: boiled beef and white beans. Even with an extra dime per man, the steward would be able to afford little more than the dried fruit, yellow sugar and eggs for a currant loaf, a poor enough substitute for the blazing plum pudding the servants would carry into the festive dining room of his brother's home. Yet there were those who would object to even a slice of currant loaf. Mustn't spoil the convicts, they would say, cornering him at some official function, champagne on their breath. They'll be so happy in prison, they'll never want to leave.

The bit of cake was the only gift the inmates would receive. It hadn't always been so. Hughes well remembered the parcels that had once arrived throughout December. Families and friends had been ingenious in their generosity. They'd sent photographs of wives and mothers, the image split from its paper backing and lovingly reattached with a dollar bill layered between. He had once taken fifty-two dollars in coin from a beautifully dressed, cooked hen; five dollars from a fig. A small pot of blackberry jam, not three inches high, an innocent-looking thing, and inside, a slim roll of tin foil wrapped around a roll of silk that held a tightly furled ten-dollar bill. He had pried open walnuts to find tiny vials of morphine, miniature whiskey flasks.

If Christmas in the penitentiary had been a little less austere, perhaps the inmates would not have been so diligent in procuring their own holiday cheer, but be that as it may, the parcels had had to be stopped. The poking and prodding and reaming out of every gift had absorbed the entire Christmas month, and when the presents that passed his inspection were finally delivered, they were mangled beyond use.

The afternoon was fading fast. Outside the North Gate, the procession of carts and automobiles thickened in the street as Hughes waited for his taxicab. How often he'd found reasons to return to Portsmouth. The sight of the penitentiary never failed to renew his sense of purpose. And something about the little village outside its walls inevitably freshened his spirit too.

Amid the shoppers, workers and veterans hurrying along the sidewalk, he spotted a band of university students, arms linked, staggering home from one of Portsmouth's taverns. *Good Christian men rejoice, with heart and soul and voice* ... The melody filtered through the bars of the North Gate, and with it came an idea. If he could not feed the inmates' bodies, he could at least nourish their souls. A Christmas concert! The tradition was as old as the first village schoolhouse. It smacked less of luxury than cake, and if the program were performed by the inmates themselves, it would be both educational for the participants and uplifting for those in attendance.

Perhaps he could even interest some government department in lending a projector and some film reels, something interesting but not too stimulating. Almost anything would be a novelty, especially for those who had been inside the prison since moving pictures were invented.

If he could have opened the window, Hughes would have tossed a coin or two towards the carollers. It embarrassed him a little to find cause for celebration in what was modest by any standard, and as nothing compared to the Christmas that his own family would enjoy. But any break from the routine would be welcomed by the inmates. And—this would impress the Minister—the concert would not cost the Department of Justice a cent.

•••

Friday P.M.

My Dear little friend Peggy —
I'm about to make an attempt at scribing you a long Kite but, I
will not guarantee you that it will be very interesting. Mostly its
always foolishness, eh?

So, I surmised correctly when I said I thought you's were
Scotch. I once had a lady friend who was Scotch. Her name was
Geraldine McIntosh & I thought a whole lot of her, & for a while
was sure her & I would be <u>even more</u> than true friends, until one
day she told me her Ma did not want us to keep company any
more because I was a Roman Catholic.

I sure would love to see that piece of potery about the teachers
you were referring about. I'll bet it would be real interesting! I
can't understand them teachers making Peggy do "C.B." [con-
fined to barracks] They should be ashamed of them selfs. I would
give them—! if I had a chance. At least, I would come & break
your way out, ha ha!

The Chocolate was delicious, & Peggy, thanks ever so much.
I still taste it, & my stomach has gone bugs. Yesterday was the
little Irishman's birthday (The boy I hit on the fingers) so I gave
him a little.

At present I am sitting on the edge of my bed with a blanket
over my shoulders & a white rag around my head. It's aching,
but just a little. I was wishing yours was better & now I have it,
but its not bad, & thank God that's all my Ailments. Outside of
Asthma & a little Headache, I am sound. So far this place has
not injured my Health, but many a poor devil dies in here with
consumption. Stone is a very bad article to work near.

They do some beautiful work in here, though, make some
very expensive monuments for the Government. You remember

Dr. Hanley who died only some few months ago. Well, no doubt, they will make some real nice monument for his grave, for he was very well liked by all the men in here. I've often heard some of the old timers talk about different Drs that was here. I wonder if your Grandpa was ever mentioned?

As no doubt you noticed, they have moved the Palace back a few feet & put another gang to work up there. They don't like working on the Hill, they say it is so windy & cold. Our Boss was saying to me, after I said how kind he was in not putting us up there in that cold wind, "Oh don't you worry Joe, we will have you up there in a very short time now." Little does he know how he pleased me when he made that remark. The three men who are working up there at present are a fairly good bunch, especially one little fellow with a lump over his eye.

There are, Peggy, all classes of men in this institution in every walk of life, from Judge on down to petty thiefs, but we are all one in here. We all go through the same punishment, no matter who or what he was B/4 he came in here. We have a Toronto Lawyer, also a minister working out in the quarry but, as I say, do we not all look alike? This minister, Peggy, is a consciousness Objector & only one of the few that are left in here. He expects to be liberated any time B/4 Xmas.

But, sure dear, even the Author of this book, R. W Chambers, done five years in a state penitentiary. And is he not a fine Author? He can make one love a Character & at the same time have murder in one's heart towards the villain. If you notice in the back of this Book I put a stroke with a pencil the book I would recommend any one to read.

As you see this is my 25th sheet & did I not promise you a long Kite? You know my little friend that I am trying my best, &

you must understand that, after all, we are true friends & trying
hard to keep up this most kind & interesting friendship. I am
going to worry you again B/4 Xmas for a few more dollar's worth
of Tob & then I will not bother you for a while, so until monday
A.M. I am, Peggy, your true

Friend Josie

(*Trust me*)

DaDy, long, legs

• • •

The streetcar into Kingston was crowded with Saturday shoppers. Vapours rose from their rain-soaked clothes, clouding the windows and obliterating passing landmarks: the penitentiary, Kingston Collegiate, the university tower. The streetcar, thought Phyllis, could be careering along the tracks to anywhere, its cargo of gift-buyers content to compare Christmas plans and pass comment on the unseasonable weather, leaving their fate to the smiling conductor who wore a sprig of holly in his cap band.

With her mother ill again and Marion visiting the wounded at the soldiers' hospital, it fell to Phyllis to do the Christmas marketing. Winnie had offered, but Phyllis was not about to let the child bride usurp so much. Suet and raisins, filberts and citrus peel for the plum pudding, butter and fine confectioners' sugar for shortbread; cranberries and candles for the Christmas tree. The bare essentials of the Halliday tradition, for the family could not afford a lot. Five months on strike pay had used up most of their savings; what they hadn't spent on necessities, they had given away to those more needy than themselves. It might be a frugal Christmas, but it would be a happy one, with Jack alive and home again.

Princess Street was busy. As she stepped from the streetcar into the crowd, Phyllis was struck as never before by the number of young men on the sidewalk. During the years of the war, it had seemed as if Kingston were a city of women, children and old men. Since Armistice, the young men had been drifting back, and now they all seemed to be downtown, wandering past the store windows in their greatcoats, loitering on street corners, hands cupped around their cigarettes. Phyllis had often seen Jack downtown with the others, leaning against the gas lights in front of Routley's or Cooke's. Several times when she was running errands for the convict, she had happened suddenly upon a knot of returned soldiers and had barely had time to turn away before Jack caught sight of her. She'd learned to take her business to tobacconists on the city's side streets, but she had a good excuse if she bumped into her brother downtown today.

The angry scars, empty sleeves and bleak faces of the veterans she passed robbed the season of some of its joy. Most of them, like Jack, had nothing to fill their days. The government had promised them their old jobs after the war, but there was no law against hiring back a man one day and letting him go the next. Jack and his friends had come of age as soldiers: the only tools they'd comfortably held were rifle and bayonet. Now some had taken up the government's offer of a farm in the West; a few found work in their home towns; the rest lived off their war gratuities and waited for prospects to improve, clustering around the city lamp posts, sharing two cigarettes to a match, living the vague dream of peace but unwilling or unable yet to abandon the trenches where their friends and brothers lay.

The Christmas displays in the shop windows delighted Phyllis, though she knew for Jack's sake she should have turned away in disgust. Only those who'd stayed home and profited from the war could enjoy such goods, he said. Pyramids of tangerines, kumquats, and coconuts lined the aisles at Carnovsky's. Tiered boxes of chocolate-covered cherries and cane-sugar Kewpie Dolls filled the window at Cooke's. In the drugstore, stereoscopic views of Niagara Falls, the Swiss Alps, Italy and France before the trenches were dug and bombs cratered the woods. And at Routley's, polished mahogany humidors spilling plump Havana cigars.

The man who does his full day's work and keeps his mouth shut is one of the bulwarks of any nation today. He is the world's best citizen. Angrily, Jack had tossed the editorial aside. And a man out of work who dares complain, he said bitterly, is the world's very worst. This was the payment he got for leading mules into no-man's-land and heaping his cart with blasted shreds of human flesh.

The pall of Jack's mood had been lightened a little by news of the end of the coal miners' strike. Soon factories would work six-day weeks, the trains would run again, the Locomotive Works would take on new orders and, perhaps, hire Jack and his friends.

Phyllis could not hold such thoughts for long. The window display at the College Book Store distracted her. Stacks and stacks of R. W. Chambers's new novel, *In Secret*. Daddy Long Legs would surely love that. But such a gift would be impossible to explain. As would the sweater she'd thought of knitting, or the mittens, or the warm scarf. He could take nothing of her inside the walls.

At Woolworth's, Phyllis stopped to buy two Chinese silk handkerchiefs, plain ivory, and embroidery thread in lavender, sapphire blue, chartreuse and marigold, gifts for Marion and Winnifred. Then she sat down at the Lunch counter and ordered a cup of hot chocolate. The walk in the freezing rain had chilled her through.

How difficult it was to give to someone who could not receive, she thought. The only safe gifts were those that could be consumed.

Candies. Tobacco. As much as he appreciated them, such tokens disappeared without a trace, leaving nothing of her to keep with him from day to day.

She had already decided on one thing, at least. She would offer to do more for him, to buy whatever he needed whether he had money or not. She would put it to him discreetly so as not to make him feel demeaned. She had even bought a small account book to keep track of what she spent. He could settle what he owed next summer, when he was free and they met face to face.

But such a gesture was too practical to serve as a Christmas gift. Phyllis drained her cup, licking the thick white porcelain to catch the last grainy bits of chocolate-soaked sugar with the tip of her tongue. She had to think of something else, something that would gladden his heart.

The idea hit her on the way home to Portsmouth. Her preparations absorbed the rest of the day: popping popcorn and stringing it with cranberries to make a red and white pattern on the thread; gathering pine cones from the trees in the park, painting them bright colours and stuffing the crevices with dried, cracked corn; packing suet into balls the size of her fist, shaking them in a frying pan on the woodstove to melt the surface slightly, then rolling them in sunflower seeds; looping the popcorn chains around the branches of the cedar at the back of the yard, hanging it with polished apples, the suet balls and painted cones.

When Phyllis saw the tree early the next morning dusted with pink snow and dappled with blue jays, cardinals and the brilliant black and gold of evening grosbeaks, it was, she decided, the most beautiful Christmas tree, the most perfect gift.

• • •

Sunday P.M.

Kind One:

First of all, I must say I was pleased to receive such a nice long Kite from you. You want to believe me, when I say I enjoy them.

No! no! no! no! my little Friend, you never in any way whatsoever hurt my feelings. Don't be afraid Peggy—I am good & bold & will not hesitate a moment in asking you to leave me a little smoking, if the time should come when I would not have the coin to spend.

Oh, oh, oh, you have no idea, little one, how grateful I feel towards you in all you have done & are doing for me. If you insist on trying to please your generous heart in spending some of your allowance on a big Tramp like me, get me a stick of chewing gum, just one stick, remember now, just one!

As you see, enclosed $5.00. Ask for smoking like a good girl, McDonald's Smoking Tobacco. You can make it in two bundles. I can handle it that way easily! & it will all be over so much quicker. No Peggy, there is no danger whatsoever! I have a good place to keep same but its like money on the outside, give, give & of course there are very few in here who ever have much to give. But the poor devils, no doubt if they had it they too would be the same as I, sure they would!

I was sure you would be fond of that Book. Was it not great? If at any time you should like another, just say so. Its a pleasure for me to know that I can do this little favour for you. Knowing it pleases you, it also pleases me.

Here I am writing & chewing gum. It's delicious & the kind I am fond of & believe me it will not owe me much when I get done with it.

This puts me in mind of the boy I was telling you about some time ago, that came from Renfrew & is in for stealing a Bottle of milk or some such petty larceny. Well he don't cry any more & now he is reconciled to the place & is well acquainted & almost Tuff. Any-how, I gave him a stick of that gum the other day, & he was very curious to know where & how I come to get that, so I told him the Warden gave it to me, & that he would give it to him if he asked for it. He really believed me & was about to put his name down to get his allowance of Gum. Luckily, I was there to stop him. He will not be so inquisitive in the future, but he is at a loss to know how I can get Tob etc, poor kid

(I am going to have a smoke)

With the onset of cold weather the prisoner had switched from chewing tobacco to cigarettes. It was like jumping from penny-ante poker to a high-stakes game. A man could indulge in a discreet chew now and then with little risk of detection, but lighting a cigarette was like burning a signal fire in a cell. The smoke drifted down the range into the nostrils of the guards lounging by the woodstove in the Dome. A convict could pay them off to temporarily lose their sense of smell, or he could wait until a waft of the bittersweet fumes told him another convict was lighting up, or he could take his chances and smoke beside the Judas slit, exhaling into the narrow stone corridor in the hopes that a guard had not chosen that moment for a surreptitious prowl.

The prisoner waited until the guard passed on his rounds, then he knelt beside the toilet, pried loose a brick and slid out the works. The penalty for possession of this little wooden box was steep: a week in the Hole, shackled to the bars, wrists padlocked as high as a guard could wrench them.

The prisoner held the works in his hand. He had often wondered who had first conceived of this marvel of ingenuity and efficiency. Inside the box was a flint, a nodule of the hard, dark grey rock that studded the limestone like raisins in a rice pudding. Most of the quarry gang earned a plug now and then selling shards of the brittle rock to convicts confined inside the walls.

Beside the flint lay a stiff scrap of burnt cloth, a corner of his coat which he had told the guard he had ripped on a rock. It had given him great pleasure to scorch the checkered cloth on the side of the Palace stove, and it gave him an extra measure of pleasure each time he lit a cigarette with the defiled scrap of prison issue. The moving part of the works was the "zipper," a round button of hard steel fashioned in the blacksmith shop. Two holes were drilled in the centre; through them passed a knotted loop of cord.

The prisoner took a cigarette out of his hiding hole. There was not enough time between the guard's rounds to roll a cigarette and smoke it too, so he always kept one prepared in advance. He balanced the cigarette and the flint on the toilet seat and crouched beside them in the corner. He held the box with its curl of punk cloth in his left hand and looped one end of the zipper cord over his middle finger. The other end he clenched in his teeth, stretching it taut. With his right hand, he gave the steel button a spin. It moved back and forth, propelled by the twist of the cord. When the steel was whipping around at top speed, the prisoner bent so it spun against the rock. Sparks flew. He manoeuvred the punk box so a spark landed on the cloth, igniting the charred fibres. He dropped the zipper in his lap, raised the punk box to his mouth and blew gently until the ember glowed. Then he put the cigarette to his lips, touched the thin taper to the orange glow and sucked deeply.

The heat from the burning tobacco rushed down the prisoner's throat and filled his lungs. With each inhalation, the smoke seeped deeper into his body. By the third draw on the cigarette, he felt the top of his skull lift off gently; thought escaped. He was pure sensation, twitchy and warm. He smiled and leaned back against the wall. After each suck on the cigarette, he puckered his mouth against the grate and blew his smoke like a lover's kiss deep into the blackness.

He rolled his cigarettes thin to keep his smoke short, make his tobacco last. Some cut their tobacco with shredded paper or dried grass but he preferred a real smoke, even if it meant indulging himself less often. He took one last drag. It tasted faintly of stone dust and skin, so tight were his fingers and lips to the burning tip. He dropped the tiny butt in the toilet and flushed.

I've reread the last few pages of my Kite & I was going to tear them up, but on 2nd thought, I think perhaps you will not mind me being so personal for as you say, we are well acquainted & understand each other perfectly, is that not so, Peggy?

Darn this snow. Say, could the messenger come in through our gate? There will be a path from the gate to our place of connections as the guard, also the water boy has to go out that gate 3 & 4 times per day. You say you always leave same in the mornings as you are afraid of the dogs carrying it away. I believe it would be safe to leave it there shortly after dark the evening B/4. I am only saying this because I believe you would much sooner not have the little messenger seen coming & going so often in the daylight & also, if it should snow at night, his tracks would be covered up B/4 the morning.

Say, did you hear the fog horn blowing last night? Does it not sound lonesome & dreary. Oh, Peggy, I will never forget that sound. We hear it all summer & are always glad when it stops, for one can hear the sighs that echoes through the nights, through every range of cells, & it speaks plainly of the misery felt.

We had some-thing new to-day for dinner. We had hash. At least, that's the name it goes under. One must shut his eyes & eat it. If at any time you should lose Watch you will know where he is. Yes, & they think it a real luxury. Oh, but I will be glad when my time comes, to be able to sit down to a real meal once again, but this is part of the game (punishment) and we must accept our little adversities here with stoical good grace, in the advent of enjoying future prosperity with a keener relish.

There is a piece of potery which I thought was real nice & I learned it off. Do you like potery? I love it. Any how, I am going to try & remember it as best as I possibly can. I will put it on a separate piece of paper.

Peggy, let me know please if my kites are too long & if they are dry. You have a great habit of saying, "This Kite is dry." I never think so. I am always more than pleased to hear from you. Only hope we can keep up the good work, & hoping the Snow will not interfere with our future connections, etc by-by,

I am Peggy, as B/4

Your friend, DaDy l.l. (Josie)

(Trust me)

• • •

Phyllis cut a length of lavender embroidery thread and wound it around the pages of the poem. *Oh Love! Pain's other name, Why cannot you remain?* Someday, she knew, they would sit on the quarry rocks together and laugh at this cruel Christmastime, and the shadows that fell over their present lives would dissolve in the moon's soft, white light.

• • •

The prisoner had been skittish all morning, waiting for the call. It was so rare in the penitentiary to know of an event in advance that he had all but lost the knack for anticipation. Most things happened without warning, like a clap of thunder out of a blue sky, but he had known for two days that he would have a visitor today. The officer had not told him exactly when, of course. The authorities always took care to preserve a thin edge of unpredictability. It kept the convicts on their toes.

At the midday break, he hurried through his meal to give himself time to spruce up a bit. He balled up his nightshirt in his fist and rubbed at his shirt and the front of his trousers to clean off the worst of the stone dust. He washed his face and hands and rubbed his teeth vigorously with salt. There was nothing he could do about the week's growth of beard. Or his shaved head. Or the smell.

The guard came for him in the chapel. Although it was barely past noon, the sun was so low in the winter sky that the yard was already steeped in the indigo shadow of the wall. The bell tower on the North Gate caught the sun and shone like a church spire against a sky as blue as the Blessed Virgin's gown. Walking alone with the guard towards this beacon, towards the outside, the prisoner dreamed for a moment that this was the day of his release.

Visits took place within the prison wall where it widened to accommodate the North Gate. In the middle was a wide, arched passage for the stone carts, supply trucks and prison gangs marching two abreast; to the right, the entrance for prison personnel and beyond that, the armoury, hung with rifles, handguns and clubs; to the left, the room where convicts met their families, within the same barrier that separated them every other day of the year.

The guard motioned the prisoner through the small door on the left and locked it behind him.

The visiting room was a long, narrow compartment. It looked

more like a dog run than a room: if a man were to pace back and forth he would have to pirouette at each end to turn around. The door to the prison yard was at one end and at the other, a wire partition stretched from floor to ceiling. Beyond the partition was a gap of three feet perhaps, then another wall of wire and another long, narrow compartment, the mirror image of his own. In the space between the two wire partitions sat an officer on a straight-backed wooden chair.

The prisoner tried to compose himself. It was bad enough that Ruth had to see him unshaven, rumpled and dirty. He wanted to show her by his bearing, at least, that he was well. That he was better than he looked.

When the guard opened the door to the other compartment, Ruth rushed immediately to the wire. The penitentiary had no mirrors, neither in the cells nor in the bathing room, but the prisoner could see himself reflected clearly in her eyes. He grinned to reassure her, and himself, that he was still the man had been.

How are ya, Sis? How's Ma? And Bro, didn't he come?

Thirty minutes. Every word hurled across the gulf between the wire walls, past the officer who, it seemed to the prisoner, took delight in interrupting every other sentence with a reprimand. That is forbidden here. You can't say things like that. And finally, If you persist in talking this way the visit will end.

Then their time was up. The prisoner watched helplessly as tears ran down Ruth's cheeks. He had tried to make the best of himself for her, but a few minutes with a polishing rag could not undo what eighteen months of cold, stone and bad food had done. Prison wore away at a man, like water dripping on a stone. It was not the gross indignities that changed a person, it was the bitter twist the penitentiary gave to ordinary things. Even these visits, granted as a privilege, were calculated to humiliate, forcing him to expose himself in this condition to a woman he loved, wiping out her happy image of him and replacing it with this haggard face and gaunt body, calloused fingers poking through the wires of his cage.

No guard could be spared to deliver the prisoner to the quarry that afternoon. He was locked in his cell where he passed the rest of the day engulfed in the despair that the visit unleashed. All his carefully erected walls, bursting at the joints. He cursed the penitentiary, he cursed the police and the judge who had put him there, he cursed his bad luck, he cursed himself. That he had caused such pain. That he had so much to bear. After the anger came the tears. Alone in the cell block, he wept. The Warden had been right. He deserved what he got. He was nothing. Nothing at all.

•••

Thursday A.M.

Dear little friend:

Peggy B/4 I forget, you notice my signals of late are not very loud, such as taking the hat off, etc. It has been so cold this last few days, it has been necessary for one to pull the cap down over the ears & thinking perhaps it may be noticed, I've been very particular, for on no account would I want any one to labour under the delusion that I was signaling to my little friend Peggy. Still, I'm always pleased to see you standing there.

A man that was doing life went out yesterday after doing some where around 8 or 9 years. He always claimed to be innocent. They say Father McDonald was responsible for his getting released. He sure is a fine man, a perfect Gentleman & good to us all. I am going to confession & communion on Xmas. It will not do me any harm, do you think so, Peggy?

Say, what is your front name? I often think it might be "Myrtle" but it's only a guess.

I wonder what made me think that? Brr-Brr, it's cold. I'm going to have a smoke, & go for a walk, up & down my cell— 15 min later, here I am again. While smoking & walking up & down, I was just thinking, would it suit you better, if I was to have a little parcel come to you, instead of the cash. It could be opened & given to me according as I would need same. It would come from Ruth & from Detroit. If you would rather have it this way, so much the better. Our only danger in the whole connections is our little messenger. As long as he is not noticed by anyone, our danger is nothing. But then, I suppose the quarry is like a graveyard when we are not out there.

Well Dear Peggy, as you notice, my Scribling is getting worst. That means my fingers are commencing to get stiff. So until our usual morning, I will close with best wishes to you & ma.

I am Peggy
Affectionate Friend

PS. Head ache is stopped
(Trust me)

DaDy, long, legs
Josie

• • •

On Thursday, December 18, the solar system formed itself in a perfectly straight line: Neptune, Saturn, Jupiter, Mars, Venus and Mercury stood in a row on one side of the sun, Uranus on the other. Scientists had not predicted the means, but they had all agreed: on this day, the world would come to an end.

Phyllis felt unsettled all day. Not that she really believed the Earth would cease to exist, but neither did it seem provident to completely discount such a once-in-a-lifetime phenomenon. Nevertheless, nothing unusual happened, and by the time she sat down for supper with her family, she had put the astronomers' prediction out of her mind.

It was a quarter past six before she noticed that the penitentiary bell had not yet been rung.

Perhaps something is the matter with the bell, her mother suggested.

By half past six, when the bell had still not tolled, Phyllis was certain: there had been an escape. No one said it aloud, but the words reverberated through the air like the refrain of a half-remembered song. Was it him? Was it him? Was it him?

The family lingered over the apple crisp, retelling all the old escape stories, one by one. How the first man had gone over the wall before there was even a wall, just a plank fence to contain the convicts as they built their cells. The trail of walkaways: men in outside gangs who had put down their tools and drifted off through the village, into the countryside, some of them returned within hours, some never heard of again. Those who had left but couldn't stay away, like Dr. Dill, who had escaped when the oldest guard now at the penitentiary had been a young recruit, climbing over the stone wall on a makeshift ladder, taking the mail boat to Ogdensburg, finding himself safe but so homesick for his family that he had sneaked back to Canada and within three weeks was again behind bars.

There had even been escapes from solitary confinement. When James Halliday had been Keeper, a convict had broken a hole in the arch above the door of his cell in the Prison of Isolation. He'd shifted the flagstone to one side, shimmied through, picked the lock on the cell next door, then with his accomplice, had sawn through a window bar and climbed out into the yard. They'd stolen discharge suits from the tailor shop, ladders and ropes from the carpentry shop and gone over the wall in the southwest corner near the penitentiary wharf.

Not too long ago, a Russian in the farm gang had escaped on horse-back into McAdoo Woods. But the escape that sent shivers up their backs had been from the quarry right next door. On a midsummer's day in 1870, one of the convicts working the lime kiln had sidled up to the guard and taken a handful of carved bones from his boot. As the guard leaned over for a closer look, another convict smashed in his skull with the ironwood stake from a sleigh. The convicts stole the guard's coat, his watch and his gun and headed into the woods on the far side of the quarry. The commotion of the officers storming by the house with their rifles drawn had sent Grandmother Halliday to her bed and thus was Uncle James born. The convicts were captured in less than a fortnight and one was hanged for murdering the guard, but the other, John Smith, was in prison for the rest of her grandfather's time, carving dice and figurines from old soup bones.

Though murderers walked their streets every day, the people of Portsmouth did not live in fear. Safer to live right outside the gates, they reasoned, than even a few miles away. A convict on the run rarely lingered close to the walls. He made for the United States, the dense woods or the anonymity of city streets.

Phyllis herself had witnessed the capture of two escapees. It was one of her earliest memories, huddling in the doorway of Halliday Electric while the Chief Keeper of the penitentiary chased two convicts down Princess Street. Major Hughes had recognized the men among the shoppers and run after them, shouting and waving his arms. A clerk at Routley's, observing the chase, handed him a gun and a box of bullets as he raced past. Everyone scurried off the street, into doorways and lanes, poking out their necks when no shots were fired, to see the Major with the convicts up against the wall, their hands held high. As Phyllis heard the story recounted yet again, she wondered which parts she'd truly witnessed and which she'd imagined from years of supper-table recollections like these.

That night, she lay awake, listening for footsteps in the snow, a spray of stones against her window pane. The trees, cracking with cold, drew her to the sill again and again, but though she stood long and stared, she saw no one in the yard below.

The next morning, on the streetcar to school, Phyllis learned the truth. Three convicts had slipped away from their guards as they were being transported from the penitentiary to the Asylum. One of them, Frank Cassidy, was a desperate man. The year before, on his way to the penitentiary, he'd leapt from the window of a train. This time, he was last seen crossing the ice.

Daddy Long Legs was still inside.

• • •

Sunday P.M.

My Dear little fiend Peggy —
Oh many many thanks for the Kisses. As soon as I got in a nice
quiet place where no person could see me, I at once put a Kiss in
my mouth & opened your Kite. Believe me, I enjoyed myself for
a few minutes, eating candy & reading. I am always anxious
for our appointed days of connection to come. The one particular
thing of all was your name—Phyllis. You say it is not a nice
name! I think much different & I will never forget it.

I was up on the Hill Sat A.M. & I don't know if you seen me or not, I was behind the Palace & was trying hard to get your eye, for I wanted you to see me going through the performance of eating one of your Kisses but <u>darned</u> if I could get your eye, & of course I did not want to stay up there too long for fear of any one getting wise. However, I had a real good look at you. But not at them eyes. I'll bet you have blue eyes, (I have). Am I right this time? Sure I am.

Quite an experience your Dad had. I've had some experience with cars. But, I am very fond of a nice machine. Are you, Peggy? & if I should ever have the pleasure of being in the position where I could afford one, it would be a <u>good one</u>, or none at all. I love a nice Cadillac car. How do you like my taste? Made in Detroit at that. Sure there is <u>nothing</u> in the world from stopping me to accomplish such, is there, Peggy?

Father McD was telling us some time ago, of receiving mail from a man who done four years in here. He left here with absolutely nothing, & today in his town, he is one of the most important of men. He gets twenty eight hundred a year as manager of this firm where he is employed, also has a daughter working in his offices. Father McD also states that this firm knew of him being here. But does it not show <u>once again</u>, where <u>Honesty is the</u> best policy. Well, he can accomplish such good, <u>why</u> not others?

Father McD was telling us today of the entertainment we are to have on the 29th. Something that has never happened in all his time as Chaplin & he says he was <u>more</u> than surprised when he was informed to the effect that we were to have important people coming from Ottawa & bringing with them, Orchestra also a moving picture apparatus & that it was the Dept of Justice that was the instigator. Does it not show that after all, they do think of us &

worry over our well-fare. Also, that they are trying to reform us &
have us leave here much better men than when we came in.

No doubt they (some of them only) are coming at last to the
conclusion that skill & patience will succeed where force fails. A
kind word goes a long ways, especially in our present unfortunate
position.

Say Peggy, when you are finished with the Book please put
a couple of envelopes in it please. Always wanting some-thing,
ain't I? I will not wish you the usual complements of the season
until my next episode, Wensday A.M.

Well, Peggy my little Pal, for now good bye & always keep
faith & confidence in your True Friend, Josie

DaDy Long Legs

(Trust me)

● ● ●

Securing one end with his thumb, the prisoner wound a strand of black horsehair round the tip of his little finger. Carefully, he slipped off the loop, picked up two lengths of horsehair from his lap and knotted them in alternate half hitches around the loop. Over and through. Under and through. Most evenings, he could finish one loop of the horsehair chain during each of the guard's rounds. Four loops between supper and lights out. But on this night, the cold made his hands clumsy, and the thick, wiry hairs were forever leaping capriciously from his fingers.

The rest of the gifts for the Halliday family were carefully planted around the cell. A bone knife for the boy, safe in the hem of his night-shirt. Knitting needles for the mother, slipped into one end of the mattress on his bunk. A hair pin for the girl, carved from bone and inlaid with brass, wedged between the pages of the Bible. Only the father's watch chain remained. The clasp and buttonhole clip, fashioned out of brass in the metal shops, had cost him a week's supply of tobacco. OK had procured the hair from the cart horse's tail. But the pattern he had chosen was too ambitious. The prisoner held the chain up to the light and counted the lacy, black links. Forty, including the one he worked on now. A little short, but it would have to do. Tomorrow was Christmas Eve, his last chance to deliver the gifts.

Footfalls sounded on the catwalk of his tier. The prisoner pulled the blanket over his lap, leaned against the wall and hung his head as if in a deep doze. As soon as the steps receded, he pushed the blanket aside and resumed his knots, over and through, under and through, the looping of the horsehair drawing him back to the sweet secrecy and joy he'd once known.

• • •

Augusta Halliday opened the cast iron door of the Quebec heater. She threw in a piece of split elm, poked it deep into the coals and added another. A smouldering fire Christmas morning was bad luck: only a brightly burning fire would bring prosperity in the coming year.

The Halliday house was still. Gussie was the first to rise, as usual, though it seemed odd to wander alone through the dark, silent house on this particular morning. Christmas should be bright and noisy, a joyous celebration of Christ's birth. In the dim predawn light, in the absolute quiet, the sense of foreboding that in recent months always weighted her heart, now spread unrestrained through her ample body until she thought she would faint with the fullness of it.

She'd had this feeling during the war, while Jack was in France. And especially when the telegram arrived from the British hospital.

Last Christmas had been filled with relief and thanksgiving, the Armistice still fresh in their minds. Jack was safe; he'd survived. He would come back to them whole, his lungs a little scorched but otherwise unharmed.

How naive she had been. How could the mothers have believed their boys would return as they had left—jaunty, handsome, a little wiser perhaps, but still their happy-go-lucky Harolds, Edwards and Jacks? Oh what a lovely war, they'd sung. And Jack in the bugle corps: he'd hardly seemed a soldier then. But it was strangers who'd returned to the village. Vacant-eyed, world-weary, four years of war pressed like sleep creases into their boyish cheeks. After the first embraces, silence. Even those who'd come back with their limbs intact, without visible scars, were wounded beyond cure.

Jack was one of the lucky ones. He had no work, but at least he had his family. So many of his friends had conducted their reunions with loved ones at the graveside, their homes emptied by influenza.

The Hallidays had a lot to be thankful for. The Locomotive Works was in full production, there was money coming in, everyone was healthy and at least William had work. Yet Gussie could not shake the heaviness from her heart. She had never felt so tired in her life. She busied herself in the kitchen, cutting the grapefruit for breakfast, putting on the kettle for tea. Her exhaustion came less from the body than the soul. She was tired of worrying. Tired of watching Jack's face for flashes of remembered pain; tired of listening for Phyllis, weighing her words for lies.

Everything was changing. Everything had changed. It was as if for the four years of the Great War, they had all held their breath, and now it was being let out in one long sigh, a great exhalation that toppled everything they knew and valued, leaving the world empty, bereft. Though her son had survived, what Gussie felt was loss. After the war, their lives were supposed to return to normal. It hadn't happened. And now, she was beginning to understand, it never would.

Gussie could hear the family stirring. She struck a match, and one by one, lit the candles on the tree. As she bent to the lowest branch, she caught sight of the rough brown paper of the convict's gift to her and though its message was kind, she read it with a premonition of dread.

May the hours as they go
Only good on you bestow
With all good wishes for a happy "Xmas" & may the new year bring you health & prosperity.

• • •

Xmas P.M.

My Dear, Kind Good little Friend Peggy—
While I am in this present mood of gratitude I wish to assure you how pleased I am at receiving that beautiful Box of Sweets & above all this lovely little Xmas card. I am sending it back to you, & I want you to put it in my next letter to my Sister, for to me, its value could not be estimated in this world's treasures. By sending it to Sis Ruth, I know I will never lose it.

Tell me Peggy, have you any idea of the great good you have been doing, & its value to one placed as I am? Great artists are prompted into their fields of labour by having such kindness rendered to them. This has been my pleasure & privilege, even though I am as degraded as base (to the world's eye) in being in such an unfortunate position as I am.

You say your eyes are not blue. Do you know what brown eyes denote? As one advanced in Phrenology claims,—Those with dark hair, brown eyes, ruddy complexion are of the sanguin temperament & are very loving, and are not fickle & changeable. But, Peggy, they say Jet Black hair denotes pride. If you say your hair is Jet Black, I will never again believe in Phrenology for you are certaintly opposite to that Statement.

This AM after Mass was over Father McD came out of the vespers & asked us to say a prayer for one boy's mother who died some few days ago. This boy was sitting near where I was, & he took it very hard. When you see tears in one's eyes in this institu-tion, you can rest assured that it's because one is really overflown with grief. It must be an aughtful shock to have it told you your Mother has died, especially when it comes at this time of the year.

Also it reminds us that even we in our predicament have many blessings to be thankful for. For instance, I would rather be in here twenty years than have it told me my Mother died. Oh, that she & all other good mothers may be blessed with a long & Healthy life. So I am going to ask you & your Ma to say a prayer for this Boy's Mother that her soul may rest in peace for all eternity.

My Dear little Friend, I don't want you to labour under the delusion that in expressing my opinions so openly, I am trying to impress you that I am _real good_. God forbid Peggy, no. Only as I said in previous kites to you, that it was my honest intention to try & accomplish some-thing good with the remainder of my life after leaving this institution.

At this very moment, they are playing a Victrola & you have an idea of what my feelings are, so please Peggy, if I have said any-thing that seems out of the usual, in regards to being too _personal_ please blame the music, & believe me when I say I am very down-hearted.

So, for this one & last lonesome Xmas day in this Hell, I will now lay back & listen & think of both the past & oh that beautiful future. I have no one to talk to, for we must keep strick silence, so I had to tell my little Pal, knowing you would sympathize with me. It honestly has done me the world of good to have the pleasure of having a friend to tell my troubles to. Good-bye.

Friday A.M.

I have just read my previous writings of that one unforgetful day (Xmas 1919) & I was going to tear same. But, on 2nd thought, as I mentioned several times B/4, we understood each other perfectly.

Many thanks for the pleasant greetings for the New Year & that you also stated you were anxious to see me released so I could once more be united with my friends. <u>MANY MANY THANKS</u>.

It will not be necessary for me to know your address as Sister Ruth will have same, & of course I can get it from her as soon as I arrive there. If for any reason I should be released any time B/4 my sentence expires, I will immediately on my arrival drop you, to your address, a post card & a short time after, write you a Kite. I am always afraid of being under this Deportation Act, that is the one particular reason I have all my mail addressed to the Canadian side. I have been notified that there are a great number of men from this place to be released between now and two weeks hence. I don't suppose there is any chance for me. It is very hard to get out of an institution in Canada, much more so than to get in.

Peggy once again I must use them two saddest words in our language, (Good Bye) & hoping to here from you as usual, I am Peggy

> *Your Faithful Friend*
> *Josie*
> *DaDy Long Legs*

(Trust me)

• • •

At midnight on the last day of the year, the bells of the Church of the Good Thief tolled: 1919 was done with; a new decade was begun. Phyllis crossed her arms and joined hands with her mother on one side, Jack on the other. Everyone in the room did the same, all her brothers and sisters, her grandmother, her uncles, aunts and cousins, until they formed a circle that wavered around the room. They began to sing, their voices, warm and husky with the spices of the wassail cup, mingling in chorus, sweet and robust, full of comfort, hope and joy. *Should auld acquaintance be forgot . . .*

The prisoner, listening to the silence of his cell, imagined distant voices raised in song. Happy New Year, he whispered to the wall by his bed. And the stones echoed back to him, Happy New Year to you.

WINTER, 1920

Let thy Friend no Secret know,
For when that Friend
Becomes a Foe
The Whole World will
Thy Secret know.

———————

DADY LONG LEGS

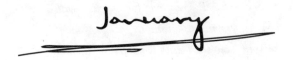

January

The temperature on January 1, 1920, hovered at precisely zero degrees Fahrenheit. The oversized thermometer outside the Kingston police station never wavered from early morning, when it was noted by constables coming off the New Year's Eve shift, to the end of the day when it was hastily checked by holiday-makers veering their horses and wagons onto the ice for the last crossing to Wolfe Island before dark.

The mercury wasn't the only thing stuck at the start of the decade. The world itself seemed becalmed. The century had endured a rocky adolescence: the Great War, Bolshevism, suffragettes and strikes. The departure of 1919 was celebrated with relief. Yet the new year was welcomed with caution, like a stranger reluctantly invited into a household that had recently suffered difficult guests. The twentieth century was about to come of age, and no one knew quite what to expect.

• • •

In China they have such a thing as professional mourners. These people are hired to wail and mourn at funerals.

But we don't go in for that sort of stuff in Canada. We detest "calamity howlers." We're strong for optimism with a big O. We look upon the pessimist as a traitor.

The word "unrest" doesn't scare us. Nor the word "red" or Bolshevist. We're Canadians. We believe in our strength, in our people, in our government, in our future.

And we greet 1920 with the faith that conquers.

DAILY BRITISH WHIG
New Year's Editorial

• • •

Phyllis sat by the attic window, wrapped in an old quilt. She'd made a nest for herself amongst the trunks and boxes, draping faded damask to soften the hard edges at her back, unrolling a piece of carpet at her feet. The air was chilly and smelled of dust, dry cardboard and musty woollens, but at least she was alone. She opened her diary at the flyleaf.

Phyllis Gertrude Halliday. King Street. Portsmouth, Ontario. New Year's Day, 1920.

She blew lightly on the ink and turned the page.

Resolutions, she wrote in large letters across the top.

Each year she vowed to improve herself in a dozen predictable ways. These ritual pledges she listed first, almost without thinking yet with conviction, like grace said before a meal. To be kinder, more thoughtful, less stubborn, more respectful to her parents, more diligent at school, more devout at church.

Her passion and zeal, she reserved for fresh promises: To be true to the convict. To bring him solace in prison. To welcome him when he was free.

Into the fold of the first page of the book, Phyllis pressed the pale mauve ribbon and the note he attached to her Christmas gift:

My little Pal
Hold this as a remembrance from Joe untill such time as I may
(with the help of God's grace) be in a position when I will be able
to offer some thing real nice.

Phyllis wiped a spot clear on the frosted glass. Through the lattice of willow and alder, she could see the convicts working in the hollow of rock below. Men small as mechanical toys moved between the limestone ledge and the carts. They lifted their arms up and down, hammering the drills with syncopated rhythm into the stone. The sound drifted up to her, a split-second delay between each downward stroke and its resonant Clink! She sat mesmerized, as if the incongruity between what she heard and what she saw would be resolved if only she waited long enough.

Phyllis often watched the convicts from the attic. She couldn't tell which was Daddy Long Legs, but she knew he was there, hammering into the rock that flowed like a grey subterranean sea under the foundations of her house, making the floor beneath her quiver when the stone was finally cleaved.

The clear space on the window glazed over with ice. Phyllis blew on the glass, wiping at it with the corner of the quilt. Something was happening below. She scrubbed at the glass again. One of the guards spurred his horse across the quarry floor, up the winding path to where the Palace stood. The closer she leaned to the glass, the more she obscured her view. The guard was off his horse, running to the Palace, his greatcoat flapping. Phyllis scratched at the frost with her fingernails. The guard had a convict up against the wall.

The letter. ·

Phyllis strained to see the men's faces but they were too far away, too blurred to make out.

The book.

With one hand, the guard searched the convict, across his chest, down his thighs, between his legs. Then the men and the Palace dissolved in the ice laid down by her quickening breath.

Phyllis did not see the convicts scramble into line or quick-march through the quarry gate; the outriders, with their rifles drawn. By the time she ran downstairs, pulled on her overshoes and hurried down the path, the quarry was silent, no one in sight.

● ● ●

The next day, the convicts did not come to the quarry. During the night, snow began to fall and the temperature dropped. By Friday morning, the streets of Portsmouth were scalloped with drifts. Thick white piping highlighted the dark folds of limestone in the abandoned stone pit.

The temperature continued to slide. The snow stopped. Still the convicts didn't come.

The Week of Prayer began. Epiphany came and went.

The quarry lay silent, shrouded and empty.

Phyllis watched and said nothing. She gave no letters to Gordon to deliver; she left none in the Palace herself; she didn't dare check to see if what she'd left on New Year's Day was still there. Her days constricted to a simple routine around the constants of school, home and church. She became an exemplary student, a model daughter, as if at last her resolutions had worked an effect. She no longer waited each morning by the quarry road. She told no one what she'd seen. In the house she moved quietly, spoke softly, making space for the knock at the door. Outside, she grew alert to shadows, to unfamiliar faces turned her way, to footfalls behind her in the snow.

That no one came for her, she took as a good sign. If prison officials had identified her, they would have arrested her by now. Their absence could be interpreted another way, of course. That they needed more proof. That each day's reprieve added weight to the evidence they compiled.

At night, Phyllis dreamt of flight. Of manoeuvring her father's car along a narrow track through a swamp, hands rigid on the wheel, her foot barely reaching the pedals. Of stalling, the key unwilling to turn, the car sinking, running board and fenders sucked into the bog, wet earth creeping up her thighs. And the convict, sauntering down the road ahead, oblivious to her cries, Help me! help me! oh, help me please!

She pushed the clammy sheets away from her legs. The sensation of mud, heavy and cold against her skin, stayed with her all day. And though her fingers kept the collar open at her throat and she pushed her hair from her face again and again, she could barely hold back the panic that rose to smother her.

•••

You could tell a Red, they said, by the way he dressed: grey over-coat of medium length, black fur collar, a soft felt hat. And you could tell by the way he walked: skulking down streets in the wrong part of town, eyes darting side to side as he traced a route too circuitous for a bloodhound, or the Red Squad, to follow.

They met in secret, in back kitchens and barns, never more than ten at a time, or cells of five if they suspected spies, straggling in from taverns, phone booths and railway stations where, in exchange for a whispered password, they learned where they would gather that night.

They slipped back and forth across the border, pamphlets sewn into the linings of their coats, books stashed in the false bottoms of their carpetbags, importing inflammatory messages, sometimes cash, and now and then American comrades, desperate for a way out.

Hughes had never seen one, at least not that he knew. Yet, if the *Daily British Whig* were right, Bolshevists were everywhere. Disguised as metalworkers and ministers, they'd built the barricades in Winnipeg; as Finn and Russian farmers, they were settling the West; at May Day picnics they preached insurrection and free love; at Armistice Day parades, they heckled the men who'd defended Christian values in the trenches of France. With their propaganda pamphlets and their wild foreign talk, they'd convinced honest men to lay down their tools and walk away from their jobs: postmen in Ottawa, British Columbia loggers, miners in the North, hydro-electric workers at Niagara Falls, Kingston machinists and shipwrights. Canada was being flooded with the scum of central Europe. The unrest they stirred up had already packed the prisons full. And now the Bolshevists themselves were at his penitentiary gates.

Scores of Reds are flocking to Canada to escape the net thrown out by the U.S. government, warned the editorial in the *Daily British Whig.*

Four days before Christmas, the Americans had deported hundreds of radicals to Russia on a ship they'd christened the *Soviet Ark*. On the second day of the new year, another five thousand had been arrested and jailed, a quarter of them in Chicago and Detroit, both cities known as Bolshevist strongholds, both just a midnight boat ride across the border to Canada. But J. Edgar Hoover had passed his secret lists to Ottawa, and now a thousand Reds awaited their fate in Canadian county jails.

The only thing worse than a corrupt man, thought Hughes, was a zealot. And now a thousand zealots were but a judge's gavel from his penitentiary cells.

A few socialists had already filtered into Kingston Penitentiary: three men convicted of possession of banned literature—police had found the journal of the Social Democratic Party, *The Philosophy of Socialism* and *Preamble of the Industrial Workers of the World* on their bookshelves—and a couple of radicals, founders of the still-born International Workers' Association, convicted of conspiring to organize the violent overthrow of the government of Canada. A few others had been convicted of making treasonable statements: eastern Europeans and Scandinavians mostly, agitating among the miners and loggers in the North. Hughes had followed these cases closely. The socialists had already been after the guards to unionize and he had no doubt they would try to work their wiles on the inmates, too. Half a dozen couldn't do much damage, but a thousand . . .

Deport them, he'd told the Minister. Nothing less would do.

Since the Winnipeg General Strike, police had had the power to arrest foreign-born Canadians and deport them without trial. Section 98 of the Criminal Code outlawed groups that advocated political change by force: those who attended their meetings were guilty of sedition unless they could prove their innocence. Fourteen organizations had been banned, including all foreign-language groups, cultural associations with a socialist bent and the Socialist Party itself. Socialist reading matter—the *Communist Manifesto, Das Kapital,* Darwin's *On the Origin of Species,* Plato's *Republic*—was forbidden. Strong measures indeed, but the Great War had just been fought, revolution was in the air, these were dangerous times.

Unless the Dominion Government promptly enforces the immigration laws, the seat of the Soviets in America will be transferred from the United States to Canada.

Hughes was dedicated to reform, but he would not countenance revolt. It was British institutions that made Canada a civilized nation. Of these, the penitentiaries were his to protect. He would not see their high stone walls hung with red Bolshevist flags like the Czar's Winter Palace.

Hughes could hardly imagine the kind of prison an anarchist would devise. One without cells, no doubt. Without guards. Stripped of hierarchy, of individualized punishment. All for one, one for all. A Bolshevist prison would be like the great, open wards of a hundred and fifty years before, when criminals and their families had bedded down together on straw, sustained by relatives or by what they could beg at the grates that looked out on city sidewalks. Prisons then had been holding pens where wrong-doers awaited the gallows or the transport ships that would remove them permanently from society. Punishment was simple vengeance, with no possibility of redemption for the man or woman who had committed the crime.

The Age of Enlightenment had given Canada its penitentiary system. Although Hughes was too modest to say as much, he thought of himself as the latest in a proud lineage of radical, progressive penologists, a lineage that began with John Howard, the man who first applied the pragmatic principles of the Industrial Revolution to the criminal soul: subjected to humane, scientifically calibrated punishment, any wrong-doer could be reclaimed; thieves and drunkards and vagrants, converted within the "factory" of the penitentiary into productive, working men.

Howard advised removing convicts from the open wards of the old gaols, those nurseries of crime, and installing them in buildings designed for work and contemplation, where each man had his own cell, barely big enough for a hammock and a loom. Convicts never laid eyes on another human soul: their meals were delivered through a slot in the door; they exercised in private yards and wore masks when they were transported down the corridors. Every aspect of every day was strictly regimented, from the clothes the convict wore to the amount of work he was expected to do and the food he ate. Through rigid discipline applied to the body, Howard believed, moral behaviour would be reformed.

Jeremy Bentham stood next in the line of enlightened penal reformers. To Howard's principle of penitence through solitude and hard work, Bentham had added vigilance. He designed the Panopticon, a prison that married form and function, moral intent and practical purpose. A state institution with the all-seeing eyes of God. A maze of individual cells tiered around a central tower where an inspector watched both the inmates in their compartments and the guards making their rounds. Like an invisible spider in the middle of an intricate web, the inspector observed every move without himself being seen.

Howard and Bentham went too far. Total solitude drove a man mad. But the principles that they articulated—individual redemption through work and solitude under constant vigilance—were still the noble backbone of the penitentiary system. If the system was less than perfect, it was not the principles that were at fault. Rather, the men charged with implementing them were flawed. If Hughes could remove the corruption, like scraping off the rust from a poorly used machine, refit it, oil it and put it in the hands of skilled, trained men, the penitentiaries would function again as its designers intended, protecting society while remaking those who threatened to disrupt law and order.

But the Bolshevists were bent on destruction. They would reduce society to rubble so they could fashion the world anew.

Ship them back, thought Hughes, closing the newspaper and creasing it sharply at the folds. Back across the border, back to the United States. Back to Moscow and Mother Russia, back to the steppes. Just keep the foreign agitators away from my penitentiaries. Let me make my own reforms.

• • •

PRISON POPULATION GROWS

The penitentiary population of Canada is steadily on the increase. Two years ago it totalled 1,400; today it is up to 1900.

Asked as to the reason for this condition, General St. Pierre Hughes, superintendent of penitentiaries, attributed it laconically to "unrest." The situation certainly has become much worse since the war.

DAILY BRITISH WHIG
January 13, 1920

• • •

The prisoner struggled awake to the fading reverberations of the third strike of the gong. He lifted the back of his hand to his fore-head. It felt white, neither hot nor cold but a bloodless white. He raised his head off the pillow. The pounding in his skull drove him back.

He could hear the morning noises of the men: cell slippers shuffling on stone; bedclothes rustling on iron bunks; the scrape of hinges against brick; great hacking coughs, spitting, pissing. The sounds this morning were curiously muffled, as if coming from a great distance or through a barrier, a dense wad of gauze, perhaps, or a weight of water.

The prisoner forced himself upright. He could not formulate a thought, but he knew this much: he had to work. No work, no remission: no time off his sentence for diligence. He pulled on his trousers and shirt and leaned against the cell gate, cooling his throbbing head on the bars. The rapid click of steel on steel as cell locks flipped open exploded like Gatling guns in his ears. Wedged between OK and the little Irishman, he made it down the catwalk and through the breakfast line-up, but his hands shook too desperately to hold a tray. The smell of oatmeal porridge made his stomach heave.

Back in his cell, the prisoner collapsed on his bunk. A little more rest, he thought, that's all I need. The quarry gang had been put to work renovating the North Wing, converting the Keeper's Hall to cells. It was a little warmer there. Easier than breaking stone.

When the gong sounded again, the prisoner struggled to his feet. The blood drained from his head; a prickly blackness swept in. He fell back on the mattress. It was no use. When his head cleared a bit, he reached for the signal stick and poked it between the bars, balancing it on the lock so the black end protruded. The guard who arrived to collect the convicts for the quarry gang tossed the stick back into the cell and made note of the prisoner's number in his book. Sometime later, maybe minutes, maybe hours, the bars of his cell swung open.

G852. Sick call.

The prison hospital extended at a right angle from the tip of cellblock C, as if the penitentiary's designer had thought to turn the cruciform of the cell blocks into a swastika but, unhappy with the effect, had given up after the first stroke. The hub of the two-storey building was a rotunda where the sick and new arrivals to the penitentiary waited their turn in front of the Surgeon. Flanking the rotunda were the doctor's examining room, the dispensary where medications were doled out—cascara to move the bowels, tussives for catarrh, heroin drops for the grippe—and the operating theatre where throats were lanced and herniated intestines were pushed back inside ruptured abdomens without benefit of anaesthesia or sterilized instruments.

The prisoner slumped against the wall of the rotunda. Last winter, a quarter of the men had fallen ill with influenza. The whole prison had been quarantined. There had been no visitors for months. The doctor himself had died with it and hadn't yet been replaced. Every so often, a medical man came out from the city, but so many were sick with the 'flu that was sweeping Kingston for the second winter in a row that for days on end no one came.

G852.

The doctor sat dwarfed behind the sick-call ledger. Just a boy, thought the prisoner. A medical student from the university, his arrogant manner betrayed by two bright spots of colour on his cheeks.

G852.

Yes, sir.

Are you ill?

Yes, sir.

Have you been vaccinated?

Yes, sir.

The prisoner started to explain about his head, how he was burning up, and sweating, and couldn't eat, and was this the 'flu, might he be dying after all . . .

That will do. The doctor wrote in his book with one hand and waved the prisoner to one side with the other. Next.

The prisoner knew enough not to insist. It took all his energy to hold himself upright. He prayed the doctor would send him to the hospital. His chances were good, he thought hazily: he had rarely signed up for sick call. It went worse for a man who stood too often in front of the doctor's desk.

He'd learned that lesson early. In his first months in penitentiary, he'd waited in the rotunda with the man who sat next to him in the stone shed. The man was often absent, and over the weeks, the prisoner had noticed how the man's body had withered, his features sharpened with pain. Yet on the day they sat together in the rotunda, the doctor would not hear the man's complaints, would not give him medicine, ordered him back to work. When he collapsed on the hospital steps, the yard officer grabbed his shoulder, jostled him to consciousness and pushed him roughly into line. The man whispered that he could not go on. The guard lifted him up by his shirt and shook him, his head bouncing from side to side. The prisoner had shouted at the guard to stop, grabbed his arm and spent twenty days in the Hole for his trouble. By the time he got back to the stone shed, the man was dead.

The doctor stood up and closed the ledger. The guard herded the prisoner and two others through the rotunda and up the stairs to the hospital ward. At the top stood Hospital Overseer Wilson. He'd been charged with O'Leary in the Royal Commission, though nothing had come of it. Behind Wilson stretched the hospital ward that was his personal domain: an interior corridor of thirty-six cells, a window and a toilet at each end of the hall, and on one side, a kitchen where the patients' food was prepared by the overseer and his convict-nurse assistant. Each cell was the size of a door frame: a canvas cot, a bucket commode and a water pitcher took up every inch of space. Men suffering from tuberculosis, syphilis and diphtheria bedded side by side with those incapacitated by broken bones, lumbago and haemorrhoids. Unventilated even by Judas slits, the ward stank of stale blood, suppurating flesh, diarrhoea and the carbolic Wilson boiled in pots outside the cells to disinfect the air and mask the smell.

The prisoner noticed none of this. He pulled off his clothes, pushed them through the bars to Wilson. He crawled onto the mattress, pulled the blankets over his chest and fell into a deep, burning sleep.

Day and night blurred into a single sweaty dream. The prisoner awoke, mouth dry, lips cracked, his brain on fire. He tried to lift the pitcher of water to his mouth, but it was made of stone. He called out for the convict-nurse—help me, help me, help me please—but no sound came from his throat. Or if it did, his cries were lost in the skein of howls and pleas and groans that wove through the night. He collapsed into sleep and startled awake again, freezing now, his body slick with sweat. Unmindful of the rules, he pulled the blankets tight around his head, curled into a ball and cupped his fists around his privates, rocking from side to side, burrowing into the straw mattress until, on bare canvas, he sank again into sleep.

Someone took his temperature. He raised his head off the mattress, as he was told to do, and swallowed a bitter oil. Once a day, he struggled awake to the sound of his number shouted over and over again. Wilson threw a pill between the bars, and he scrabbled through his bedclothes like a blind man, finding it by touch, swallowing it with his spit. Once, he awoke to a voice high overhead, asking if he wanted to go out. He stared at the looming figure, concentrating on the words. Go out. Where? Why? After long deliberation, he shook his head, but the man was gone.

The fever passed. He felt light, as if the heat of it had dried the blood in his veins. He was no longer delirious, but he drifted in and out of a warm, heavy sleep. Night and day fused into perpetual twilight in the tiny cell, a cosy, comfortable gloom punctuated by the muffled flap of the convict-nurse's rubber-soled shoes on the linoleum floor. Trays of tea and bread materialized outside his bars, sometimes a section of orange to suck or a rag twisted around a nipple of crushed ice. Now and again he stumbled on his knees to the bucket to empty his bladder, but he never left the cell, and his mind never wandered beyond its walls. He loved this grey cocoon of stone, the heavy pulse of the bell, the sweet, interminable sleep.

When the walls took on substance, when he pondered once more the world he couldn't hear or see, the prisoner knew he was getting better. His tongue was thick with thrush, his skin reddened and raw where his bones had pressed against the canvas cot. His blankets were foul with sweat. The stench from the bucket caught his breath. It had been days, maybe weeks since he'd had a bath.

One morning the doctor appeared with Wilson in front of his bars. We will give you your clothes, he said, and see if you can walk.

The prisoner pulled on his pants and shirt. He stood up. Wilson unlocked the cell door. The prisoner passed through into the hall. His legs quivered. He clutched at the bars. The window at the end of the corridor pulsed with light.

Walk up and down today. Tomorrow you can go out. You are losing your good remission here, the doctor added sternly.

The quarry. The prisoner had not thought of it for he knew not how long. The days had slipped past him, unremarked. Peggy. As the mist of illness dissipated, the bits and pieces of his life came back into view. And he remembered: The book. The kite. The overzealous guard they called the Scout whipping his horse across the quarry to the Palace gate. The search. The prisoner had not seen the girl since.

Hand over hand along the bars of the cells, the prisoner made his way towards the brightness at the end of the hall. Flaking layers of paint coated the window frame and sash: it had not been opened in years. He leaned his forehead against the cold glass, his eyes focused on the carcasses of cluster flies trapped in ancient webs that joined the inner and outer panes. His head swooned from the exertion of the walk.

When the wooziness passed, the prisoner looked past the filth into the prison yard that stretched, brilliant under the white sun, between the cell blocks and the walls. A man in red and grey checkered clothes came out the door of the cell block, a guard in military drab close behind. Side by side they walked along the shovelled path, their heads and shoulders bobbing, disembodied, above the snowbanks as they approached the staff entrance to the North Gate. A woman and a child moved out of the doorway, into the sunlight. The convict opened his arms and they went to him; he held them tight, bending his head to the woman's breast. He kissed them both, stroking their hair and kissing them, while the guard stood to one side, his back to the family, his eyes fixed on the cell-block door, stamping his feet in the snow.

Later, lying on the straw mattress in his tiny hospital cell, the prisoner wondered if what he had witnessed had been a vision, his fever returned. If not, if what he'd seen was true, then what had it cost that man to touch his lips to those he loved?

●●●

They could come for her at any time. Like a mantra, Phyllis repeated the warning to herself every waking hour, as if the incantation could forestall her fate.

With small gestures, she sought to prove her innocence. When the streetcar passed the prison, she looked the other way. And when she walked to school, she took Union Street, bypassing the stone walls altogether. She stopped picking up the mail, stopped going out at all, except to school and to church, and even then she avoided routes that might cross paths with the convicts, though sometimes, out of the corner of her eye, she caught a glimpse of their red and grey checkered uniforms as they shovelled snow on a distant street or cut ice far out on the lake. She had not been near the quarry's edge since the first morning of the year.

But no matter what she did to avoid suspicion, Phyllis's heart was not at ease. She felt hunted, like a fox pursued by dogs that never gave away their position by braying or crashing through the underbrush. Hers were silent stalkers who watched and waited for her to make the mistake that would prove her guilt.

She tried to pray for deliverance, but she had no right to God's grace. She had sinned. There was no escape.

Except perhaps one, she thought as she walked home from school in the late afternoon dusk. On a winter's evening just before Christmas, an evening much like this, Ambrose Small had walked out into a snowstorm and had not been seen since. The photograph of the millionaire stared at her from every telegraph post she passed. Five feet, nine inches tall. Fifty-three years old. One hundred and fifty pounds. Blue eyes; brown hair; reddish complexion.

Phyllis had once seen Ambrose Small, the Toronto tycoon, at the Grand Opera House in Kingston, one of the chain of moving-picture theatres he'd owned. Her father had taken her to a matinee musical and while they waited for the program to begin, he had pointed to a man moving briskly down the aisle. There goes one of the richest men in the country, her father had said in a tight voice she'd never heard before. She'd been surprised that such a wealthy man would look so ordinary, short and stubby in his dark tweed suit, like a shop clerk or a teller in a bank.

According to the newspaper reports, on Tuesday, December 2, 1919, Ambrose Small had had an early supper of pot pie at the Hotel Lamb, as was his custom, then he'd said farewell to the proprietor and walked out the door, turning towards Yonge Street, the heart of the city. He had just closed the sale of all his theatrical interests in Ontario; a cheque for a million dollars lay in his breast pocket. The wind was blowing and the snow fell in thick, wet flakes.

He never arrived at his destination. As soon as he was reported missing, relatives and friends wired resorts in the south, all the smart seaside places. Circulars were posted on city streets, broadcasting his description. Telegrams were dispatched to Cuba and the islands. No trace of him had been found.

With his quick little steps, Ambrose Small had headed into the night, into the veil of snow and out of sight.

If the richest man in the country could disappear, thought Phyllis, who would miss a seventeen-year-old village girl?

• • •

Father McDonald wrapped his cassock closer and bent his head into the storm, away from the penitentiary, towards the Church of the Good Thief, where he had been priest for twenty years. He always passed through the North Gate to the street with an unsettling mix of relief and shame. Relief that he could now minister to those who might indeed improve their lot; shame that he was free to go. For in the inmates' place, he suspected, he would be as crass and dejected as they.

The Roman Catholic chaplain had just come from the hospital, or what passed for a hospital in that wretched place. It was full to the point of bursting. Influenza. Cholera. Rheumatism. Consumption. Bronchitis. Pneumonia. Diphtheria. The winters were always bad.

The men worked outdoors in almost any weather, rarely with adequate clothes, and they returned at night, wet, cold and exhausted, to cells only slightly warmer than the outdoors. Those who worked inside were not much better off. Windows were sealed shut, ventilation was bad, the prison overcrowded. Dozens of men squeezed together in the shops, breathing each other's exhalations. The stone shed was the worst. Stifled with limestone dust, the lungs of the men who worked there were unfit to fight the viruses that ran riot among them. A quarter of the inmates were tubercular, only the very worst of them in the hospital, where they coughed up mouthfuls of blood that soaked into the straw of the mattresses on their cots. More than half the men in the prison, according to one of the doctors, had gonorrhoea. Dozens had active syphilis sores, ulcers in the mouth and on the tongue, glands enlarged, their skin erupting. And at least once a year the penitentiary lost a man to marasmus, that slow wasting away that seemed to have no cause other than the poor unfortunate's inability to adjust to the place where he found himself.

Most of the men worked as long as they were able, or as long as the officers could force them to, before they fell to their knees in a faint. According to prison regulations, being too sick to work was the same as refusing to work: a man forfeited his remission, either way.

In the hospital cells of the penitentiary, Father McDonald was called on to minister to the bodies of the inmates as often as their souls, swabbing the worst of the ooze off the sores, bringing the men oranges to suck and lifting a cup of water to the lips of those too weak to help themselves. Overseer Wilson was lazy and corrupt: he observed not even the most basic rules of hygiene. Father McDonald had watched in horror as Wilson wiped mucus off a syphilitic, then passed the same cloth over the face of a fevered man. The linoleum was sticky with grime, the chamber pots were emptied sporadically and never cleaned, and as if that weren't enough, amid the smell of infection, vomit, blood and carbolic wafted the sour odour of the cabbage that Wilson boiled for his dinner in the hospital kitchen across from the sick men's cells.

It is difficult to conceive what characteristics of the building set apart for the care of the sick at Kingston Penitentiary warrant it being designated 'hospital,' the Royal Commission of 1913-14 had written in its Report. *There is nothing in the building or equipment which justifies the name.* And nothing since then had changed.

The chaplain's grim, pale face was barely visible in his voluminous, wind-whipped cloak. He had a slender Irish countenance, with a shock of light hair swept to one side in an impatient, boyish way. His forehead was broad, clear and high, but his eyelids were weighted at the corners, as if by the thoughts he'd pondered, the sins he'd heard confessed, the wretchedness he had seen. Altogether, he would have had about him the anxious, sensitive air of a philosopher or a poet, were it not for his mouth, a firm hard slash. Mike McDonald felt the world deeply, but he saw it clearly too, and he did not shrink from the view. He was a man prepared to fight.

The priest had been forthright with William St. Pierre Hughes, when he'd solicited the chaplain's opinions on penitentiary reform: *Religion is a mighty and all essential factor. If good men need it to help them sustain them, bad men need it even more.* Without God, the inmates would leave in even worse condition than they entered. Hire God-fearing officers, he urged. Rid the library of base, infidel, sentimental, licentious print. Teach the inmates a trade and refurbish the prison chapel so that there, at least, a man could rise above the pain and sorrow of his life.

Father McDonald was often tempted to break the rules to improve the inmates' lot. The laws of God and human decency superseded prison regulations, forged as they were by common men, however well intentioned. He knew other chaplains who had delivered letters from inmates on their deathbeds, bought medicines that the prison could not or would not supply. And they had been dismissed for their Christian charity.

He had not yet succumbed, but tonight, as he struggled home through the snow, the pleadings of the convict rang fresh in his ears.

Please, Father, tell the people in the house by the quarry that I am all right.

Nothing else. No letter, no money, no favour but this.

Just tell them I am okay. Nothing happened. Tell them I'm sick, but I'm on the mend. Please, Father.

The simple things were the hardest to refuse. Ask him for a ladder and a rope and his reply would be immediate and firm, but this, what was the harm in such a message, after all? An innocent request in the light of others that had been pressed on him over the years. Still, the regulations were clear: *The chaplain shall not write any letter for or on behalf of a convict except with the permission of the Warden.* There was no Warden, but the chaplain was quite certain that this wasn't a message that G852 would want official ears to hear.

Father McDonald mulled it over as he walked up the hill to the church, straight into the teeth of the northwest wind. By the time he pulled open the carved oak door and shut the storm behind him, he'd made up his mind. The convict's request must be denied. Not for fear of countermanding rules—Father McDonald answered to a higher authority than the Department of Justice—but there were battles to be fought at Kingston Penitentiary. He must not squander what power he had on such a trivial matter.

The convict had conveyed an urgency that was curious, thought the chaplain. But the cocky young American was prone to overstating his case. He would be up and about before long. Whatever his dealings with the Hallidays, the priest concluded, they could resume soon enough.

● ● ●

Friday P.M.

Dear little friend Peggy:
Now the only thing that will stop me writing this evening is my
health. I am yet weak & my hand gets tired often. But I am going
to make a big attempt at telling you just how things happened on
that never to be forgotten A.M.

It was like this. There was a fellow working in the Quarry, I
will call him S. He was of a very obstinate nature & was always
in some sort of quarrel with the officers.

On that morning, I was working down below, so I told OK
to get that book & bring it down to me. The Scout seen the Book
and thought sure it was S who got the same, & not being in
favorable sides with S, he was pleased to have the opportunity
of putting him in severe trouble, so he made a wonderful piece of
Short time on his Horse to the Palace. We had to tear the paper
out of the book. I got the Kite & cake, read the Kite & tore it up,
eat some of the cake. Well that was all to that part of the trouble!
& so help me God there was never any more said about it. But I
know it must of looked real serious from behind the curtains, &
I tryed & tryed to reach you with a message to let you know that
everything was ok but it was impossible. If I had known your
address, it would of done me no good. I couldn't send anyone
with a message. So there I was, continually thinking & worrying
of how you & Ma felt. I knew you would be expecting to be called
up any-time. I raised my cap many & many a time even though
I never seen any-one in sight. However, suffice to say you have
nothing in the least to worry about. As I said B/4, if you or the
House was under any suspicion, I would of learned of it long ago.

Not for years more in here would I ever get you in wrong. If for one moment you really believe after this explanation that you are held under suspicion, please notify me in your next, & then we will have to practice safety first, eh. However, here is hoping for nothing but future good luck.

Say Peggy, you do have some wonderful dreams. Quite a coincidence you dreaming me being sick & sure enough I really was good & sick. Oh never did I say my prayers so feverently as I did when I was so sick. Dear friends, excuse such miserable uninteresting explanations as I am not very well yet, recuperating slowly. Good bye for now, will leave it to your judgment if I should write again & on what days. Always the same as B/4

DaDy, Long, Legs

(Trust me)

• • •

It had been more than a fortnight since the convicts had been to the quarry when she saw them from the streetcar, rounding the corner by the blacksmith's shop and without thinking, against her new resolve, Phyllis stepped off the trolley, walked towards the work gang and there he was, last man on the left, thinner than she'd remembered, fumbling with his cap and grinning at his boots: a letter was waiting.

Phyllis congratulated herself on her calm, her daring. On resisting the urge to confess. On her faith in the convict, her trust in herself. She had given herself over to instinct, or whatever unseen forces direct a life, and everything had turned out for the best. A private triumph, one for her and Daddy Long Legs to share.

Phyllis didn't add the letter to the Ovaltine tin but tucked it in her camisole and kept it close through the night, a talisman against her dreams. The next morning, after her sisters left, she read it over and over again as she lay in bed, nursing a sore throat that raised, once more, the spectre of the 'flu. The epidemic was spreading like an ill wind from the west: fifteen thousand cases in Illinois; in Toronto, fifty-five deaths in one day, two in Belleville. Kingston and Portsmouth had so far been spared, but schools had been closed and social events cancelled as a precaution. Stay warm, advised the doctor, eat well and rest.

Phyllis was asleep when her mother laid an envelope on the table beside her bed. The postmark was Los Angeles, California. A month before, she'd clipped an item from the People's Forum page in the *Daily British Whig. Your future foretold. Send dime, birth date for the truthful, reliable, convincing trial reading by psychic Hazel Hart.*

Phyllis felt at her breast for the convict's kite. The timing of the two letters was too close to be coincidence: the convict easing her worries about the past; the psychic pointing the way ahead.

Dear Friend:

I thank you for this opportunity to send you a TRIAL READING of your CHARACTER, and sincerely hope you will be pleased with it.

I am especially glad that you have come to me at this time. I see much in your CHARACTER to build on, and a bright future ahead of you, if you can but understand yourself and those with whom you come in contact.

You were born under the sign of Leo and many of the best and greatest people the world has produced were born under this sign.

You are kind hearted, generous, sympathetic and magnetic and would give up all comfort and even your life to care for and nurse the sick. Your great love and tenderness make you loved by all and give you a charm and personality which is felt wherever you go.

You have an emotional nature and are very intuitive and possess so much magnetism that you as a rule, go thru the world without much friction.

You are wonderful to inspire others to do good. You are fearless and courageous and have the power of mind which enables you to bear up under all danger and difficulties. Courage is a noble trait and commands the highest admiration and respect.

You are exceedingly wise, for you do not yield or take advice from others.

There is no limit of great things in store for you, altho you have had many sad and sorrowful experiences.

You have latent power and capabilities of which you are not making the best use. You are letting good opportunities pass by, because you have not the courage to rely upon your own judgment.

Why not seek a remedy? KNOW YOURSELF. Why not let me help you to better your life by sending you a GENERAL READING based on the Zodiacal signs at the exact time of your birth.

Those contemplating marriage should not fail to have a READING, for no man or woman should think of marrying unless they know their own tendencies, weaknesses, etc.

I am now offering a full READING for ONE DOLLAR, which also entitles you to ask THREE questions on any matter pertaining to yourself

May I expect to hear from you?

Three questions:

When will the convict be released? When will he come for me?

The third was barely a flutter in her heart. She could not ask it, even of herself.

• • •

monday, <u>noon</u>

my dear little Pall: —

So <u>sorry</u> I am to learn of your sickness, & it come so sudden. I am going to say a prayer for you this evening, & ask our God to bless you with a quick recovery. I am a great believer in prayer. Are you Peggy?

You say it is your bronchial tubes that are affected? Dr. E. B. Foot says that trouble in the bronchial tubes is caused by constipation; mostly in the Duodenum (which is the little stomach which receives food from the larger stomach & further digests it). He claims it is at all times absolutely necessaraly to have the bowels in perfect working order. Cure is very simple, in as much as it is only one ½ pint of hot water every morning B/4 any food is on the stomach. This I <u>practice</u>! & never need any other physic. He also claims to have all fresh air available, especially in a sick room. The coldest day, the window should be open. The lungs are full of air sacs, the air in which is designed to purify the blood. The blood in the veins passes very, very close to the air, only a thin sort of membrane separating them, so you can see the need of pure air. Kidneys are designed to collect the poisons from the blood & past them out through the bladder. When these become tired—as when we have so much to do that there work is left undone—we get rheumatisms, lumbago, head-aches, dizziness, & lots of trouble.

But I cannot dwell on such a vast subject, time bids me hurry on. Suffice to believe that it is at all times necessary to keep the bowels in perfect working condition. I hope you do start that hot water in the mornings & in a very short time you will not complain of being ill.

This AM I got your little parcel, paper & Kite. More than pleased to receive same, <u>many many thanks</u>. All right Peggy, if you please you can leave same this evening & say Peggy, can I worry you for an envlope? I got another letter all ready, but no envlopes. Would you not think, the way I demand any-thing I ask for, as though it was compulsury for you to do so, but, please Peggy, I don't know of any other way, so leave it to my ignorance.

Now little one please get better quick. They are coming to open up the gates so <u>pro-ten</u>, by-by (take good care of yourself)

<u>DaDy Long Legs</u>

PS. Will answer your loving kite to-night

Josie

(Trust me) Hurry. Excuse Scribling.

The prisoner folded the pages quickly and slipped them inside his boot. The convict-runners were taking their places at the far ends of the catwalks. The grind of the iron flywheel disengaged the double bars that spanned the tops of the cell doors. A sharp command. The slap of boots on concrete as the runners raced the catwalks, flipping open the cell locks, one after the other, click-click-click-click. For their amusement, the guards often laid wagers on the morning race. The prize for the fastest tapper: an extra ration of molasses with his bread.

The prisoner stepped outside into a Christmas picture post-card. Fresh shoulders of snow shrugged up against the stone walls; the paths across the yard had been erased by a blizzard in the night. Instead of breaking stone, the quarry gang was assigned to clear snow from the village streets. The news unsettled the prisoner: he'd have to wait another day to plant his kite.

The twenty-five convicts were stationed along Front Street between Aberdeen Park and the penitentiary's North Gate. The prisoner stood at the head of the line, in front of the Portsmouth town hall. Snow stretched before him, unmarked, to the harbour ice that rubbed up against the railing of the sidewalk on the far side of the road.

The prisoner slid his shovel into the snow, carved out a neat block and threw it over his shoulder into the park. As he bent to the snow, his gaze slid along the penitentiary wall that bounded the bay and slipped out across the lake to a thin, ragged line that hung suspended where the ice and the pale horizon dissolved. Simcoe Island. Somewhere between the dark fringe of trees and the harbour, a cluster of figures appeared to walk on water.

The penitentiary at Portsmouth was Canada's Alcatraz, though it was built not on an island but a point. The lake at the prison's back, the authorities surmised, would deter most convicts contemplating escape and force the truly desperate to take their leave by the road, overseen by towers and armed guards.

They hadn't counted on the alchemy winter works on a landscape. The prisoner could see a wagon far out on the lake, hauling a harvest of ice blocks towards Portsmouth on a road laid across the water with spruce saplings, frozen into place. A narrow channel separated Simcoe Island from Wolfe Island. And from there, less than two miles across the solidified St. Lawrence, lay New York State. By land roads, on foot, the penitentiary at Portsmouth was days from the American border. But across the ice, freedom was mere hours away.

The prisoner kept a steady pace with his shovel, edging across Front Street from the park to the harbour.

He'd walked away from prison before. He hadn't intended to

escape, though the thought was never far from any convict's mind. He'd been nine months into a two-year sentence at Burwash, the experimental Industrial Farm in the wilds of northern Ontario. Instead of walls, thousands of acres of spruce, hemlock and pine kept the convicts confined. Instead of breaking stone, they chopped down trees. And instead of cells, they lived in barracks, though the guards still carried rifles and the rules of the game were the same.

He'd been assigned to the kitchen gang, but he'd been caught stealing food and, as punishment, was set to scrubbing floors. Fair enough. But when a black man had laughed at him down on his hands and knees, and the guard had joined in the joke, the prisoner had finished his job, taken his grimy bucket outdoors, dumped it in the yard and kept on going, into the underbrush, through the trees, until the branches closed behind him and the barracks disappeared.

It had been so easy. As easy as stealing the motorcar that had landed him there in the first place. Try the handle. It opens. Turn the crank. No one comes running. Jiggle the wires. Jump in. Drive away.

There's only one trick to it, he thought, his breath coming hard from the weight of the snow. Just act like it's yours. Like you have every right.

The prisoner stopped shovelling, picked off his cap and used it to wipe the sweat from his forehead. He felt weak. He wasn't yet himself. This life was no good: prison wore a man down.

He'd almost pulled it off. The guards with their dogs hadn't chased him far. They must have figured he'd come back on his own or get lost and be gone for good. But luck had been with him. He'd happened on a hunt camp with a good barrel stove, a stack of cord-wood by the door, cans of beans in the cupboard and warm clothes hanging on the wall. He'd cooked himself a fine supper, had a good night's sleep, then followed a hunter's trail to the main road, where he'd hitched a ride south with a traveller selling ladies' hosiery and lingerie. They'd stuck together, driving and drinking, selling a little here and there. He'd made connections in the south and sold a little liquor to keep himself flush. He'd meant to work his way back to his family, but when the police picked him up with whiskey on his breath, he'd been too broke to pay the fine. After a month in the St. Thomas jail, on the day before his release, his luck ran out: the Warden spotted his face on a poster and he was shipped back up north to court.

If he hadn't walked from Burwash, he'd be a free man now.

The prisoner stared out across the frozen lake. A light snow had begun to fall, obliterating the islands near shore.

• • •

Thursday evening

Hello there —

I suppose by this time, you are well aware of the unfortunate fact that I've been moved down off the Hill. I feel so bad about it, that its on my mind. But I will not be down for all time, perhaps for a month or so. It will not in anyway interfear with our usual connections. I will be up to empty the Ashes & I only hope you will happen to be around. That will be about five minutes or so after we are out. No doubt you seen me empty them this A.M.? As you see, I will not be beaten by my own game (where there is a <u>will</u>, there's always a way).

Our Boss, the stout man more commonly known to us as the Knowledge Box, for he thinks he knows it all, well, he will be back from his vacation next Wensday or Thursday and he does not allow so much running around. But him & I get by fairly well. He is not ½ bad, just give him his own way!

You were quoting in yours of late, something like this—I often wonder how it was you placed confidence in us people in not betraying you, when you asked us to do that favour. Well, every one knows that a high fore Head indicates the intellectual type, that a pronounced chin means determination. These & a few other signs give a complete picture of a person & you can read them as you read this scribling! For instance, one must either sympathise or condem us, it must be one or the other! & it is very plainly seen. Did you not notice how I signed my Kites at the time, An Adventurer, & was I not an Adventurer? But I was <u>almost sure</u> you were in favour of one placed as I am.

Yes Peggy, I did indeed notice you with the sleigh, also seen you fall, poor Peggy. Surely you did not hurt yourself. One of the fellows near me at the time seen you fall, & he laughed. Immediately there was <u>blood</u> in my eyes. I could of killed him there. But he never noticed it & of course I daren't say anything, for it would not do. However, you being so short you did not have far to fall, ha. ha.

No Peggy I don't like the winter, did you ever see an American who did? I dread the cold & especially the wet snow, although I am very fond of skating & playing hockey! Do you skate? That & base-ball is my favorite sport (outside of Dancing). I am "bugs" about dancing! I've seen me dance all night & work the following day, & dance ½ of the same evening. Oh, I do love dancing!

Oh, I had <u>some</u> supper to-night. You see its like this: I have tobacco mostly all the time & there is a fellow in the officers mess who sells me food about three or four times a week, so you see, I don't fair too bad after all. Now that I am talking about tobacco, if I leave another $5.00 will you, etc. & if that is too much at *once, we can make three or four trips as B/4. Say Peggy, that fellow down at the little store is no good, so when you are coming home from school, get it somewhere else. I know him from experience, many & many a $ he has got from me, I guess he got a hundred $$s from me, but I was told by a friend (officer) that he would betray one in a minute, so safety first, eh.*

Now Peggy, don't think for a moment I am directing what you should do. Oh but what's the use of me talking like this. I am sure you understand me thoroughly. Do you not? You certainly do!

It may seem to your eye a small deed, but to one placed in the predicament that I find myself, it is more than I could commence to thank you for. Tobacco in here is far more luxurious to our eye than money outside! & if as you say you will be pleased to have that little ring that I mentioned in one of my Kites, rest assured it will be some-thing you will be proud of. It might not come immediately after my release, for perhaps I may have the pleasure of giving it to you personally!

Yes Peggy, the little boy I was refering to must stay inside the walls for the winter anyway, & by next spring he may possibly get out in the Quarry. He has what we call in here only a sleep, a short time. Well, is it not short when we look around & see men in here for 15-20-25 years, also for life. Some have been here long B/4 you & I were born & will be here as long again.

You have read in the good book concerning Noah & his Ark. They tell us he lived to be twelve hundred years old. I was just thinking, if he ever got into any trouble & got two hundred years it would be only short time for him, a Sleep, ha. ha.

Well Peggy, my fingers are commencing to get stiff & sore & I know you must be tired of this nonsense. So until I hear from you again, I am going to close my face, say my prayers & go to

bed & dream of the days that are to be & the day of my release.
So good bye, & believe in me as a True & Trustful friend always

Dady long l.
Friend "Joe"

PS. I often wonder how you can make out such scribling!

• • •

In the frontispiece of Phyllis's diary, her mother had inscribed:

Remember too that God on high,
Is hearing all you say.

Although Phyllis read the inscription every day, she could not decide if it was intended as a warning or as reassurance that she was never truly alone. There was comfort in the phrase only if a person did not mind being overheard.

If God was such a persistent eavesdropper, then He must have listened to her prayers, yet never once in her life had He replied. Perhaps the trick was in deciphering the signs. God's messages in the Bible were dramatic and direct. Blazing wheels in the sky, olive boughs in the mouths of birds, water transformed to wine, bodies raised from the dead. But Christians in the twentieth century had to make do with twinges of conscience or a pastor's word as to the true path of righteousness.

Perhaps, thought Phyllis, God speaks in ways we have yet to understand. Marconi, on Signal Hill in Newfoundland, had reported hearing strange voices in the crackle and hiss of his wireless set. Indecipherable messages from other worlds, he'd concluded, most likely from Mars. But maybe he'd been hearing the words of God. Who could say for sure?

Phyllis preferred Ouija. It spelled things out for you.

Phyllis consulted Ouija about practically everything she did, and although she never kept close account of the results, it was her impression that Ouija was right more often than not. She kept the board close at hand, sandwiched between the wall and her bed, the heart-shaped table under the edge of her pillow. She was quite certain that her parents, broadminded as they were, would not approve. The newspaper called Ouija a national pest, a serious menace, but it also told the story of a woman who had written an entire novel dictated to her by the Mystical Oracle.

Phyllis positioned the board in front of her on the quilt and poised both hands lightly over the little table as if she were about to play the piano. Her fingertips hovered, barely grazing the wood.

She closed her eyes. She could feel the energy gather in the pads of flesh under her fingernails. The table began to move. It circled tentatively, as the question formulated itself in her mind. She always began a session with the Oracle by asking a question to which she knew the answer, a surreptitious test.

Would the convict be released this year?

The table nosed straight for YES.

Another question took shape in her mind. The table jerked skittishly back and forth across the arch of the alphabet, then sidled up to the star and the sliver of new moon that cradled NO.

She would not finish school.

When would the convict get out of the penitentiary?

The table stabbed its front leg on M, then in quick succession:

Q, W, E. Four letters. They spelled nothing, though there were two four-letter months, June and July. She asked for a date.

The table swirled out of control, zoomed through XHLUSTEMOPGVMDILGF. Ouija didn't stop. KVKUFD MVLK ASDGODFB, it said, JDSIUTU IWEB XKL.

Phyllis tried again. When will the convict come for me?

The little wooden heart dove for her ankles, between the twin stars, and careened off the board, right through GOODBYE.

February

On the first day of February, the cold that had held January rigid snapped. Smoke from chimneys rose straight into the milk-blue sky after a month of crouching low over village roofs. Motorcars cranked to life. Children, housebound for weeks, were shooed outdoors to play. In twelve hours, the mercury in the thermometer rose forty degrees.

The air warmed but in the quarry, cold hunkered in the rocks, playing tricks with the detonator caps, shearing the limestone at odd, unpredictable angles.

The prisoner worked the top ledge, a bench of limestone as wide as a dance floor. A fresh burden of rock, recently blasted free of the quarry face, had been marked off with a square and straight-edge into dimension stone of a size the derrick could lift. All day the prisoner worked his section of the line, slowly perforating it with holes sixteen inches apart, an inch and a quarter in diameter, four feet deep. The Irishman held the drill bit steady while the prisoner brought down the hammer: a hundred blows with an eight-pound sledge would sink the bit one inch.

The skill was in starting the hole, keeping it round and plumb as it penetrated the stone. The short drill first, struck with light blows, the other man twisting the bit an eighth of a turn after each blow so the bore deepened in a smooth cylinder. Too much torque and the hole would be rifled with sharp grooves where the rock could give way, splitting helter-skelter in all directions instead of along the neatly perforated line.

Most of the year, the convict who held the bit also tended chuck, pouring water down the shaft to suspend the debris that clogged the drill. But in winter the men drilled dry, stopping every so often to clean the chiselled rock out of the hole with a wooden rod, one end frayed like a broom to trap debris. As the hole deepened, the men switched to heavier hammers and longer bits until the Irishman was turning a shaft as slender and weighty as a water pipe full of lead, lifting it up, hand over hand, again and again, to daub out the bore.

One and a half holes a day; a week to drill the line. Only the penitentiaries still cut limestone this way. Commercial quarries used steam-driven hammer-drills that punctured the rock in a fraction of the time. But at Kingston Penitentiary, time was not money. The harder the labour, the better: it was the convicts who had to pay.

When the line was drilled, the prisoner pounded into each hole a pair of feathers: tapered lengths of iron, flat on one side, rounded on the shoulders to match the curve of the bore. Between the flat faces of the feathers he fit a steel wedge called a plug. He plugged and feathered all the holes, then he moved down the line, striking the head of each plug with his sledge, one after another, forcing the feathers apart, gauging by the ring of metal the strain against the rock. Controlling his blows like a drummer, he eased the plugs deeper, slowly spreading the feathers until the rock gave up and shattered, sharp and smooth along the straight-edged line.

Limestone split willingly along the rifts, the horizontal layers laid down as true as lintels, half a billion years before. It also cleaved neatly along the joints that opened perpendicular to the layered rock beds. Some joints were obvious, the work of insinuating moisture and cold; others, like the one the prisoner had just tapped into, were barely discernible fissures opened when the primordial ooze suddenly shrivelled in the sun, the same sun that evaporated the sweat on the prisoner's brow.

That this blue-grey rock had once been mud on the floor of a warm lagoon, the prisoner had no doubt. The inner planes of a freshly split block of limestone were soft with rock-sap, smooth and glistening, resilient as flesh. Exposed to the air, the rock hardened quickly. By the time it arrived at the stone shed, where the prisoner had first come to know it, the limestone was dusty white, resistant to the hammers of the men who sat on benches reducing the rough blocks to gravel or shaping them into neat architectural forms—window sills, foundation caps, a plinth to support a courthouse column, steps up to a church.

Darwin's theories, wondrous on the pages of the prisoner's library book, became credible in the quarry. The prisoner imagined himself knee-deep in the shallow water where the rock had been born, at the edge of a great Paleozoic sea. Ancient organisms of fantastical shape swam at his ankles, the forefathers of jellyfishes, sea-urchins and fairy shrimp. Multi-limbed creatures scuttled scorpion-like across the mud; archaic snails clung to underwater plants, their shells coiled like rams' horns. All this before creatures breathed air on bare land, before amphibians, before reptiles, before trees and ferns, before dinosaurs, before mammals, before Man. Five hundred million years before the prisoner stood on the quarry ledge, soft-bodied, boneless creatures had dropped their feces and shed their shells in the mud. Year after thousands after millions of years, layer on layer, lives turned to stone.

The prisoner had spent long hours in his cell, fingering the chiselled face of limestone that framed his bars, searching for a shell, a fern leaf, a bit of bony skeleton that had been trapped in the ooze, their shapes preserved for eternity, the hieroglyphic remains of some ancient life form locked in the stone. But there was none. The limestone of Portsmouth, laid down on granite, was pure, even-grained and fossil-free. No record of the living things that had made it. No record of the nameless men who cleaved it from its granite bed and shaped it. All in all, a most desirable building stone.

• • •

The period of unrest that followed the war has been succeeded by a period of reckless living. Lavish expenditure, the demand for luxuries, a disinclination to work and the constant seeking of worldly pleasures mark the present day.

Above all else, this country needs a nationwide revival of old-fashioned prayer-meeting religion—a religion that makes men realize that if there is a heaven, there must also of necessity be a hell—a religion that makes a man realize that every act is recorded on his own conscience and that though it may slumber, it can never die.

DAILY BRITISH WHIG
Editorial

• • •

Elbows akimbo, back erect, Phyllis moved in time to the tune she hummed, sliding between the beds, across the muted ferns and flowers of the pressed linoleum on the floor. Quick-quick-slow; quick-quick-slow. Her left hand on a tightly muscled shoulder, her right foot poised perilously between imagined male limbs. The Catholic church would condemn her; Presbyterians issued warnings against what she did, *the propriety or moral tendency of which is open to serious doubt.*

The foxtrot Phyllis danced was tame compared to that other new animal dance, the tango, with its languid steps, partners gliding across the dance floor like panthers through a jungle, smooth as sweat. Phyllis had never seen anyone dance the tango, or the shimmy, or the Castle walk, though she had read about them all, seen in the music shop pictures on the covers of piano scores, Irene and Vernon Casde, stiff-backed, the air between them charged, women draped across their partners' arms, hair brushing the floor, their bodies limp, legs entwined.

Phyllis's life was more schottische than tango, a predictable round of church and school and family, with an occasional Sunday School banquet, as a kind of fandango, thrown in. None of the girls she knew were shaking their shimmies or baring their knees. They wore their lisle stockings sensibly gartered at the tops of their thighs. Though when she was alone, as she was this afternoon, home again sick and by herself, she would dance in her nightdress (as short as any flapper's), feeling the air waft up between her legs, her breasts sway, nipples brushing against the thin cotton fabric where she had embroidered a flamboyant P in bright pink, for Peggy.

And often, when she placed the tobacco and cigarette papers in the hiding spot in the Palace, her hand paused on the package as she considered taking some for herself, to try this pleasure, too, that the convict so enjoyed. Through the window of the Opera Cafe, she had seen women smoking, seen the way they held the cigarette to their lips like a kiss.

The church condemned that, too. She had read with alarm the petition posted by the Women's Christian Temperance Union urging the government to pass a law prohibiting the selling of "smokes" to the "fair sex." Cigarettes, dancing, picture shows, even the comic supplements in the Saturday *Daily British Whig*: harbingers, apparently, of a sinful age.

••

The Ovaltine can lay open between her knees, the letters of the past four months scattered over the quilt. The patches of buff-coloured paper, evenly striped with dark waving lines, blended into the patterns of her past: the gingham from the jumper she wore on her first day of school; a piece of her mother's wedding suit; the faint blue stripe of her father's once-best shirt. Fragments, smooth and coarse, stitched one to the other as if they belonged together, as if they made sense, as if something useful could be fashioned from the random bits and pieces of their lives. The rolls and rectangles of penitentiary paper, stubbornly inconsistent in size and shape, fit right in. Phyllis leaned back against her pillows. From this perspective, hardly a word on a page was legible. Squinting, she could make out ... *say Peggy* ... *wanting* ... *too much trouble* ... *get me* ... *please*.

The convict's letters had changed. Although she would never be able to reconstruct precisely the order in which they had been received—the notes, mostly undated, had been hopelessly jumbled in the tin—she could trace their evolution by their form. The slight, tentative furls of their first connections. The letters that swelled through the autumn, each one fuller than the last, fattening as the weather sharpened until by Christmas they were plump as geese, so many pages of that familiar sloping scrawl with its odd capitals and misspellings that she had to tie them together with bits of ribbon and string to keep them from flapping free and mixing in the tin. But lately the kites had grown lean, a single page folded flat, sometimes just a scrap of tissue so flimsy that she had tucked the last few together inside an envelope to prevent them from being overlooked or lost.

Their most recent exchanges had been businesslike. Not unfriendly, exactly, but perfunctory and to the point, his messages scratched quickly on the back of hers. They made her feel necessary without being needed, like a servant or a clerk, delivering the letters from Sis with their regular allowance of cash, picking up his kites folded around a coin or dollar bill, making his purchases, rendering accounts.

Wednesday noon

To Daddy:

<u>No hurry</u> for that dollar, I have still $1.30 to your credit after leaving this chocolate. This morning I had $1.55 of your money & I bought the chocolate at noon which leaves still $1.30 for you, whenever you want it.

Friend Peggy

3:45 pm

Say P, that chocolate was so tempting that OK & I eat it all! I'm sending another 25¢ & will you invest the remainder of cash in same kind, as I'm sure Sis will be writing one of these days, & then OK & I are going to have another feed of cheese. Pigs, aint we?

Your friend

DaDy

(Trust me)

Will send $1.00 to-morrow.

Wednesday P.M.

To Daddy: I got the 25 cts. which you left this P.M. & I am leaving 5 bars to-night. You say you want the remainder of your money $1.30 in chocolate bars. Will I leave them in your mitts a few at a time or in the Palace all at once, also would you like all nickle bars?

Friend Peggy

No P Dear, not all chocolates. $1.00 Mc Chewing & 30¢ chocolate Bars. But if you got some never mind. You could leave chocolate & chewing Tob in my mittens, say two at a time. Bye Bye

Troublesome Friend DaDy

PS. OK asked me if I could get him a little weed. He would like two packages of Bull Durhum & some zig-zag papers. OK wants to plant it, as he believes there is going to be a famon. But I'm in no hurry. Any-time will do!

DaDy

Thursday P.M. <u>noon</u>

To Daddy —
I am leaving the 6 Bars (30¢) this noon. I will leave the tob this P.M. but will I leave it in the Palace or mitts?

Hurry, Peggy
The 1 o'clock bell has just gone so I have to be off. P.

*P, use your own good judgment as to where you think best. I
received candies all ok. Did you get the $1.00 at noon hr? I'm as
usual fine, but don't know what to think about Sis. I ain't heard
from her this week. So bye, bye.*

(Trust me)

Friend DaDy

Lying in bed she reread all his letters, one by one. The final
exchange, when she got to it, did not seem so cold and distant after all.
Rather, it was the comfortable give and take that marked her parents'
conversations over the breakfast table or in the parlour at the end of
the day. The long, loving kites in which he shared his desolation and
his hopes reassured her: an understanding stretched between them,
firm and fast.

With both hands Phyllis scooped up the letters and let them tumble
through her fingers to the quilt. The dry, brown papers with their faint
purple markings stirred her as nothing ever had.

•••

The prisoner leaned on his sledgehammer and watched Beaupré's
entourage move across the quarry floor and up the makeshift ladders
to the bench. From a distance, they looked like a company of vaude-
ville clowns in their baggy red-checkered suits: one convict with the
powder keg on his shoulder, another scrambling after the coil of fuse
wire as it rolled this way and that over the uneven ground, a third
carrying the long-stemmed funnel before him like a mace, and behind
the three of them, the stout-bellied Beaupré. Except for chasing down
the occasional convict runaway, blasting day was as important and as
exciting as a quarry instructor's job got.

When Beaupré reached the top bench, he took a notebook from his breast pocket, ripped out a page, sprinkled it with a pinch of black powder and struck a match. The powder ignited in a burst of smokeless, white light like a photographer's flash. It was a magician's trick: the black grains were gone, the paper untouched. Beaupré held it up against the sunlight, scrutinizing the surface for yellow stains, black smudges and scorch marks, indications that the explosive contained too much sulphur or too much charcoal, or that the powder had been dampened by the midwinter thaw.

The prisoner waited for Beaupré's ritual to play itself out, his thoughts on a short leash, ready to snap back at the quarry instructor's command. Much of his workday was spent like this. Waiting for the guard to bring a drill-bit extension. Waiting for the rest of the holes to be bored. Waiting for the cart to return for a refill of stone. Waiting to be counted, to be searched. For the signal to come and go. Long, idle pauses punctuated with spasms of drudgery.

Beaupré nodded to one of the convicts. Cautiously he fed the stem of the funnel into the drill shaft, careful not to touch the fuse wires that dangled out the top of the hole like the split tail of some deep-burrowing rodent. The prisoner had already scraped the hole with the long-handled spoon they called a wiper, then twisted a gob of hay around the handle end to dredge out the narrow shaft until it was dry. The detonator cap with its dangling fuse wires was in place. Beaupré measured a tin-can of black powder from the keg and poured it through the funnel, burying the cap. Then he gave the signal to extract the funnel and his motley band of convict-assistants moved on to the next hole.

The prisoner scooped up a handful of dry sand and tipped it slowly into the drill hole. With a wooden tamp rod he gently pressed down the sand, then added a handful of damp clay, tamped again, alternately adding clay and tamping, each thrust of the rod a little more vigorous than the last until at the top, he hammered the end of the rod hard against the clay, plugging the hole tight and flush to the surface of the rock, the two ends of fuse wire that trailed from the black spot at his feet the only evidence that the stone was charged.

One by one the line of drill holes was fused, charged and tamped. By the time the line was finished, there was enough explosive under the convicts' feet to fell a regiment. All that lay between them and death were the detonator caps: slender copper capsules no bigger than a finger joint, filled with fulminate of mercury and sealed with a sulphur plug. The two fuse wires poked through the sulphur into the mercury, their bare copper tips bridged by a platinum filament. One sharp blow and the mercury would explode. A yank on the wire and the filament would break. A little friction, a little heat, a ton of rock blowing up in a man's startled face.

From the moment a detonator cap was lowered into the first drill hole until the blasts shattered the rock, the convicts worked quickly and with care, invoking their own rule of silence. For these few hours, theirs was the most dangerous job in the penitentiary, the price they paid for the fresh air and relative freedom of working on the quarry gang.

Beaupré moved along the line of trailing fuse wires, stripping the cotton casing off the ends, baring the copper with his knife. Convicts joined the fuse wires in series, twisting the brightened copper strands together, raising the joints off the ground on little stone cairns to keep the wires dry. To the wires in the first and last holes, Beaupré attached the leads that trailed across the stone bench, dangled down the rock face like abandoned climbers' ropes and snaked across the quarry floor two hundred feet or more to the magneto, a narrow, upright box the size of a biscuit tin, positioned several yards behind the Palace.

A trip of the foot, an error in timing, a crazy man at this moment could kill them all.

The guards rounded up the convicts and herded them to the opposite end of the quarry, where they congregated like ordinary workers taking a break. The tower guard climbed down and took up position on the rise of ground behind the men, his rifle cocked.

Beaupré stood alone by the magneto. He pumped the handle a couple of times. Then with exaggerated care, he connected the lead wires to the magneto terminals. He stood up and looked back at the convicts and guards, ahead to the wall of stone, then he stooped again. Lifted the handle to its full height. Pushed down slowly for half an inch. The quarry was so still the prisoner could hear the magneto sigh.

There she blows, yelled Beaupré. And he pushed down on the handle with all his weight.

Before the penitentiary invested in electric detonator caps, the end of each fuse wire had been wrapped in candle wicking soaked in kerosene. The fuse wires themselves were threads of black powder pressed inside spun jute yarn, waterproofed with coal tar. A convict would run from fuse to fuse with a torch, daubing each wick with fire, then race for cover as the flame sizzled along the slender powder train, heading for the charge, the guards placing bets on whether the man would make it to safety before the rock exploded at his back.

Now, as swift and stealthy as a sideways glance, the electric current flashed across the quarry floor, up to the stone ledge, then shot down each shaft in succession, whizzed across each tiny platinum bridge, left red-hot in its wake, heat exploding the mercury, starting the chain reaction of the blast.

The black powder pressed in each hole had the constituents of gunpowder—saltpetre, sulphur, and the charcoal from alder and willow trees—but in hair-trigger proportions. Each grain of powder, heated by the mercury explosions, combined chemically with the next: grain to grain to grain with lightning speed, molecules igniting, fusing, converting to gas in a sudden, single burst, the powder's full power released in the blink of an eye, the push of a hand.

Black powder was the feeblest of explosives, a popgun compared to the land-mine power of dynamite. Even so, a hurricane would be mild compared to the force of the black-powder gas trapped inside the limestone shaft by the tamped plug of clay. A thousand mighty fists pummelling the narrow cylinders of stone, pressing against the drill-hole walls like a madman, straining for a weak point, hurling into the rock in every direction, most destructive where it met the most resistance, shattering what stood in its way, blowing stone into the sky ahead of it, boulders of limestone raining on the bench.

The stone split along the line of bores like a drum roll. One . . . two . . . three . . . four . . . The men counted the deep-throated booms, felt the ground under their feet shudder with the passage of the blasts. They didn't need to see the rock to know their job was done. Too much powder, and the explosions split the air like thunder-claps; too little and they sounded like toy pistol shots.

So much could go wrong. Had the sides of the drill shafts not been smooth, had they not stopped short of the stratified rock at the rift, the gas would have pressed into the nicks and natural fissures, splitting the rock into flagstones and shards instead of a smooth-faced block. Sometimes the cold sucked the power from a charge and the explosions failed to dislodge the rock. Sometimes a charge didn't go off at all.

Every man on the quarry gang counted the blasts. When there was one too few, they would wait, whispering among themselves, comparing the tally. Wait for the last cap to go off. Wait, knowing that it might explode as they climbed back on the bench. Knowing that if it didn't,

THE HALLIDAY FAMILY

(TOP) *Father and Betty in the garden*
(LEFT) *"Fetching Vixens" Phyllis & Marion—Fall, 1919*
(RIGHT) *Our darling Mother*

Jack's wife, Winnie, and Gordon, the "messenger"

Dear Jack (second from right, middle row) *in the Bugle Corps, on his way to war with his commanding officer Major St. Pierre Hughes* (far right, middle row)

PORTSMOUTH, ONTARIO

(FROM TOP)
*Aerial view of
Portsmouth—1919*

The Penitentiary

*Front Street from the
North Gate to the Church
of the Good Thief*

CONVICTS FROM THE PENITENTIARY

(FROM TOP)

Returning through the North Gate

Marching through the village

Unloading the coal barge at the penitentiary wharf

IN THE QUARRY

(FROM TOP)
The "Palace"

The Scout by the quarry crow's nest

Breaking stone

"Xmas," 1919.

my little "Pal"

Hold This as a remembrance
from "Joe", untill such time as
I may (with the help of "God's" grace)
be in a position, when I will be
able to offer some thing real nice, So
with wishing you the usual
compliments of the season (happy
"Xmas", & a prosperous new "year)"
I am your friend "Joe"

"PEGGY"

In the quarry with Watch—Spring 1920

William St. Pierre Hughes, Superintendent of Penitentiaries

Warden Ponsford

the men who had drilled and tamped the defective hole would have to go back and drill another a few inches away, hoping that the reverberations of the hammered drill wouldn't set off the original charge before the new one was set. Or they'd be forced to scoop out all but the last three or four inches of clay in the dud hole, lay a new cap, fuse and powder on top of the first and tamp it all back in place, a double dose of explosive in the rock under their trembling feet. Knowing that this time, too, a defective splice, a dislodged fuse wire, a bit of moisture seeping through the sulphur into the detonator cap might kill the charge again.

The prisoner breathed easy: every charge was accounted for in the rain of rock.

For the rest of the day, half the quarry gang worked at the block, sledging wedges between its backside and the rock face. When the block was lifted out, they would stay on the bench for another week, maybe two, clearing the rubble from the newly exposed face, sledging the boulders to manageable size, then heaving them to the quarry floor and piling the debris, stone by stone, into a mountain of rock that awaited the arrival of spring and the machine that would crush stone for the village roads.

All through the preparations for the blasting, the prisoner had watched for an opportunity to pass a plug of tobacco to OK, but Beaupré had been busy among them, watching every move. Once the quarry settled back to its routine, Beaupré retired to the Palace to have a smoke with the other guards. They still kept the convicts within sight, of course, but their vigilance would be relaxed as they congratulated themselves on the success of the blast.

The prisoner caught OK's eye. He made a slight tossing motion with his hand. OK nodded. The prisoner bent as if to tie his bootlace, fingered the tightly wrapped plug out from under the arch of his foot and flicked the packet in the direction of OK.

Nine times out of ten, no, ninety-nine times out of a hundred, thought the prisoner, OK would have fielded the low pitch and in a single motion tucked the plug inside his mitt.

Nine hundred and ninety-nine times out of a thousand, Beaupré would have been sucking on his pipe, staring off into space, considering a job well done or anticipating his evening's entertainment. He wouldn't have seen the dark little square arc through the air, silhouetted against the stone.

Nine hundred and ninety-nine times out of a thousand, had Beaupré seen such a thing, he would have looked the other way, not allowed the shape to register in his brain, taken another draw and counted his blessings.

He wouldn't have tapped out his pipe on his heel and stalked out of the Palace, across the quarry floor.

He wouldn't have let the prisoner ruin his otherwise perfect day.

• • •

In winter, the outside officers at Kingston Penitentiary looked like Russians with their black fur headpieces and greatcoats that swept to their ankles. In summer, they wore peaked caps like trolley conductors and khaki tunics with epaulettes. Only the Warden went about in civilian suit and tie; the rest of the staff kept military style.

For Beaupré, taking a position at Kingston Penitentiary had been like joining the army. The work was secure, the qualifications minimal: over twenty-one, in reasonably fit condition, able to read, write, do elementary sums and handle a rifle. He'd secured his job as had most others on the staff. A word to the Reeve, who spoke to the local Member of Parliament, who passed his name to the Minister of Justice, who informed the Warden that when a new officer was needed, Peter Beaupré was his man.

Beaupré didn't come from one of Portsmouth's penitentiary families. His father had been a shipwright, then a publican, though all his life the men in Portsmouth had called him Captain. The nine Beaupré children were raised in rooms above Captain Beaupré's tavern at the edge of Hatter's Bay. At night, when he was a boy, Peter Beaupré had looked across the water to the penitentiary walls and wondered what went on in there. When he came of age he'd worked as a shoveller on the coal boats that plied the lake in summer, but by the time he was twenty-five he had three children of his own and was in need of steady work. In Portsmouth, that meant a penitentiary job.

On Beaupré's first day inside the walls, the tenth of January, 1885, the Deputy handed him a pocket-sized edition of the Penitentiary Act and told him to read it through. When he finished, the Deputy Warden told him to read it through again. On his second day, he was put to work guarding a convict gang.

What Beaupré knew about handling criminals, he'd learned on the job by watching other officers, slowly sorting the confusion of official rules into those that were hard and fast, those that could be bent and twisted, softened, let slip. The convicts serving long time helped him out, too, whispering in his ear when a cell gate was left ajar, tipping him off as to whom it was wise to watch.

For thirty-five years, his daily routine had been driven by the prison bell. At ten minutes to seven every morning but Sunday (half an hour earlier in the summer months), he was in the Keeper's Hall for roll call. In the early days, he'd supervised the breakfast parade and taken morning count while the convicts ate in their cells. But after twenty years as a keeper, he'd been promoted to quarry instructor, in charge of a gang of his own, so that now, while the convicts ate, he considered the orders for quarry stone.

When the bell tolled at eight, he picked up his work gang, escorted them through the North Gate and through the village to the quarry, where he dispersed the convicts to the shelves of rock they would work that day. While they hammered, he moved among them, supervising the quarrying and watching for misconduct among the men. At half past eleven, he lined up the gang, took them back through the North Gate and the body search, to the kitchen where they picked up their trays and returned them to their cells for lock-up and another count.

At one o'clock, he picked up his gang again and took them back outside, directed their labours until sunset (or five o'clock in summer), then back inside the walls for one last line-up and search, back to the kitchen, back to the cells, supper in hand, for the final count. The sentries climbed down from the towers, the officers, instructors and guards came in from the ranges and shops, the Chief Keeper took the evening roll call, verified the convict count and sounded the bell at six o'clock. Eleven hours after he'd arrived at the North Gate, Beaupré was free to leave.

Seventy-one officers guarded the convicts by day; thirteen at night. One man on the North Gate, two patrolling the yard, the rest making forty-minute rounds past each and every cell, listening to the men call out in their dreams, passing through the pale green light of the Dome, waiting for the sun to rise so they, too, could sleep. The men on nights worked thirteen-hour shifts and every two weeks, when they changed from nights to days, they worked twenty-four hours straight. Beaupré had lobbied hard for his quarry instructor's job: it meant he was always home on Sundays, holidays and nights.

Even so, it wasn't an easy life. A penitentiary officer, like the convicts in his charge, was bound by rules, drafted mostly from the barracks. When officers moved across the prison yard, it was to be at a quick-march. They were to stand at attention at their posts. They were not to lounge or chat with one another. They were to address their superiors as "Sir!" They were to carry out any and all commands immediately, without question. They were to salute the Warden and his Deputy when they passed.

An officer's relationship with the convicts was also strictly prescribed. No familiarity. No profane or insulting language in front of the convicts or among themselves in the prison yard. A dignified demeanour, no matter how sorely they were provoked. And an officer was never to censure another or hold conversations within earshot of a convicted man.

The rules followed Beaupré out through the North Gate at night, into the village, into his home. When he'd first gone to work at the penitentiary, officers had been required to live within the sound of the prison bell and even though that regulation had been dropped, when the alarm bell sounded, Beaupré had to hasten to the prison no matter what he was doing or where he was. He was not allowed to discuss penitentiary affairs outside the stone walls. He was forbidden to recognize a convict after his release. And if he did anything, anything at all *unbecoming to the character of an officer of the institution*, he could be dismissed out of hand.

In drafting the code of conduct, the authorities failed to take one matter of fact into account. It was men who wore the uniforms, on both sides of the bars. Bored, angry men. Conniving, jealous, vindictive men. Kind-hearted, sympathetic, susceptible men. Had all the guards been angels and all the convicts automatons, the system might have worked. But an officer of the penitentiary at Portsmouth was sergeant to a pack of wolves, as cunning as they were desperate, scheming every minute to get even or get out.

The fundamental tenet Beaupré had learned as a new recruit: if a convict could break one rule, he could break them all.

And its corollary: if one convict could break a rule, then so could they all.

Beaupré had come to the penitentiary wide-eyed and alert. But in a system built on silence and inspection, it wasn't enough to be observant: nothing less than vigilance would do. An officer had to notice everything. The drape of a pant leg, a blanket's bulge, the way two men contrived to brush against each other as they passed, a convict stooping to a shoelace that wasn't undone. Beaupré had trained himself to look and never blink. His eyes had narrowed, become sensitive to the flicker of intrigue. He'd grown wary, learned to nurse his doubts, suspect the worst. Even in the prison chapel, sitting high on his stool between the stained glass windows as the men bent their heads at prayer, he'd listened for whispered conspiracies, watched for a sharpened fork, a sliver of tobacco palmed hand to hand. Always on the lookout. Creeping in stockinged feet down the spy corridor, squinting through Judas slits, curiosity stiffening to certainty, the muscles behind his eyeballs strung taut as fence wire, the skin of his face grown pale from what he saw and couldn't see. Finally, that extra sense taking shape somewhere in the back of his skull, a sense peculiar to prison guards, and from then on he knew, without so much as a glance, when a rule was being broken, as if, like a twig underfoot, it broke with a snap.

Eleven hours a day, Beaupré held the convicts to their work and to the rules, and for the most part, kept the rules himself. He was good at his job and he was fair. The convicts didn't give him much trouble. They seemed to like him: they called him Knowledge Box. Yet he never forgot for a moment that every day, he risked his life. Eight sets of locks separated the convicts in their cells from the village, but four times a day Beaupré's quarry gang walked the streets: at those times, he and his officers were all that stood between murderers and rapists and the women and children of Portsmouth.

At the end of every month, in return for his efforts, his pay packet held half what a Portsmouth tradesman earned. Every dollar of Beaupré's wages went to feed and clothe his children and keep a roof over their heads. Not a penny extra to set aside. And when he walked out through the North Gate one last time, he knew, the Department of Justice would give him nothing but a fare-thee-well. An officer at Kingston Penitentiary worked until he dropped, from exhaustion, old age or a convict's knife.

And so Beaupré did what men did on the other side of the bars: he did what he had to do to get by. If the Deputy Warden wanted to see a certain number of convicts in Warden's Court each week, he'd write up a man for talking, or insolence, or negligence at his work, for oversleeping, for dropping his tray, for whatever came to mind. Rules were broken every second of every day; it hardly mattered whether a man was innocent any one particular time. He was guilty by virtue of the uniform he wore. And it was a good idea, every now and again, to remind a convict of where he was and why. Remind him that rules weren't signposts to help him walk a straight path, they were traps, set and ready to be sprung, maybe not today, maybe not tomorrow, but someday, at the whim of the officer in charge.

And if the convicts' never-ending guile had given him a nervous tic, kept him bug-eyed, stripped his nerves raw, curdled whatever milk of human kindness flowed in his veins, then they owed him a little entertainment in return. Who was harmed, after all, by a bet laid on a convict-runner or by an innocent little lie, telling a convict that he would be released the next day, bringing him his discharge suit and convincing him that really, truly, even if he hadn't heard it yet, the guards all knew, he would be a free man soon, congratulations, too, and watching with a smirk as the day passed and the convict broke down, a grown man snivelling, the toughest of characters heaving girlish sobs, as the truth sank in that he was not today, maybe never, going home.

And why shouldn't a guard take home a little something extra, after all he endured and the risks he took? A few dollars from selling tobacco, a trinket carved in bone, a gift in exchange for looking the other way while a deal was made, while men performed their acts of love or vengeance, a surcharge now and then for those who liked to watch. It was safe, as secure as money in the bank. No one would believe a convict who told such a tale; an officer could make a man suffer in the attempt. A scrap of newspaper or a boiled egg would be found in his cell, hidden behind the books on his shelf. Enough to send him to the Hole. And on the way, the convict's ribs might fall against the iron ring of keys that hung on a guard's belt. The convict's cheek-bone might make contact with a boot, raised to break the poor man's fall as he tumbled down the stairs in a sudden, unexpected faint.

Beaupré had not participated in the *sub rosa* convict economy— the "trucking" —or its enforcement, but he knew such events trans-pired. A man couldn't work in a place all his life and not be privy to its darker side. He had seen more than he cared to remember, and remembered more than he wished to know. But he kept these mat-ters to himself. He'd always held himself aloof, as much out of fear as good conscience. In all these years, he'd never set himself up as judge over other men and how they chose to survive. His tactic had paid off. His mail had not been seized, his bank accounts had not been scrutinized by the Royal Commission in 1914. He'd not been called to testify. Long ago he'd made his peace with O'Leary. He knew that the Deputy gave certain officers hard postings to force them from their jobs; that he rewarded his favourites with plum assignments; that jobs could be bought and that the right to traffic with the convicts had its price. But Beaupré stayed out of O'Leary's way and did his job. It may have been as Major Hughes had charged, that being Roman Catholic had served him well in O'Leary s eyes. But Protestants like Alexander Atkins had prospered, too.

Hughes was right about one thing, though: under O'Leary, the military order of the place had collapsed. Sentries read magazines in the towers, leaned on the railings and gazed out at the lake. Officers sucked on cigarettes as they strolled across the yard. At night, guards lay their heads on folded arms and let their eyelids droop. Rare was a uniform with all its buttons; the officers' boots had lost their shine. With neither a Warden nor a Deputy to cross their path, most had forgotten how to salute. But it hardly mattered, really. The officers did their job. The convicts worked steadily. They served their sentences. Few escaped. Most survived.

Beaupré strode across the quarry floor, his eye fixed on G852. What propelled him towards the convict was not devotion to rules but a gathering wind of change. He'd been hired thirty-five years before, when a medical examination swept the penitentiary clear of another Warden's cronies. Now doctors were examining the staff again. Beaupré was no fool: he knew what it meant. In a few months, he'd be sixty. His only hope of keeping his job was to apply the rules with diligence and trust that Superintendent Hughes—a man he'd known as self-righteous but fair—would take note. The saints forgive him, but he couldn't afford to squander his sympathy on the young French American.

•••

MUCH EXCITEMENT CAUSED BY
MEDICAL EXAMINATION OF PRISON OFFICIALS
NOBODY KNOWS WHO IS GOING TO GET THE AXE —
DEMAND THAT ALL OFFICIALS BE PLACED ON EQUAL FOOTING

The medical examination of officials at the Portsmouth Penitentiary has caused the greatest excitement. Nobody knows who is going to "get the axe" and all things are reported to be more or less demoralized in consequence. Only twice within memory has a general order for medical examination been resorted to. This was in 1885 and again in 1899. In both cases the examination was used as a method for weeding out to make places for political hangers-on. In the present instance, however, there is no essential difference, except that the work is being done apparently by the Civil Service Commission; and the fact that the order has been made applicable to every member of the staff is causing more or less suspicion of favouritism and consequent resentment.

"If one man past 60 receives notice that his resignation would be demanded, why should not every one over that age receive the same notice?" This statement was made by an indignant official whose record is beyond question.

The action of the commission is not going to be overlooked when parliament meets and some sensational revelations are promised unless all officials are placed upon an equal footing and the same rule applied to those employed in the penitentiary branch at Ottawa as well as those at the institutions.

DAILY BRITISH WHIG
February 18, 1920

• • •

The prisoner sat on the bench in the Keeper's Hall, waiting his turn with the others. He had already waited for hours, lying on his bunk, listening to the damp swish of a convict's mop wiping the flagstones in the deserted range. Sometime before the midday break, a guard had appeared outside his cell.

G852. Warden's Court.

The prisoner had joined the line of convicts, each man's business written on his face clear as an affidavit. The polite, guarded hopefulness of the convicts making petition, requesting permission to change work gangs or to write more than one letter a month. The dread anticipation of the convicts who'd just been admitted, new fish on their way to hear the rules that would shape the next two, five, twenty years of their lives. The resignation of those who'd been written up on report.

The fish went first, then the supplicants. Those who would be punished were saved for last. The prisoner had ample time to consider the Acting Warden's options. He could erase the remission the prisoner had earned, the days he'd whittled off his sentence with good behaviour and diligence in his work. Or he could sentence him to hard bed: sleeping on the iron springs with a single blanket or none at all. Bread and water diet. Each was a little harder on the body than the last. Shackling to the bars during working hours. Flogging with the paddle. That was the extent of what the law allowed: to be lashed until he bled. The Warden wouldn't go that far. But he could send him to the Hole.

Under the thin soles of his cell slippers, in the stone basement under the Keeper's Hall were the punishment cells. The dungeon. The Hole. Convicts who were ordered segregated from the prison population—too violent, too perverse, too bent on escape—were held in the Prison of Isolation, a separate stone building behind the hospital. But a convict who was in need of a little time alone, whom the officers wanted to deal with in private, the Hole was designed for him.

The prisoner had heard stories of what went on down there. Savage beatings. Punishments not prescribed by law. A secret enterprise between convict and guard, conducted away from the open range of cells. No one to witness, no one to hear. A man went to the Hole as he went to his grave, alone.

That he might not be punished at all did not occur to the prisoner. He had long since learned the fundamental lesson of prison life: that loss of freedom did not mean restriction of the body; it meant submission of will. They could do with him what they would. It was a contest he could have avoided. It was not one he could win.

How would they make him suffer? How much could he stand? Fear nudged him, grabbed at him, wouldn't leave him alone. He looked away from his feet pressed against the wooden floorboards, looked for a scrap of blue sky beyond the window bars, something to stitch his mind to other things, but the fear was all over him, clutching at his bowels, squeezing his gut. He had always known enough to stay out of the officers' way. He hadn't known enough to be afraid.

G852.

The prisoner stood up. He steadied himself, then walked into the office ahead of the guard. Beside the man acting as Warden sat the Acting Deputy, Corby, the officer who used to run the black-smith shop where he'd earned a small fortune turning a blind eye to the manufacture of wheels and boxes for the works sold up and down the range. At one end of the desk stood Beaupré looking out of place without the backdrop of pale, layered stone. Beside the prisoner stood his escort guard. He was outnumbered, four to one.

G852, you've been reported for possession of contraband, namely tobacco, and for insulting an officer. How do you plead?

The tobacco charge he'd expected, but the other surprised him, though his face registered nothing. For a first contraband report, a convict could expect to lose remission and suffer bread and water for a couple of weeks. An insult charge was a ticket to the Hole.

Warden's Court was a misnomer: there would be no trial. No one defended the prisoner, and he was not allowed to speak, except to enter a plea. Only the officer's evidence was heard. And he was not presumed innocent: he was guilty the moment the report was filed. Passing sentence was the only business of the Warden's Court.

The prisoner considered pleading guilty to the contraband and not guilty to the insult charge. That was the truth. He had admitted right away that the tobacco was his. But truth counted for nothing here. If he dared tell his side of the story, it would only go harder for him. The less said, the better.

Stand up straight and answer the charge! How do you plead?

The guard at his side jabbed him in the ribs with his stick.

Guilty. Sir!

The man acting as Warden turned towards Corby and Beaupré. They spoke together in low voices as if they had a secret to share.

Now then, you plead guilty to possession of tobacco, a substance banned inside the penitentiary. Tell me, where did you get this tobacco?

I found it.

Someone planted it in the quarry for you, is that not true? Who is your connection? Who gave you the contraband?

I told you. I found it.

G852, you understand that you are under suspicion of dealing in contraband. That is a very serious charge. We have been watching you. We know what you are up to. Until now you have had a fairly good record at the penitentiary. We want to help you. Tell us who your connection is and it will go easier for you.

I told you already. I found it. The prisoner looked the man straight in the eye. I don't know where it came from. Maybe somebody dropped it. I don't know. I found it, that's all.

Perhaps a few days in isolation will restore your memory. Take him away.

The guard marched the prisoner out of the office, past the other waiting convicts, through a narrow wooden door, all but unnoticeable, the entrance to a storeroom or a closet perhaps, down a flight of cement stairs, through an iron barrier, then left, into a narrow hall.

The stone cellar under the Keeper's Hall held nine cells flanked by a corridor on cither side. The cells were larger than the ones on the range, as wide as they were long. There was a small sliding window at eye level to the left of the door and another on the opposite wall, both screened with wire mesh, the glass painted over. A wooden door was padlocked over the bars of every cell. Here was total privacy, the antithesis of the range, where a man was exposed at all times. Visibility made a man vulnerable; invisibility invoked the terror of what could be done to a man alone.

The walls, ceiling and floor of the cell were painted a slick, uniform green. The room was a concrete box, absolutely bare. No toilet, no sink, no bed. If he needed to go to the bathroom, the guard informed him, he was to yell. An officer would take him to the toilet at the end of the hall. Twice a day, he added, someone would bring him bread and a mug of water.

Put your hands through the bars.

The prisoner did as he was told. He refrained from pointing out that the Acting Warden had said nothing about shackling or a starvation diet. He would do as he was told and hope for the best.

Higher.

The prisoner withdrew his hands and put them through the grate

above his head. The guard snapped cuffs on his wrists, then secured
the bolt on the iron gate.

Take a good look, said the guard, grinning widely. It'll be a long
time before you see another face.

The wooden door closed inches from the prisoner's face. He heard
the padlock snap to, heard the guard's footsteps fade on the cement,
heard the barrier at the bottom of the stairs shut, a muffled clang,
listened for footsteps, almost indiscernible now, the door at the top
of the stairs slammed, he imagined, though he never heard it close.
Whatever sounds he heard from that moment on would be his own.

Almost no light made it through the painted windows of his
cell. A ten-watt bulb screwed in the ceiling raised the illumination
to a more uncomfortable pitch: too dark to discern anything without
squinting hard, too light to be free of the desire to look. He stared into
the fibres of the wooden door for a while, then twisted his upper body
to survey the limits of his concrete cage. Graffiti covered every surface. Scratched into the paint, with what, he wondered. A man's bare
fingernails? He strained to read the messages, the ones closest to him
first, then the marks farther along the wall, spending long minutes,
maybe hours determining if F14 might really be F19 and whether a
sentence was 130 or 150 days.

He did not know how much time elapsed before his shoulders
began to ache. There were no sounds, no shadows to gauge the passage of the hours. He shifted his weight from one foot to the other,
pressed his palms flat against the wood, curled his knuckles, leaned his
forehead against the bars, held himself straight, threw back his head,
flexed his neck, his knees. He imagined he was lying on his back in the
warm sand, lifting his arms to the sun. A person could do that forever
on a hot summer's day.

Hours passed. Days perhaps. No, probably hours. His arms went numb. He called out for the guard, called out again, and when no one came, he relieved himself, wetting his trousers. He let his thoughts roam free. Let his mind range in search of something, anything that would make him forget where he stood, make him stop wondering when it would end.

He thought with longing of his cell. His book, his blankets, his plant of tobacco (they'd probably found that, too), his fold-out chair. Until now, he'd counted his loss of liberty from the moment he'd walked through the North Gate. But he'd adjusted to the constraints of penitentiary life, become accustomed to the bars, to the surveillance, to the line-ups and searches, to the toilet exposed to passersby, to the never-ending light, the silence and the cold. He had not realized that freedom was such a layered thing, that there were still so many freedoms to lose. To go to the bathroom when he felt the need, to see the faces, meet the eyes of other men, to work, to see the sky, to take a fork in hand, such a civilized thing, to be shaved, to bathe, to pace the length of a room, to lie down to sleep, to sleep, to breathe. The freedom to breathe.

They could take that too, he thought, if they chose. It wasn't likely, though. A dead man, even in prison, was not easy to explain. Besides, there was no point to the punishment if the prisoner died. It was his spirit, not his body, they were out to kill.

How is your memory now? The wooden door had opened. The prisoner squinted with the light. Corby's face appeared in silhouette, cut by the bars. Will you tell us who gave the tobacco to you?

I told you. I found it. The prisoner believed himself now.

That's a cock and bull story and you know it. You'll stay here until you tell us something reasonable about how it came into your possession. Tell us who gave you the tobacco, and we'll let you out. Your release is in your own hands.

One day bled into the next. He was unshackled, taken to the toilet, shackled again. He dozed and startled awake, a thousand times, uncertain where he was, or why, the facts of the matter coining to him slowly, as if through a fog. Nothing happened. Hour after hour. No detail to look at outside himself. Not one thing changed but the ache of his muscles. No rhythm of night and day, just an endless present that went on forever, had gone on already how long, the words yesterday, today and tomorrow running together in the pale muffled room, damp wool against his legs, arms numb, thoughts splintering off every which way, his sanity, that hard nugget of himself, exposed and crumbling, chiselled away.

A guard appeared. A mug of water outside the bars. His hands, swollen, clumsy as if wrapped in thick mittens, tipping the mug too far, water slopping on cement, licking the cold metal bars to salvage the drops, gnawing a round of bread jammed in his fist.

If the prisoner's trade had been with an officer, there would have been someone to take his side. Someone to whisper, Go easy on him, eh? But the prisoner had gone outside for his connection.

That was it. He swallowed the dry bread in the half-dark. They were out to teach him a lesson: if deals were to be done, it would be through them. That he had tobacco didn't matter. Where he got it, did. The plug was proof: he still thought for himself. They hadn't broken him down. They knew he wouldn't give them the information they asked for. Naming names would never get him out of the Hole. He was being punished for his cheek. A lesson to new fish and others: don't act on your own. As if you were free to choose. As if you were still a man.

They explained it to themselves another way, of course. Break his body to save his soul.

The prisoner rested his temple against the bars, read the writings on the walls. Convicts had survived the Hole for weeks, for months, for years. But there was a limit to the officers' power over him. He could not be held beyond the term of his sentence. March, April, May, June, July, August, September. Seven months yet to go. Seven months of bread and water. Seven months shackled to the bars. Seven months in the cold, the smell of damp cement and urine, the rising stench of him. The interminable light. Seven months. He could do it. If worse came to worst, he could do the rest of his time inside the Hole. Spring would come. The stone would warm.

On the second day, or the fourth, maybe later, the cuffs were taken off. He slumped to the floor, the release of his arms shoving hot swords through his shoulder blades. He curled into the corner on the cement floor and slept. When he could once again feel his limbs, he forced himself to get up and walk, crossing the room wall to wall, corner to corner. He stared at his feet as he walked, watched how one toe moved forward, then the other. He swept his arm through the empty air, as if clearing cobwebs from his path. It was a marvel to him. That something had moved. That he could cause a foot to take a step, make an arm describe an arc. That he had chosen to do these things, to defy the force of gravity by standing erect. What a triumph! That in this cement box, in this pale green light there were still liberties, layer upon layer of freedoms, deep moist beds of private will they had not penetrated yet.

When his drinking cup arrived, the prisoner dipped the corner of his shirt in the water and washed his face and hands. Then he drank. His release, he was certain, would be imminent.

● ● ●

Valentine's Day, 1920, fell on a Saturday, which meant that the midwinter tea-dance at Kingston Collegiate Institute was held on the Friday. Phyllis did not attend; she was still confined to her bed.

She didn't mind. There was something ominous, she decided, about celebrating Valentine's Day on Friday the thirteenth. Friday, the sacred day of Venus, the goddess of love, a good omen for affairs of the heart, but also the day of Christ's crucifixion, which put a blight forever on the week's end. All Fridays were unlucky, but the thirteenth especially so. Phyllis avoided the number assiduously, on the calendar and off. She would beg off sick from a family celebration rather than set thirteen places at the table. She was careful never to put thirteen chocolate kisses in the bag she handed to the clerk, or to plant thirteen crocus bulbs in a bed. And when she peeled apples for a crisp, even if thirteen fit perfectly in the dish, she would slice one more and heap the fruit to overflowing so as not to tempt the fates.

Phyllis wasn't sorry to miss the dance, to forego the humiliation of sitting alone, her back pressed against the wall, sipping tea while the others flirted, giggled and danced. She wasn't one of the popular girls: she lacked their easy air. She couldn't say, Mind your biz or He's a scream, in that offhand way the city girls had, tossing their bobbed hair and throwing each other knowing looks. She could rouse herself to anger, to indignation and scorn, but she lacked a capacity for the casual, the ability to utter nonsense then laugh, as if nothing she said or did could possibly matter.

At school, she kept mostly to herself, excluded from the city-girl cliques, unwilling to cast her lot with those who came to Kingston Collegiate from surrounding villages and farms. She kept herself distant from teachers, too, refusing to collaborate with them in the subtle struggle of wills by which classroom discipline was maintained. She was not a student teachers openly complained about. She was neat and quiet, her homework most often attempted, if not particularly well done. But more than one on the Collegiate staff had wondered about this remote, compliant girl, sensing inside her a rebellious spirit, glimpsed only rarely, like an image reflected in a mirror, but sometimes suggested in a disdainful rounding of the shoulder, a stubborn set to the mouth, a sly shift of the eye. Never enough to convince themselves they'd underestimated the homely village girl.

Phyllis sifted through the valentines that had arrived in the mail. Their messages mocked her. *My love I'm giving with a kiss, Dear little girl, to you.* All of them from aunts and cousins, from other Portsmouth girls. At breakfast, Jack had given Winnie an enormous lacy red heart and kissed her in front of them all; even Marion had come back from the Mowat with a hand-drawn valentine from her beau. But Phyllis had received nothing from a boy, except perhaps the card with the young man on quaking knees, one hand pressed to his heart, the other outstretched to a slender, dark-haired girl, her face demurely turned aside. Scattered around the page were hearts inked in red. *Heaps of love from—guess?*

The writing was cramped and unfamiliar, but Phyllis was not intrigued. She looked forward to only one valentine, though when she finally persuaded Gordon to check the quarry, he had returned empty-handed.

Phyllis could have sent Daddy Long Legs a valentine, of course. Nineteen-twenty was a leap year, and according to the custom, a girl had the right to choose her own partner. If the object of her affection declined, he was obliged to soften the blow with a silk gown and a kiss. Had Phyllis been a light-hearted sort of girl, one who could shrug her shoulders, hold a gown to her waist, arm folded across the fabric like a lover's, and cheerfully present her cheek for the promised kiss, had she been able to see it all as an inconsequential game, she might have sent him a painted cardboard heart. But even on the sunniest of days, Phyllis was one to note the black shadow that dragged the ground behind her like a desultory Siamese twin. And of late, her outlook had considerably darkened.

The doctor had not meant for her to hear.

Don't let on how serious her condition is. If she knows, there won't be anything in the world that can save her.

Phyllis had always assumed she would die young. Her earliest memories were of mustard plasters and bitter infusions sipped slowly, the bedcovers tucked tight under her chin. She had been too sick too often not to have considered an early demise. The idea did not upset her. It was simply her fate, like her high forehead and her muddy brown eyes. She imagined for herself a pretty, lingering death, her young body wasting away, cheeks flushed bright pink, dark hair curling against crisp linen, her family teary-eyed in the parlour, awaiting the news that yes, finally, it was a blessing really don't you think, she was dead.

Sometimes she altered the ending. The doctor, called in as a last desperate measure, finding exactly the right cure, a miraculous recovery, her gratitude, his pride and joy at making her well uniting them forever.

There won't be anything in the world that can save her, he had said.

Phyllis had not let on that she'd heard. She'd kept her eyes tightly closed, her breathing even, as if she slept. But when her mother had returned to the makeshift bed set up by the stove in the kitchen, she'd not been able to hide her trembling. Her mother had taken it as an effect of the girl's malfunctioning heart and sent for the minister, who held her hand in his and said a prayer. When he assured her she would get better soon, Phyllis had nodded and smiled. She made no sign that she knew the truth, though the trembling wouldn't stop. At night, while the rest of the family slept, she lay awake on her bed and wept.

Lord, spare my life, she whispered. Please, God, please don't let me die.

By the end of the week, she was better. Her breath came more easily, the tremor subsided. Saturday morning she sat propped against a bank of pillows, looking pale but quite pretty she thought, in her peach-coloured bed jacket with the embroidered flowers and lace trim.

In the afternoon, with her mother's permission, she sat at the piano. She was not particularly musical, not as naturally gifted as Betty or Marion. The tunes she played sounded forced, the notes spastic and uncertain, a trail of sound that didn't quite know its way. Haphazardly, she fingered the keys. Before, illness had been the aberration, now recovery seemed a temporary respite.

A bright foxtrot like the ones she heard in the music store might have lifted her spirits, made her forget for a moment her terrible fate, but in her house there were only songs of God. She opened the hymnal and began to play, revelling in the dark exhortations of the sacred music, singing the words to bridge the gaps while her fingers fumbled for the chords.

Throw out the Life-Line! Throw out the Life-Line!
Someone is drifting away.
Someone is sinking today.

•••

On Monday afternoon, the first flakes of the biggest snowstorm of the year began to fall. That night, the wind rose, whipping the snow into drifts that plugged every road in the district. The postal stages were stopped in their trades. A drift six feet deep and thirty feet long sloped from the university to the edge of the lake. The convicts were sent out to clear the streets of Portsmouth; in Kingston, unemployed veterans did the same. Husbands shovelled the snow from the roofs of their houses before they left for work, fearful that in their absence, the rafters might collapse. Wives took on the shovelling of the walks, calling to each other gaily as they stooped to the unfamiliar task. A holiday feeling caught them up, loosening their tongues and brightening their eyes, as often happens in times of minor natural disasters such as electrical interruptions, flash floods or sudden, high winds that rip branches off the trees and fling them to the ground. Not tragedies such as fires that threaten lives, but the natural phenomena that pull women from their pastry boards, cause men to drop their briefcases and lunch pails, herding them outside to their garden gates, daily routines abandoned as they chatter to one another, excited as children, telling stories of other storms, recalling the damage that was done and how they had survived.

Although her mother urged her to rest, Phyllis was caught up in the fresh possibilities of the day. She insisted on going to school, if only to escape the doctor's words, which had grown bold and followed her now into every corner of the house. She had another reason, too. The afternoon before, as soon as the storm subsided, she had bundled up to walk to the veterans' hospital to meet her mother, her first outing in more than a week. As she'd turned the corner to Forty-foot Road, she'd almost walked right into a red and grey checkered figure bent over a snow shovel. It was him. Daddy Long Legs. Not an arm's length away. From the way he looked at her, Phyllis knew: after a week of silence, a letter would be waiting.

Her mother had been right, of course. Going to school was a mistake. She had survived the morning, but by two o'clock, her head hurt, her chest felt laden with burning coals. She had barely enough energy to pull on her coat and boots and make her way to the streetcar stop.

The trolley was all but empty. She settled into a seat near the back, thankful for the peace and quiet. She had slipped into the quarry during her noon hour and found the note he had promised with his glance. She had read it over quickly, a brief, sharp infusion to carry her through the rest of the day, but she wanted to savour it now, relive their meeting face to face, dream his future with him.

Tuesday P.M.

Hello —

Quite a stranger, ain't I? But as we know the snow is the cause. How are you & all. I am pleased that I've had the opportunity of having a good view of you, now I'll never forget your features, & will be able to tell my sister when I go home all about my little friend Peggy & of how kind she was to me, & leave it to me for laying it on thick. Anyway it's in my line of business to lay it on heavy. As soon as I get in proper trim (after leaving here) I'm going back at my line, for honestly, I like that kind of work. I think it runs in the family, for there are two besides my-self in the same line of business. But fortunately, they have more common sense than I will ever have! I wrote a letter to the Firm that I was working for when I fell . . .

A commotion at the front of the streetcar made Phyllis look up. Some men were getting noisily to their feet. She had noticed the group when she got on. They were the only other passengers in the car and she had wondered, briefly, what business such men could have in Portsmouth in the middle of the day. Foreigners, with sallow skin and curly black hair. Labourers, perhaps, looking for odd jobs. She could smell the warm odour of damp wool as they passed, moving awkwardly, without speaking, single file to the door at the back of the car. She glanced up and saw, dangling in front of her eyes, the thick iron chain that fell from the wrists of the man shuffling by her side.

The pages on her lap fluttered to the floor. She bent quickly but they were trapped in the slush under his boot, under the iron band that looped the sole and circled his ankle, that fixed the chain from wrist to foot.

The man paused, made a motion as if to stoop, but a voice called out roughly, Move on!

The streetcar had stopped in front of the penitentiary. The men stepped down, clustering in the alcove behind the pillars of the North Gate. The iron grating of the door swung open to receive them. As the trolley pulled away, Phyllis glimpsed the arched stone corridor that burrowed through the wall, bars silhouetted against the snow, but that was all.

She picked up the trampled pages from the floor. The ink had bled; the words seeped into the slush. Only the page she held survived.

• • •

Hughes's brief trip to check on the progress of the medical examinations at Kingston Penitentiary had turned into an overnight stay because of the storm. Even after the weather cleared, trains were delayed, which left him with a morning of unexpected time. He could have lingered over his tea and oat cakes in the officers' dining hall, but he was drawn to the penitentiary routine, the cell blocks and the ranges, to the inmates who absorbed so many thinking moments of his day.

Hughes sat in the corner of the Keeper's Hall watching the Chief Keeper admit the five new inmates. Manslaughter, assault, sedition. Some of the crimes were new, but the men wore an aspect that was familiar to Hughes: he'd seen it on the faces of the hundreds of men who had been in his care; it had undoubtedly marked the first man brought inside these walls.

Hughes had passed several hours the night before reading the convict register, marvelling at the number and variety of inmates who had served time in Kingston Penitentiary. The first entries were dated June 1, 1835: Matthew Tavender, three years for grand larceny; John O'Rorke, five years for the same crime; John Hamilton, three years for felony.

On their second day inside the penitentiary, that first handful of convicts had been sent to work in the quarry. Their labour was a matter of necessity—the prison had to be built—but it was also meant to punish.

Imprisonment in a penitentiary shall be with hard labour, whether so directed in the sentence by which such imprisonment is adjudged or not. Every convict, except during sickness or other incapacity, shall be kept constantly at hard labour, of a kind determined by the Warden, during at least ten hours, if possible, exclusive of hours for meals, of every day, except Sunday, Good Friday, Christmas Day, and other such days as the Governor General sets apart . . .

That clause in the Penitentiary Act of Canada was borrowed from Britain's Penitentiary Act, the first in the English-speaking world. John Howard, who had helped draft the original, advocated work *of the hardest and most servile kind, in which Drudgery is chiefly required and where the Work is little liable to be spoiled by Ignorance, Neglect or Obstinacy.* Work such as sawing stone, beating hemp, chopping rags. British authorities had been ingenious in meeting the challenge of finding hard labour of sufficient quantity and drudgery. A man named Samuel Cubitt had invented the tread-wheel, a huge revolving cylinder like the paddlewheel on an oversized riverboat but with steps where the slats should have been. Inmates would mount the steps, turning the wheel as they walked. Sometimes the footpower ground corn or raised water but as often as not, the men ground nothing but air. Convicts had been set to turning hand cranks weighted at thirty pounds pressure, a thousand revolutions per hour. To hammering bricks into powder. To sewing pillowslips and shirts, then ripping them apart, seam by seam, stitch by stitch. To pulling down buildings, only to re-erect them and pull them down again.

In the first days of the Provincial Penitentiary at Portsmouth, hard labour had been easy to come by. Ton after ton of limestone had to be quarried to raise the walls, three feet thick, twenty-five feet high, three thousand feet long. The cell blocks, the Keeper's Hall, the hospital, the Prison of Isolation, the boiler house, the laundry, the kitchen and dining hall, every building had been raised row by row with hand-quarried stone. Wheelwrights were needed to make the axles for the two-wheeled carts to haul the stone; liverymen, to manage the horses; masons, to lay up courses of brick for the inside walls; carpenters, to nail together the tables and shelves. As inmates were brought to Hatter's Bay from the outposts of the colonies, they had to be fed and clothed: tailors were assigned to sew the uniforms; laundrymen, to keep them clean; shoemakers, to cobble the leather boots; farm workers, to tend the gardens and feed the sows; cooks, to boil the pork; and dishwashers, to clean up after the meals. Doctors incarcerated for quackery and abortion cared for the sick; teachers convicted of raping their students sorted books in the library. Men who entered the penitentiary without a skill quickly learned to sew a straight seam, thicken gravy, push a mop, pull a calf. There had been more than enough work for them all.

Before the first sentence had expired, however, the work had petered out. Four hundred men at hard labour ten hours a day, six days a week, accomplish a lot. The penitentiary was soon built, its spartan rooms furnished, enough uniforms stitched, of both winter and summer weight, for several lifetimes of inmates and guards. The farm, the kitchen and the laundry had kept a handful of men busy year-round, but to apply the letter of the law, something—anything—had to be found for the rest of the convicts to do.

To the pragmatic reformer, the inmates had posed a temptation that was difficult to resist. All that muscle, absolutely free, like a wild horse waiting for harness and bit. As soon as the penitentiary at Portsmouth was completed, the inmates had been set to building workshops behind the cell blocks. Entrepreneurs were invited to set up factories inside the walls, leasing inmates on a five-year contract at thirty cents a day per man. The dining-room and bedroom suites in some of Kingston's best houses had been built inside the prison. So too were the desks for the Royal Military College; the ceremonial chair for the visit to Kingston of the Prince of Wales; the scarlet tunic, grey breeches and high leather boots for the first recruits to the North West Mounted Police; the wrought-iron railings for the Parliamentary Library in Ottawa; the thirty-three-ton switch frames that shunted Canadian Pacific railway cars from coast to coast; and the stone lintels and sills for virtually every school and church within hauling distance of Portsmouth.

But the manufacturers who hired prison labour had too loudly proclaimed their good fortune. Businessmen who had to pay living wages and could work their employees only half as hard were outraged. And so just a few years before Hughes had arrived at Kingston Penitentiary, the contract system of inmates for hire had come to an end. A new clause had been added to the convict employment section of the Penitentiary Act: *The convicts may be employed in labour under the control of the Crown; but no labour shall be let out to any company or person.* Inmates still had to work, but they could not produce goods of commercial value.

The workshops had stayed open, but for one customer alone: the government itself. The inmates made uniforms for the North West

Mounted Police, for themselves and the guards. They made trousers for treaty Indians at residential schools. They made mail bags for the Post Office. During the Great War they made boots and puttees for recruits, bandages for the Red Cross, and after the war, civil re-establishment suits for veterans and a thousand ballot boxes for the Electoral Office.

The penitentiary had always absorbed a number of convicts in the constant round of maintenance, renovation, repair and expansion of the buildings on the site. But even with a steady influx of criminals to house and cook and sew for, to clean up after, with the farm and the quarry to run and a sprinkling of government contracts, there was never enough work to fulfil the letter of the law.

The men the Chief Keeper was admitting now, thought Hughes with dismay, would be sent to the stone pile. At Kingston Penitentiary, when there was nothing else to do, this was the inmates' work: to sit ten hours a day with a hammer in one hand, reducing great blocks of lime-stone to pea-sized paving stone. They sat indoors, in a shed, on long benches facing each other, sometimes thirty, sometimes a hundred and thirty men sitting elbow to elbow, knee to knee, the stone between them. Ten hours a day, they leaned over the rock, hacking at it with pointed hammers, pulverizing the stone, breathing dust-choked air. Men who arrived at the prison without skill or aptitude, or men whose spirit needed breaking, were assigned to the stone pile as their per-manent work. But rare was the inmate who passed through Kingston Penitentiary without serving some time there, as bad weather drove gangs indoors from the farm and quarry, as each job was completed before the next could be found.

When there were more men in the shed than there were hammers and places to sit, wheelbarrows were hauled out and the inmates were set to loading up the carts, staggering across the prison yard to dump the stone in a new place, moving the rock piles from one corner to another, here to there, to no purpose other than to keep them employed, a labour as pointless, as endless as Cubitt's treadwheel.

Hughes had inherited the stone piles with his Superintendent's job. They were a fixture of every prison yard. In 1918, a quarter of the inmates in Canada were breaking stone, though there was no customer for the gravel and little needed on penitentiary roads. No one remembered who started the first stone pile or when, but it would be under his tenure, Hughes resolved, that they would come to an end.

Nothing ever written regarding the 'stone pile' was to my mind sufficiently severe and I never look at the men at this work that I do not wish I could place those responsible for the necessity of its existence in their places, he had written in his first report to the Minister. He was quick to acknowledge the dilemma, of course. *It is a matter of choice between idleness and stone piles—two evils—the lesser of the two being the* stone pile.

The architects of the penitentiary system had believed that crime was bred of idleness, and that the antidote to idleness was the discipline of work. That a regimen of obedience and diligence, imposed by force, would habituate a man's mind to order and, after much repetition, order would become his preference, the routine of work internalized as moral duty and, eventually, as his own heart-held belief.

Hughes saw the sin of idleness somewhat differently from his predecessors in penitentiary reform. It was not so much that the devil made work for idle hands, but rather that idleness bred despair and discontent. Furthermore, it engendered a viciousness that could not be cured by either punishment or solitude alone. The monotony of slowly passing hours, in which neither hand nor brain was engaged, not only left the brain free to contemplate crime: it wore away the mind.

Idleness promoted mischief, too, of course. Without heavy, absorbing work, inmates could not be controlled. Hard labour was a necessary tool of prison management as much as it served to punish and reform. The great irony that had always perplexed Hughes was that although work was essential to occupy the inmates and keep them out of trouble, it was also in the workplace that the men came together and it was here their illicit schemes flourished.

The rule of silence had been instituted to prevent exchanges between inmates who worked side by side, but the men would talk, they would make deals, they would do what they could to ease their lives. The more mindless the work, the greater the talk. On the stone piles, loud, lewd conversation was constant and could hardly be stopped without reporting dozens of inmates every day. Even in productive workshops, the forge or the tailor's shop, absolute silence was impossible. Two or three guards supervised more than two dozen men. They could not be everywhere at once. Trying to keep the inmates quiet was like pushing a cork under water: the hubbub only erupted elsewhere.

And so the men talked as they worked and the trucking carried on. Inmates on garden duty grew tobacco between the rows of corn. Kitchen helpers stole bread and beans or felled pigeons and roasted them as a means of exchange. The lifer pushing the mop down the range passed contraband from cell to cell. Gangs working in the prison yard picked up goods tossed over the wall at night and delivered them, for a price.

Hughes watched the new inmates cross the yard to the stone shed. If his plan was approved, they would be among the last condemned to that mindless, debilitating labour, for he had hit upon a solution to it all—the idleness, the contraband, the erosion of discipline, the aching need for moral reform. The answer was work, as Howard had believed, but not the futile drudgery he'd proposed. An inmate who saw little or no value in what he did became discouraged, but effort that brought results would have an elevating effect. The "results" for the inmates would be cold, hard cash: Hughes would charge the government a fair price for penitentiary-produced goods and with the earnings, he would pay the inmates, not a full working wage, but a few dollars every week, enough to earn them their self-respect, to help support their families while they served their time or to build some reserves with which to make a fresh start.

And here was the genius of his plan. Inmates would be allowed to buy a small ration of tobacco each week with the money they earned. As it stood, an inmate could earn time off his sentence for working hard. But he was as likely as not to risk that remission by bringing contraband into his cell, the comfort of the moment more alluring than an added day or two of liberty, two or five years hence. In the new system Hughes had devised, an inmate could earn both a shortened sentence and his own tobacco: the twin vices of smuggling and insubordination felled in a single stroke.

He knew what his critics would say. Giving paying jobs to convicts would take bread from the mouths of honest men. Paid work rewarded criminals for their crimes, gave them an advantage over law-abiding men. Instead of paying for their sins, they would be learning a trade and accumulating a fortune, all at government expense. The scheme would prompt a crime wave as men clamoured to get into prison as a means of getting a step up in life. The critics, thought Hughes, underestimated the toll of lost liberty, of living so completely under someone else's thumb.

If penitentiaries can change a man's character so that he will never again commit crime, they will have accomplished a very great financial saving. Far greater, however, than this will be the changing of a life of sin, sorrow, failure and distress to one of happiness, success and usefulness. Such reformation will add not only to material wealth, but will add largely to the moral greatness of our country.

Hughes had spent the winter months polishing his revisions to the Penitentiary Act. By early February, he'd still had no response from the Minister of Justice to the outline for reform he'd submitted in September. Hughes was not deterred by his superior's silence. Far better to present the Honourable Mr. Doherty with *fait accompli*, every argument answered, a document that awaited only Parliament's seal.

Hughes had sent the draft to the Wardens of all seven penitentiaries. Their replies had been prompt and positive.

... *recommend that they be printed for circulation among officers as soon as possible* ... *John C. Brown, B.C.*

... *thoroughly approve* ... *W.R. Graham, Stony Mountain*

... *would recommend their adoption* ... *L.H. Chambers, Dorchester*

Hughes had also leaked a few of his proposed changes to select members of the press and the response had been overwhelmingly favourable. What he advocated was already standard practice in most of the countries of the International Prison Congress. Canada must move forward, he would argue, or lose her place in the front ranks of the civilized world.

The day before, the Acting Warden of Kingston Penitentiary had added his signature to the letter Hughes affixed to the front of his revised Act: *We the undersigned officers of the penitentiary service of the Department of Justice certify that we have read the foregoing drafts of the Penitentiary Act and Regulations and that we unanimously approve and recommend their adoption.* At the top of the list, William St. Pierre Hughes had signed his own name.

This afternoon, this evening at the latest, when the snow cleared enough that the trains could run again, Hughes would return to Ottawa and lay the document on the Minister's desk. By spring, the draft would be before Parliament. By summer, it would be the law of the land.

•••

Sunday pm

Kind Friend: —

Received OK's Tob also, Hum-Bug's.

Say Peggy, every time I've left a letter, I never mentioned it, because I am ashamed at sending them so often, & I know it soon counts up, 8 or 9 letters every week. So its up to you to invest some of that money in Stamps: I expect to hear from Sister Ruth some time this week, with a <u>very</u> small parcel. I told her to put DaDy Long Legs on same. You don't mind me doing that, do you? An aughtful nerve, eh!

Well Peggy, for now: good bye.

DaDy Long Legs.

(Trust me)

P.S. Don't spend money buying thread etc. when I can get you all that material for nothing. The Goverment is rich & anyway, it owes me something. Dady L.L. Joe

•••

The doctor was wrong. Phyllis knew how sick she was and yet she didn't die. By the last week in February, she was truly on the mend. Getting better despite the deep, bitter cold that had settled in again. The lower the temperature dropped, the more the sun shone. And it wasn't the grim, pale sun of winter that gritted its teeth at a washed-out sky. It was a bright spring sun, shining through the cold, glinting off the snow, holding out the promise of warmth.

Was it the doctor's medicines that cured her? Her mother's cod liver oil? The convict's cup of boiling water that she took every

morning before breakfast without fail? Or was it God who was making her well?

Don't let me die, she had whispered, night after night, her voice
echoing back to her as if from inside a long tunnel, please, please,
don't let me die.

Some sort of pact had been made, though she wasn't sure of the
terms. The God of her father, demanding and omniscient, would
never have answered her prayers without exacting a promise first. Yet
she had asked for help and it had been given, generously so it seemed,
without conditions, as though from a friend. If it was God who'd
given her back her health, then she owed Him something.

And so Phyllis went back to church. She had not sat on those hard
wooden benches for weeks, her illness both reason and excuse. The
day of her return was February 29. Leap year day. Twenty-four hours
stolen from another dimension, from some grand universal clock, to
add to the human year, to slow down the timepieces of the world to
match the inevitable rhythms of the earth. It was also the fifth Sunday
in February, an event so rare that it would occur only once more in the
century, forty years hence.

On this last day of the second month of the new year, the pastors,
ministers and preachers of every Protestant congregation in North
America called on the worshippers in their pews to commemorate the
success of the Forward Movement, an ambitious, interdenominational
campaign to raise eleven million dollars, a thank-offering for victory
in the greatest war of all time, a canvas for funds to spread the gospel
of goodwill, brotherhood and peace, and a call to the youth of the
land to life service in the work of Jesus Christ. At the little Methodist
church in Portsmouth, all the seats were filled.

We have not only met our goal, intoned the student pastor from
the theological college at Queen's, but we have exceeded it by three

times. Thus have we given our thanks to the Lord Jesus Christ for the victory he has granted us. By our generosity have we proved that here in the village of Portsmouth we arc recommitting ourselves and our families to the spiritual renewal that is sweeping our great nation.

Let me tell you a story, a children's story, but one that holds a lesson for every one of us here.

Many years ago there lived a famous Roman Emperor called Titus. At the close of every day, he had a habit of sitting down and thinking. And what do you suppose he thought about? Not his pleasures nor his gains nor the praises of his people, which were many. Though a heathen, he loved to do good and at the close of every day, in the latter part of his life, he thought, "What good have I done today?" If nothing came to mind, if he had helped no one, if he had done nothing to improve the lot of his people, he would write in his diary, *"Perditi diem."* "I have lost a day." For Titus believed that a day in which he had done no good was lost.

Make that your personal challenge on this special day of thanksgiving and rededication to the service of Christ. Every day, some good to someone. Every night, reflect on what Jesus has done for you and then ask yourself, What have I done for Him? Never lay your head again on the pillow knowing that you must admit to the Lord Jesus Christ, *"Perditi diem."*

Let us pray.

Perditi diem, Phyllis whispered that night as she leaned her chin on the attic window sill and stared down at the vacant ledges of stone in the penitentiary quarry.

Perditi diem. I have lost a day. How does one say, I have lost a month. Or: I have lost a year. Or (and this she could not even whisper, though she saw it lodged in the blackness between the stars): I fear I am losing my life. I am sinking without leaving a trace.

March

During the night, an ice fog crept in from the lake and settled over the village of Portsmouth. When the quarry gang passed in the morning, every limb of every tree was seeded with crystals, tiny prisms that sucked in the early morning sun and spewed it out in a spray of light that swelled the treetops full and white. As the day warmed, the ice fell from the branches, not with the sharp rattle of midwinter but noiselessly filling the air with flakes of silver, spinning and drifting, winking in the sun. The prisoner, looking up from his stone, thought he saw a girl among the willows, Peggy shimmering in the mist.

In the lining of the prisoner's inner coat lay a letter, the weight of it pressing against his skin like a promise. When they had let him out of the dungeon, he had vowed to keep the rules for the remainder of his time inside. But when he saw her note in the Palace the first morning of his return, his heart leapt. It wasn't what she wrote or even what she did for him that had come to matter so much. It was the fact of her, an indistinct figure from a world he'd all but lost, giving him leave to speak.

For the penitentiary had forced on the prisoner an unnatural parsimony of speech. He had never entirely stopped talking, of course. But when he spoke, it was in spastic whispers, his sentences stripped to essentials, conversations contracted to a phrase, a word, or less. The lift of an eyebrow. A finger crooked. The compact language of the body speaking volumes, yet never saying enough.

Even the words in the official monthly letter were rationed: seven hundred to a page. A man like Thackeray, whose penmanship was so precise he could inscribe the Lord's Prayer on his thumbnail, would have no advantage in the penitentiary: seven hundred was the limit, whether the words filled the page or not.

A certain number of words; words of a certain kind. If the subject matter, the phrasing or the tone of the prisoners letter displeased the censor-guard, the words disappeared under a heavy black line, the prisoner struck dumb, though he never knew when or why.

The first Sunday of the month was library and correspondence day on the prisoner's range. When he returned from chapel, a single sheet of prison-issue writing paper, an inkwell and a pen were laid out on his table. Beside it lay the library catalogue and his book card. An embarrassment of riches; the rare luxury of choice.

The prisoner picked up the little catalogue. Once a month the convicts made a list of the books they wished to read. One book at a time, no more than two books a week. On Tuesdays and Fridays, the convicts who managed the library, all university men fallen from grace, made the rounds of the cells in the prisoner's range. They collected the book the prisoner left on his table and set his next choice in its place.

According to official count, the penitentiary library contained more than five thousand volumes, but in fact, there was not much to read. At least a third of the books listed in the catalogue were out of circulation, the pages ripped out for punk or so mutilated that the story no longer made sense. There was little money for new books: most were donated by charitable citizens or cast off by more fortunate institutions. Thus, there were hundreds of copies of *High School Geometry* and *Pitman's Shorthand*, enough that, should they choose to do so, all the convicts could simultaneously study isosceles triangles in their cells. Half of what remained were magazines: the *Forestry Report* and *Agricultural Gazette of Canada*, monthly issues from 1912 to the present. No newspapers. A set of *Encyclopaedia Britannica*, which could be borrowed one volume at a time, except for volume nineteen, *Ref-Sai*, which had been removed so that convicts would not be tempted to improve themselves by memorizing the inner workings of a safe. Detective stories were banned, though the odd mystery got past the censors, those with neither corpses nor minutely detailed crimes. For the illiterate, there were picture books, illustrated volumes *of Jack and the Beanstalk, Sleeping Beauty* and *Babes in the Wood*. Every book on the shelves had been vetted by a committee composed of the Warden and the two chaplains to ensure that nothing would disturb the delicate equilibrium of a convicted man.

The prisoner studied the list of books. He had already read everything that was of interest to him, all of Hall Caine, all but one of R.W. Chambers. *The Maid-at-Arms*, he wrote on his card, #242.

The books that appeared in his cell usually had more than one story to tell. The inside covers and the margins of the text were scrawled with comments, praising or damning the book or the penitentiary itself. And since the books moved freely from cell to cell, they carried messages among the men. The prisoner had learned to read between the printed lines, working out the complicated codes by which one reader sent clandestine messages to the next: dots impressed with the tines of a fork, letters underlined to spell out words, sentences made up of words reshuffled into a telegram of anagrams.

As the prisoner marked off his next seven choices, he could hear the sounds of surreptitious conversation on the range. There was no keeping the convicts quiet: they would communicate with each other, crumbling the walls with whispers. The cells on Sunday were especially alive with intrigue. Faint mouse-like scratchings on the stones and spoons tapping messages on the bars in the terse dots and dashes of the Morse Code or more often, a primitive, exhausting exchange in which the letters of each word were spelled out with taps corresponding to its position in the alphabet. *Charlie . . . murder . . . and you.* Men bending low over their toilet bowls, the water scooped into the sinks, breathing quiet conversations into the pipes. Lines tossed out between the bars, dangling like spider's threads from one catwalk to the next.

The officials of the penitentiary did their best to keep paper and pencils out of the convicts' hands but the world was made of string: trouser hems, begging to be unravelled; blankets full of long, coarse threads that could be picked out of the weft; a length of binder twine pilfered from the farm; the knotted hairs of a horse's tail. Weighted at one end with a stone, the message tied in a loop (or if paper was scarce, worked in knots along its length), the string was cast out between the bars. The lifers were experts, worthy teachers of the sport: casting at an angle, directing the line just so, letting it out until the man in the cell below cast out his own line with a bent-spoon hook, reeling in the message and sending it off again, angling the kite across the range, sideways, down, sideways again, until it reached its destination, the convicts working together like a crew of old salts, all of them celebrating when the catch was brought home.

On Correspondence Sunday, the prisoner had the right to compose and send one letter. It was the rule. At the beginning of his first prison term, he had wept to see the piece of paper on his table. There had been so much to say. Now that he could write to anyone at any time, the official letter seemed a sham. Yet he always filled the page with his allotted seven hundred words. Anything less would arouse the suspicion of the guards.

The prisoner dipped the nib of his pen in the ink and filled in the lines labelled Writer's Name, Address on Envelope, Date.

Below that, the penitentiary's printed message to the recipient:

Letters to Convicts in this penitentiary should contain nothing but family, personal or business matters. <u>General news, neighborhood gossip</u> or reference to other Convicts will prevent delivery of the letter. Enclosures, such as newspaper clippings, photographs— except small size of some near relative—tooth brushes, handkerchiefs, cards, pictures, fruits, cakes, Christmas boxes, etc. are prohibited.

By Order Of The Warden.

The prisoner had no faith that the officers mailed the letters he wrote or that the letters addressed to him were delivered to his cell. He knew of a man who hadn't received a single letter during his prison term. He was convinced his wife had forgotten him, had thrown him over for another. He'd lost heart, grown bitter, no longer cared whether he earned remission or not. No one waited for him at home. When the day of his release finally came, the Keeper handed him a stack of picture postcards from his wife, sent faithfully one a week for two years. The man cursed so loudly the convicts in their cells had heard his cries up and down the range.

How the men lived for their letters! Even the pages with line after line blacked out. They would paper the walls of their cells with the words of their loved ones, kneading bread with saliva and soap (tooth powder, if they could get it) to make a paste to fix the paper to brick.

Dear Sister Ruth:—

The prisoner had to think carefully before he wrote. Only a narrow range of topics was allowed. Nothing about his friends, his keepers, the ups and downs of his daily life. And she could tell him nothing of what was going on outside. What the convicts needed most, thought the prisoner bitterly, was what was denied. News of the world. Of his friends. Family gossip. Who had made it back from the Great War alive. Who had moved away, got married, started a new life.

How is your health? I can't complain.

The prisoners pen lagged, for although he sat down every month with his prison-issue page, it affected a man to speak with a hand poised before his mouth.

Yet the words themselves never stopped. They formed in the prisoner's brain like raindrops, condensation from the mists of thought. He talked to himself: endless, silent soliloquies, debates in which he took both sides, arguing the case and making rebuttal too, words accumulating inside his skull until he thought he'd drown.

Peggy was his lifeline. With her he could speak to his heart's content. Every day he wrote, hunched over on his bunk, stringing words across the pages, their meanings often tangled in the rush to let them out. Where he was, what he was, papered over with words. He wrote to forget. He wrote to remember. An endless loopy maze of words: a shelter from the silence, a passage through the stones.

● ● ●

Friday PM

Dear little Pall —

The same occurance is repeated this Friday as was a week ago; rain all day, with the result that dissappointment is what follows.

Some few evenings ago, I was thinking of how absent minded I was at not thanking you for your thoughtfulness in cutting & saving that clipping out of the paper. (Concerning our concert.) Please forgive me for my forgetfulness. In the future I will try & bear in mind such favours.

I am pleased to hear that you have regained your speech. Also, hope you are back to normal health.

I don't know what I would do if I lost my voice. Heredity has often transmitted a talent. There are many families of Singers, & loquacity, too, is hereditary: for instance, most of the children of talkative persons are chatterboxes from the cradle. Words— idealess aimless & unbridled—appear in us to be prompted by a sort of elastic spring over which we have no control. So you see how hard it would be for me to cease to talk. The boss tells me I do enough talking for the whole quarry.

You were quothing in your last, asking my forgiveness for not coming down last Thursday evening. Little one, by all means & at all times, use your own good judgment. I believe as you were saying, that on account of the snow, you thought best not to undergo what I am sure must be an aughful exciting trip, for I have a slight idea of the thrill that must rush through your body when you are about to ascend that grand stairway.

That odd letter with the stamp on it was done by me without your kind permission. That was to a man's wife who lives in

*Kingston. He was sick in the next cell to me, & asked me one day
if I knew how he could get a letter to his wife, as he had some
important facts to notify her of & he believed it may get him out
of the Institution. I simply told him to write the letter & I would
try & have it mailed for him. You know who the other one was to.
Many thanks for this never to be forgotten work*

*So Bro & Sister have at last departed. I did have a fine little
laugh all to my-self when in yours of late you referred to your
Sister-in-Law. I would of done 3 <u>more</u> days in here to of had the
opportunity of seeing little Peggy giving a piece of your mind,
& gently permitting her to know that she was not your boss. ha.
ha. Well you are right, & keep right on sticking up for what you
believe is right; a very good practice. A familiar old phrase is as
follows—a pretended friend is worst than an open enemy.*

*How is ma keeping? Are you successful in keeping her from
going up there to work for that other woman? I am sure you <u>must</u>
miss her, for home without a mother is like porrage without sault,
not genuine, (not like home). I very often think of my poor old
mother & wonder how & what she would be doing at times. You
were saying there were plenty of young girls to do the cooking for
the soldiers. Indeed, I don't for a moment doubt your word. But,
is there not another question, Peggy? Namely, Experience. <u>Could</u>
they do the work? Not like the mothers.*

*Once again, I can plainly see that you & mother would be
pleased to see me next summer, Peggy. I give my word of honor
as a man (or a specimen of one) that I will, if God spares my
health, pay you a visit. That much would be accomplished at all
costs: That little ring I promised you with the initials of Peggy
engraved on same.*

*I will likely have a PS in this to-morrow, so until then good
bye, & God bless you all,*

DaDy Long Legs

(Trust me)

• • •

Miss Naomi Irving held the stick of chalk in front of her ample bosom
like a votive candle. *Good writing cannot be acquired in a day,* she
intoned, chanting the psalm of proper penmanship to her third-form
class. *Success comes to those who earn it.* Phyllis had heard this lecture
too many times to count. Yet she could never quite get her Os round
enough, her Ls swooping forward then back with confident grace. Her
ascenders wavered; her descenders drooped.

*Sit squarely in front of the desk, close to it, but not leaning against it.
Keep the feet flat on the floor in front of the chair. Let the arms rest on the
desk with the elbows over the edge about an inch.*

Phyllis checked the position of her body. Her wrists stuck out in
front of her as if awaiting handcuffs. How she hated these four walls,
this drudgery she had to endure before she could do her real work,
God's work, in the quarry and in the tobacconist's shop downtown.

*Sit erect, with the eyes twelve to fourteen inches from the paper. The
sides of the paper should be parallel with the right forearm. The paper
should be held with the left hand above the line of writing.*

Phyllis lifted her pen and dipped the nib in the inkwell at the upper
right-hand corner of her desk.

*The first finger should rest on the penholder about an inch from the
penpoint. The second finger should support the holder anywhere between
the root of the nail and the first joint. The thumb, curving outwards, should*

lightly touch the holder somewhere between the end of the first finger and its first joint. The hand should be well turned toward the left and rest on the nails of the third and fourth fingers, which are bent back under the hand. The wrist, which is held nearly flat, should not touch the paper.

The teacher's voice was as round and measured as the Cs that coursed across the top of the blackboard. The woman sounded as if she could go on forever, beyond the classroom, beyond life itself, preaching good penmanship with enthusiastic patience to the angels who kept the Judgement Day Book.

Back erect, feet flat on floor, eyes thirteen inches from the page, forearms free, Phyllis began to write.

CCCCCCCCCCCCCC

Count Your Blessings

The nibs of thirty pens, sixty fingernails, rasped lightly in rhythm as letters curved into words across the blue lines of thirty well-positioned pages.

EEEEEEEEEEEEEEE

Even a Child is Known by his Doings

Outside the window, the sun grilled the sky to a deeper blue. The snow would be melting. Rocks splitting. A letter waiting.

GGGGGGGGGGGGGG

God moves in mysterious ways.

• • •

Thursday noon

Hello Peggy: —
I saw my first Robin yesterday afternoon, & of course I wished. I wonder if our wish will come true? I seen you waving your hand from the window yesterday (or <u>was</u> that you?)

*I received all the Tob ok, <u>many thanks</u>. But as usual I am
going to ask for more. Selfish, ain't I?*

*Please get one pound of Burnt Amons (chocolates with nut
inside) & if they do not cost any more than $1.00 per lb, spend
the remainder of the dollar in Gum & say Peggy, would you
mind keeping the change for me. OK asked me this A.M. if
I would again ask you to get him a couple more pcks of Bull
Durham. So will that be alright?*

*Now Peggy, although I am not expressing my thoughts,
please believe me, that I do feel cheap asking you to do so much
for me, so for now good-bye.*

As B/4
DaDy <u>Long Legs</u>

*Can I worry you for a <u>couple of envlopes</u>.
(Trust me)*

<u>in a Hurry</u>
Excuse scribling

• • •

DIVORCED ON GROUNDS OF DESERTION

*The lady appeared before Judge Welch in the Douglas County
courthouse accompanied by her mother and two attorneys. She was
dressed in an old dress of no particular colour except that it was
dark, a shapeless old hat and had mud all over her shoes and skirt.*

*She said that her name was Gladys Moore and that she was
the wife of Owen Moore and that he had plumb deserted when she
was a dutiful and loving wife. She cried and took on and it was
real pitiful. As soon as the judge said she could have her divorce,*

*which he did right away as soon as she began to cry, why she
wiped away the tears and smiled as cheerful as could be.*

How could the judge not know that the woman standing before
him was Mary Pickford? wondered Phyllis. Everyone on the continent
knew the sweet face of this Canadian girl.

*It was a tight-lipped, tense little person who clenched her fists and
lifted her chin in an aggressive manner with which her screen admirers
are not familiar. Pickford was sitting in a ranchhouse sunroom reading a
much thumbed copy of Balzac, charmingly gowned in an airy cloud of blue
chiffon with blue silk stockings and blue satin pumps.*

*"I sought for a divorce because I wanted to be free." The little star was
on the point of shedding tears she was so angry. "My plans for the future
are my own."*

Mary Pickford had brushed Owen Moore aside as casually as
flicking a spider from her skirt. Phyllis could hardly bear it. She threw
the newspaper to the floor. From the girl who was Jerusha Abbott,
who had promised Daddy Long Legs, *Yours, forever and ever*, what
kind of loyalty was this?

• • •

Phyllis told Daddy Long Legs everything. Though she worried sometimes that she carried on too long, he said he loved her kites. He never
intimated that next to his, hers was a paltry life. He never dismissed her
tales as trifling. No matter how much she complained about Winnie or
worried over her health, he always took what she said to heart and
offered solace, advice and encouragement in exactly the proper measure, at just the right time. He had a way of accepting her confidences

that loosened the stays on her spirit: she revelled in her deliverance, and it bound her to him.

Oh! the beauty of the place we went to! It was all bridges
& falls and the sprays went about 10 feet in the air, and the sun
shining through them, it was simply glorious. I have never before
seen anything like it. I'll be able to tell you more when I see
you—there is too much to write. I had a splendid time, but my
heart was always yearning for home. I sure am some home-bird.

So far, my stomach is fine. I can eat anything, it seems,
but pastry. I have had one bad attack. I had to take magnesia, a
nature's remedy, & then after that soda, and the pain, which was
around my heart, bothered me all the next day. But I am fine
now & it has been a warning, so I have wiped pastry off the slate.

I do hope you take care of yourself. Mother isn't sparing
herself and I am afraid she will get sick again.

I think that postman thinks I'm in love with him, I visit him
so often. But I do love a letter. Yes, by all means, tell Ruth to
please try & write a few lines.

Peggy

P.S. I had a sick headache to-day so excuse blunders. I'm
afraid I'm getting an awful cold. My head is light & dizzy & I
have a wretched sore throat.

Phyllis wrote faithfully every day. At noon hours on designated days, Gordon delivered her notes and collected the convict's kite, but every evening, she too crossed the no-man's-land of the quarry floor, pushed open the bottom half of the Palace door and reached for their special stone. Under its weight were two, sometimes three envelopes:

thin paper folded around a coin or a dollar bill, a letter to mail, perhaps, and always a kite explaining the details of the day's transaction, sharing with her the vicissitudes of his life.

The days lengthened as they warmed, forcing Phyllis to wait until well past supper before the shadows fell thickly enough to veil her passage through the rocks. Her feet knew the route: down the path by the pump, across the road, under the chain, along the flat top ledge of limestone to the ladders, the soles of her shoes secure in the convict's footprints as she descended each level to the next, lowering herself by degrees into the pit, the sprint across open ground, over the picket fence, then crouching low by the Palace door, waiting, counting slowly to eleven, for it was on the eleventh of October that she'd found his first kite, then reaching inside, her fingers shaped to the familiar curve of stone, his letter spread open on her lap.

But as Phyllis read his words tonight, a chill crept up her neck. He had not had a letter in several days, he said.

She'd left one yesterday.

Phyllis pressed the door open as far as it would go, leaned her shoulder against the wood and reached deep inside, raking the floorboards, the rough edges of strange tools and boxes with her fingertips.

She'd already stayed too long: in the rising moonlight, the shadows were coming alive. She pulled out a pencil, retrieved her envelope from under the stone. *P.PS. I left a kite yesterday. Look for it please.* If it hadn't been misplaced, then another convict must have taken it, for if an officer had found it with the plug of tobacco inside, the quarry would have been closed by now. *It is my idea that someone close to you stole it.*

She was about to replace the kite when caution stayed her hand. If yesterday's letter had been stolen, then someone knew their hiding place.

She put the letter in her pocket, stood and brushed the stone dust from her skirt. She had only one option: to return to the safety of the roadside, for tomorrow at least. In the meantime, she'd think of another hiding place. The snow was almost gone; the Palace was no longer banked. Perhaps they could use the long dark vault between the beams again.

The next day at the hardware store, Phyllis found just the thing: a small metal box, big enough for a pound of tobacco, a packet of chocolate kisses, a book. It was painted deep hunter green with a black metal lock, nothing to catch the light but two thin brass keys. One she strung on a ribbon around her neck. The other she rolled inside the note that she hid in a clump of last year's dry grass, between the dog-house and the path to the pump.

• • •

Hello my old Pall Peggy:

As luck was in our favour, a good fellow found your parcel or letters or whatever it was! I told him OK put them in the Palace. He was going to keep them.

Yes, Peggy, this little tool box will be ok. I will not know if you get this or not. But if you leave a Kite there so I can get it tomorrow, then you can expect a long Kite telling you all. My hands are nearly frozen so for now untill I hear from you. By. By.

Cord.

DaDy long legs

(Trust me)

PS. Enclosed $1.00. I will leave my mittens in the new Box.

Friend "Joe"

I got your Kite this <u>noon</u>. DaDy.

● ● ●

March, thought the prisoner, was like a woman. Unpredictable and coy. She led a man on with her balmy breezes and sunwarmed skies, encouraging daydreams of spring, then when his blood was hot for it, she let loose a slap of snow.

On the fifteenth of the month, no sun shone. Wind-whipped clouds scudded across an ashen sky. Within the stone walls, however, summer had begun.

The authorities at Kingston Penitentiary refused to be bound by the natural quartering of the year according to the Earth's movement around the sun. Instead, they reduced the number of seasons to two, one hot and one cold. By their reckoning, the first day of summer was the Ides of March: on that day, the wake-up gong shifted to six-thirty from seven; the heat to the cell blocks was shut off; and during that week, when the convicts went to their baths, they traded their red and grey checkered woollens for straw hats and suits of brown and purple striped denim that they would wear until the leaves, which had not yet sprouted, fell.

For the prisoner, it was the season of his release.

Bye-bye, he mouthed, handing his mud-caked clothes to the change-room clerk. He would never wear the skin-rasping wool again, at least not so as anyone could see. For the prisoner had kept his second shirt. The lightweight summer cloth was too flimsy, even doubled up, to camouflage his contraband, he'd decided.

He hadn't worn his second shirt today. There was no way to hang onto it when he stripped for the bath and once he handed over his suit in the seasonal exchange, there'd be no getting his extra wool shirt back. So he'd left it in his cell, hidden under the blankets hanging above his bunk. Unobtrusively, he hoped: his number could come up any time in the endless roulette of cell searches that amused the keepers while the convicts worked. It was a risk he'd have to take every bath day for the rest of his time inside if he was to remain courier to his friends. At least he could stop worrying about the girl: the system of exchange she'd devised was more secure, and bolder, than anything he'd dare conceive.

In the quarry, when he saw how the others shivered in their summer issue, the prisoner gloated that his enterprise had forced on him the extra clothes. By summer, he would swelter in the wool. But by summer, he'd be gone.

•••

Friday <u>noon</u>

Am I not a fine one to put you kind people through so much trouble, <u>poor, ignorant, block-headed Joe</u>. But it was such a lovely warm day that I thought I would only put on one shirt, & I was in such a hurry, I just for the moment allowed it to slip my memory. Oh, I was so angry at my-self for being such a blockhead.

Ain't this one miserable day! I am not sure about your receiving this to-night for perhaps we may not go out to the quarry, but I do hope so!

This last day or so has taken away all the snow, perfectly wonderful how rapidly it does go, once it commences to. I think good old June will come after all. You know when it snowed so heavy a few weeks ago, the officers were kidding me, telling me there was going to be no June this year, (on account of me going out the last of June). But if we have a few more days like yesterday (Thursday) there won't need to be any spring.

I do feel so much better to-day. I have been fortunate enough to make connections with that party in the kitchen & got a good lunch to-day (all to your generosity). Oh Peggy, I must tell you what it was: two pieces of apple pie also a piece of cake, & a great big pork sandwich. Pig, ain't I? But, Peggy, it did taste so good!

Well, Peggy, my little Pall, time is pressing me, so hoping you will forgive & forget the big <u>Blunder</u> of being so absent minded. I remain with best regards to ma & yourself As B/4

DaDy Long Legs

(Trust me)

• • •

Is this yours?

The boy handed Phyllis a stubby roll of brown paper.

I found it over there, he said, pointing to the narrow yard between Phyllis's house and her uncle Alex's. The rain had shrunk the snow to ragged drifts that hunkered in the lee of buildings and shady alleyways.

Phyllis opened the note. The paper was dry, the ink unsmeared.

Hello Peggy:

I will leave a Kite Monday PM in our closet, that is the little red shed in the middle of the Quary, with the white fence around it. Also, I will leave a small flat stone (IN SAME) underneath will be Kite explaining all.

Don't worry! I got everything ok. My object in printing is obvious, so sufice in saying,

<u>PEGGY</u>

Trademark

So as B/4

Faitful Friend

DaDy long legs

(Trust me)

My name isn't Peggy.

I know, but you and your sisters are the only girls on the street. I thought it must be yours.

Did you show it to anyone else?

No.

Are you sure? She gripped the boy's shoulder.

Hey, let go.

She mustn't frighten him.

Well, it's not mine, she said, crumpling the paper and shoving it in her pocket. Besides, it doesn't make sense. It's just gibberish. It belongs in the rubbish.

She turned and walked straight to the house.

In the refuge of the attic, her hands shook as she smoothed the kite flat on her knee. The paper looked like the convict's; the handwriting did not. Instead of his loose, loopy scrawl, the words were printed, and even the printing was odd. Letters jerked across the page as if they'd been written on a streetcar. Her name was queerest of all: the upper and lower strokes of the E stretched towards the Y, embracing the double G. What did he mean "trademark" and why would he change his penmanship just now?

Someone was spying on them. The convict who'd found her letter in the Palace. Of course. Only he would know their private names, their hiding place. And he even knew that she was Peggy. When he'd found no more kites under the stone, he'd come right to her yard.

Desperately Phyllis read the kite again and again, searching for proof that she was wrong, that the words came from Daddy Long Legs after all. But the convict's style had been mimicked perfectly, even to the "trust me" affixed like a seal at the end of every kite. Surely, she thought, she should be able to detect a forgery, if not by the writing or the words themselves, then by the feel of the letter in her hand. Something of the convict, something indisputable and distinct, must be conveyed in his kites.

Phyllis held the paper before her, her palm flattened, arm outstretched. She closed her eyes and prayed for guidance. The strange script, the unsmudged ink, the peculiar message, its odd delivery: none of it made sense.

•••

Wensday <u>noon</u>

I don't wonder at you being so interested in this printed long lost Kite. Yes, Peggy it is my scribling & to convince you, I printed another like it in order to show you it really was mine. The only one difference lies in the pen-nib: one is a little heavier printed than the other.

This Kite was printed by me about Jan 2nd or 3rd or thereabouts, with the intention of throwing it near the House when shovelling Snow. One day you was out in the yard & OK informed me of the same, so I says, here, take this Kite & try & make her understand that you mean to leave it where she can get it. This he done, believing you were wise. Hence, that afternoon he looked & said the Kite was gone, with the result that I looked every day for weeks in our little red house. Well, Peggy I was sure you got same, but on account of our trouble was afraid to answer same, so the next time I tryed to reach you was one day when we were passing the House on our way back from the Hospital. This was some weeks later, shortly B/4 I took sick. You know the telegraph pole almost opposite your house. I threw a little Kite on the far side of the side-walk, between the inside of the walk & the fence, & only a few feet south of the small gate

leading to the house. Some one was at the window I think it was
your Sister in Law & she was looking my way, for I was leading
the gang. Hence I threw same, in above mentioned position. No
doubt, it would be there yet. Any-how, if any one did get it, they
would not comprehend same.

This is glorious St. Patrick's day & I told a lie, I said I
wasn't feeling good & asked to stay in my cell this noon hour, but
did I not have a very good reason, (namely to explain matters)
Any-how I am tired of the choir. Now its practicing for Easter
& as no doubt you know, it's all Latin in our church & that is
tiresome.

Good bye my little friend, & I do hope your mind will be at
ease, after examining both Kites.

By By

DaDy long legs

(Trust me)

● ● ●

Above the bars outside each convict's cell was a coloured card printed
with his number and his prison term: a red card for Protestants, blue
for Roman Catholics. On alternate days, choirs for the two denominations practised through the noon hour. Monday, Wednesday and
Friday were Catholic choir days. Of the two hundred convicts who
claimed the Roman Catholic faith, only a couple of dozen signed up
to sing. For the prisoner, it was an opportunity not to be missed: when
he'd worked in the stone shed, he'd rubbed shoulders with men from
all over the penitentiary, but since he'd been moved to the quarry, the
choir was the only place where he could meet and do business with
men from other ranges and work gangs.

The prisoner tucked the letter in his coat in case the guards chose that day to ransack his cell and waited at the gate to join the parade of convicts heading for the chapel. Rain beaded the tall, narrow windows across the corridor, stitching lake to sky, a seamless grey.

Down the stairs, through the Dome, up the stairs of the north cell block, past the library, above the Keeper's Hall was the Roman Catholic chapel. Father McDonald had done what he could to fashion a sanctuary within the stone walls: wooden pews, identical to those in any cathedral outside except for the cubicles that screened female convicts from the men; a Eucharist table with a carved relief of the sacred lamb; an ornate altar with six tapers, three on either side, rising towards the crucifix that hung empty and waiting. Life-sized murals flanked the altar, Mary and the Cherubim on the left, and on the right, the Holy Mother kneeling at the feet of her tortured son, an image calculated to wrench the heart of any convict who could bear to bring his eyes to rest on her weeping face. According to prison officials, this chapel and its Protestant counterpart were the most dangerous places in the penitentiary, but only on Sundays, when six hundred men huddled together in the pews, the entire population of the prison mingling cheek by jowl, watched over by a handful of guards, one beside each window and door, a slit-eyed paling of shepherds scrutinizing their wayward flock.

The Protestant chapel was larger and had a proper choir loft, but the Roman Catholics had a pump organ and a paid musician who came to the prison four times a week to accompany the choir. The convicts grouped themselves loosely around the organ, altos to the left, tenors in the middle, basses on the right. Most of them, like the prisoner, were young men doing short time; only a few of the lifers sang. In the back pews of the chapel slumped the guards, dozing off their midday meal.

At the organist's signal, the convicts lifted their music sheets and hummed the opening chord of the song they were preparing for the solemn mass of Easter Day. The strains of the music carried the prisoner back to the churches of his boyhood and his youth, to his first communion, his father's funeral. Balm to the senses; comfort to the soul.

Gloria Patri et Filio, et Spiritui Sancto,

Sicut erat in principio, et nunc, et semper, et in Saecula Saeculorum.

The music honed the rough edges from the voices of the convicts. They sang lustily, grateful to break the silence, even with these ancient, inscrutable words. On Sunday, the choir would be joined by a bellow of male voices from the congregation, loud hosannas, though perhaps not loud enough to mask the sounds that rose from the Keeper's Hall below. For in a peculiar twist of penitentiary logic, floggings were oftentimes scheduled for the Lord's Day. The rack would be dragged up from the basement and installed in the room under the chapel, wood scraping heavily through the convicts' prayers. The man condemned to lashes by the court, stripped to the waist and shackled to the frame; the Surgeon and the Deputy Warden standing by; the Warden with the cat-o'-nine-tails in hand, thinly braided leather that whistled through the pauses of the song . . . *Pater noster, qui es in caelis, sed libera nos a malo* . . . the sharp, scattered thwap, the cries of the man rising in crescendo with the convicts' song.

Alleluia! Alleluia! Pascha nostrum immolatus est.

The organist tapped the music stand sharply with his baton.

Remember men: This is a celebration. Christ is risen! More majestic, if you please!

The convicts began again, from the beginning. The song went on for pages. Before the *last Amen*, two young men in the back row exchanged a small wrapped package the prisoner recognized. Only moments before, he had traded it for five sheets of writing paper and a new nib, to be delivered during Sunday's mass. And what would its latest owner get for it, he wondered. An extra sandwich at supper. Half a dozen smokes, crouched low in the corner of his cell, blowing softly through the Judas slit. A few moments of intimate touch, even tenderness. Or perhaps, before the day was out, the tobacco would find its way back to the prisoner, payment for a letter mailed to a trusting wife.

• • •

Friday: P.M.

Dear little friend: —

Once again, its my pleasure to have the privilege of answering your beautiful Kites. It pleases me to know that you are convinced that it was my printing, but, after reflecting over the whole in general, I've come to the conclusion that perhaps after all you are correct about that mischievous boy. For one would think that the ink would be all blotted, on account of it lying out in the open for such a long time. Can't but believe that the boy held it all this time, & only pretended he found same just previous to the time he presented it to you. However, no harm done & experience is the best of teachers, it will not happen again, & any-how, even if it did take such a long time to reach its destination, after all, we know its in safe hands.

Say Peggy, was not yesterday one grand day. I was a <u>wee</u> bit lonesome yesterday, & oh how often I did wish it was the last of June or around the begining of July. I've even got the days counted.

So Sunday is the 1st day of spring. Are you not glad this winter is at last over with? Ain't it wonderful how fast the snow has vanished? It was what I've long been wishing for, & now I

am patiently looking for the ice to break up & see the boats running up & down the bay.

Say Peggy I am not to have my hair cut any-more for the
remainder of my time. You have no idea of how pleasant it feels to
be able to have one's hair, after having it cut off every month for
seventeen months. I've had mine since Jan, & its now commencing
to be long enough I can use a comb. So if you please, if there
should be a small piece of comb around the house, would you mind
allowing me to have same? The fine end, if possible, as my hair is
very fine; many thanks. But always wanting some-thing, Ain't I?

I got Tob ok. Also change, again thanks.

Did I not enjoy watching you sawing wood this P.M. But
you are bashful, are you not? I was so anxious to see you look
up & smile. OK drawed my attention to you being up there &
immediately up I went, as all the Bosses were labouring over
a large piece of stone. Your ma is always so pleasant, never
yet have I seen her but she had a great big smile. I am sure the
daughter must of inherited that beautiful gift, but I can never
get her to look in my direction. It is claimed by men of Science
(Phrenologists) that bashfulncss denotes many very good marks
in character, too numerous to mention.

In calling back to last winter, yes Peggy on several different
occasions did I notice you & ma. One special occasion was when
you were both coming from the store, by the old black-smith's
shop. I was 2nd from the front & the nearest side towards you, &
looked your ma right boldly in the face, but Peggy was reading
some article. Only once did I ever get a look at you, & that was
the day down by the Hospital, but I don't believe you would know
me if you met me. I don't believe you ever once looked in my
direction, ha, ha.

*Scarcity of paper bids me crowd in. That Guard, the one
who was talking to your Dad last fall, is on night work; they all
change every two months from day to night & vice versa. The
one up there now is to my estimation too Sleepy to see any-thing.
However, he is watched. Once again, Peggy, good by & keep in
good health, ma also.*

DaDy Long Legs

(Trust me)

*PS: Here I am sending $1.00 for one of my friends inside, he
wants two cans of Colgate's tooth-powder. Of course Peggy it's
to be an understood thing, he don't know how I get it. He is a
french-man, & a very good pall of mine, & helped me out often
when I never had any Tob. So one good turn deserves another, &
I am sure you don't mind me asking you to do this, eh? I am in
no hurry, next Thursday evening when you come down will do,
so long as I can get it Friday, for this party works in the Bathroom. Ain't I an aughtful pest. Always wanting some-thing, eh?
Oh well it's all in this game of mine in here. Nerve must never
be absent, & I don't think it is! Good bye once more my good
Friend,*

As B/4

DaDy Long Legs

(Trust me)

• • •

On Sunday, March 21, the Earth stood erect, balanced perfectly on its
axis. A still point. From that moment on, the sun would be in ascen-
dance, winter's darkness overcome by the quickening light.

For three weeks, Phyllis had held to her Lenten vows. Church on Sundays, Bible readings every morning and night, and a regimen of exercise and cleansing to make her body a fit temple for her strengthening soul.

Before her on the bureau lay two tin basins, a dish of Woodbury's Facial Soap that she kept for herself in her top drawer, a facecloth, a towel and a piece of ice chiselled off the block in the kitchen ice box. She dipped the cloth in the basin of steaming water and held it to her forehead, her chin, each cheek in turn. She could feel the pores opening like blossoms in the rough, moist heat. With the cloth, she worked up a lather of soap and rubbed it for thirty seconds into her skin using the upward, outward motion recommended in the facial treatment brochure. She rinsed off the soap with hot water, scooped cold water from the second basin and splashed her face again, then wrapped the ice in the cloth and rubbed every square inch from temple to temple, hairline to chin, as if there were some mark she was trying to erase. She patted her face dry and leaned towards the mirror. The light from the coal oil lamp smoothed her complexion, but at close range she could see six tiny red volcanoes ready to erupt. The blemishes never really disappeared: her ministrations managed only to push them under the surface, to break through elsewhere.

She dipped her fingers in the warm water, worked up a fresh lather and coated each spot thickly.

While she waited for the soap to dry, she moved to the window and stood before it, drawing her body erect, her chest well forward. She held her arms out in front of her, towards the black glass, felt the coolness washing over the clenched fists of her upturned palms.

Snap your fists together as your arms meet in front.

Phyllis could feel the muscles in her breasts contract, lifting the rounds of flesh, pushing them together.

Draw your arms backwards as far as possible, bending your elbows and keeping them as close to your side as you can.

Each time she moved her forearms, she drew a deep breath, letting it out slowly as she lifted them again, keeping the muscles tight. She felt good. She felt strong. Felt her body work. Felt, at last, that this vessel of flesh and bone might be her friend.

The deep breathing of the exercise, the steady rhythm of her arms, the tautness of her skin drying under the soap, drawing out the sickness inside, cleansing her, released her mind to wander out through the glass, over the treetops, into the quarry, among the stones.

The place that had once been her sanctuary was peopled now with ghosts. The faceless figures of the convict's friends and enemies circled the Palace, their arms reaching out to her, hands grasping. She'd done favours for men she would never recognize. How many of them, she wondered, knew her name—either the special name she shared with Daddy Long Legs or her Christian name. The convict had grown careless, throwing kites in odd places, forgetting to retrieve what she'd left, leaving letters addressed to people she didn't know in places she'd never heard of, without asking her leave or feeling obliged to explain.

Perhaps she'd been wrong about him. Perhaps he was not the man she'd thought him to be.

Phyllis raised her arms above her head, stood on tiptoe and stretched, her body erect, balanced perfectly in the lamplight. It wasn't too late to put an end to it, before he got out, before damage was done.

• • •

The spring offensive was launched.

For William St. Pierre Hughes, the careful preparations of his first year as Superintendent had been like trenchwork, tediously digging a slit for himself in rocky soil, extending it slowly along his flanks, marshalling his forces, moving them unobtrusively into position. Now the signal had been given. The first advance had begun.

The medical examiners' reports lay on his desk in a thick file with copies of the letters of termination that had been mailed to the penitentiary officers declared over-age or unfit. Eight at Kingston Penitentiary, including O'Leary, who would find the envelope bearing the Civil Service Commission stamp in his mailbox when he returned from his leave of absence at the end of the month. O'Leary was the only casualty that gave Hughes satisfaction. As expected, his first salvo had provoked a spate of newspaper articles ... *conscientious officer* ... *years of valuable service* ... the indignant tongue-clicking of the local press, tempered, he knew because he had forged it, by their greater sympathy for his cause.

A good commander kept his sights fixed on the objective, never allowed his gaze to linger on the bodies that fell at his side. Hughes had learned his lesson at the battle of the Somme, fighting hand to hand with the Hun in his own trenches, driving them back and scrambling out after them, drawn by the points of their bayonets across no-man's-land to the enemy line, star shells exploding like Roman candles above them, cordite stiffening the air.

His objective: a young, well-trained penitentiary staff, a paramilitary force, ranks swelling with a new kind of soldier, army and Salvation Army bred, equal parts policeman and reformer, strong in body, mind and soul. A staff organized along the lines of the North West Mounted Police who had fought beside his regiment at Batoche, a force in which the commanding officer could engage, discipline, dismiss and administer without interference from any quarter. Removing the selection of penitentiary staff from the hands of the politicians had been a first step. But the Civil Service Commission, in Hughes's scheme of things, was just the middle ground. For the penitentiaries to function at their best, Hughes needed full control: his own Penitentiary Reform Police Force, officers he would train in the firm, humane handling of their fellow men, officers who understood that true reformation came not from coercion of the body, but from improvement of the soul.

But that was in the future. For now, Hughes had to content himself with overseeing the hiring of men to replace those he'd found unfit. Most of the new recruits were in their twenties, untried, but more importantly, unformed. Only two were over the age limit of thirty-five, and these men filled senior posts. In positions of authority, the wisdom and judgement of age took precedence over the malleability of youth. His chaplains, after all, were both close to threescore and ten, and he himself was just three months shy of fifty-nine: a man in his prime.

Nevertheless, the two appointments had raised a fresh clatter of protest in the *Daily British Whig*.

Now comes surprise number two, in the person of an ex-guard who played one of the leading parts in the investigation that took place at the pen before the war. He finally resigned, received his gratuity and succeeded in landing a military job. He has held two different military jobs during the war. He passed the age limit years ago, but nevertheless he is back on the strength at the Kingston pen. What I want to know, is this justice from the Justice Department?

Hughes did not respond. He ignored the newspaper's telephone calls. He was like the land dreadnought, the iron caterpillar born on the battlefield where the trees of Bouleaux Wood once grew, lurching across the shell-shocked earth, nothing could stop him, emerging through the mist to the soldiers' huzzahs, crashing through the ramparts, moving forward, relentlessly, as if driven by a supernatural force, into the hurl of rifle and machine-gun fire, forward, until straddling the enemy entrenchment, sweeping fire from side to side, clearing the way for the footsoldiers with their bayonets, taking the front trench, the stone ruins of the village of Courcelette itself. Hughes, schooled in the smoky mists of the Somme, was moving forward, though he stood fixed with a steady gaze at the window of the Warden's Office inside the walls of the penitentiary at Portsmouth, resolute, indestructible, amazing to behold.

• • •

Phyllis took her mother's arm and led her across the road, weaving between the muddy patches that the spring sun had not yet dried. The street was dark. Behind them, the windows of the McGuire house were still flickering with people milling about the parlour, relatives, friends of the family, the dead boy's playmates, up past their bedtime. It was the second funeral they'd attended in as many weeks, both of the dead taken by influenza.

Phyllis and her mother walked in silence, words smothered by the fear that death could brush its wings against their family, too. Betty seemed to be getting better, but so had Eddy, the boy in the tiny coffin, so had James, the young man at whose bedside Marion had passed her winter days. Had the soldier lived, Marion would certainly have married him. As it was, she lay disconsolate on her bed, the sound of her weeping lulling Phyllis to sleep and waking her again before first light.

Above the Halliday house, streaks of pale green splashed up against the evening sky. Giants, thought Phyllis, crouched among the quarry stones, tossing buckets of whitewash into the night.

Look, Mother, said Phyllis, pointing above the house. The Northern Lights.

Gussie Halliday squinted into the blackness.

It's going to storm, she said.

...

With his thumbnail, the prisoner drew a crucifix on his forehead, his lips, the centre of his chest. Bless my thoughts, my words, purify my heart. *Dominus vobiscum. Etcum spiritii tuo. Sequentia sancti Evangelii.* Christ speaks to you: hear Him! In these words are the tidings of His life and of His teachings; and they are one.

And when they were to come to the place, which is called Calvary, there they crucified him, and the malefactors, one on the right hand, and the other on the left.

And one of the malefactors railed on him, saying, If thou be Christ, save thyself and us.

But the other answering rebuked him, saying, Dost not thou fear God, seeing though art in the same condemnation?

And we indeed justly; for we receive the due reward of our deeds: but this man hath done nothing amiss.

And he said unto Jesus, Lord, remember me when thou comest into thy kingdom.

And Jesus said unto him, Verily I say unto thee, Today shalt thou be with me in Paradise.

And the sun was darkened, and the veil of the temple was rent in the midst.

Father McDonald boomed the gospel from his pulpit, sending the deep, powerful waves of the Holy Word undulating through the chapel, stirring the hearts of the convicted men.

Inasmuch as in His human flesh He suffered more than you can ever suffer,

Since He died as you shall die, but more horribly, being given over to the dread infamy of a felon's end;

Therefore did He give you an example to follow, by revealing that Death is swallowed up in Victory,

For you, being ransomed by Him, are destined and promised to Life Eternal.

If ever there was a chance to make an impact on these men, thought Father McDonald, it was on this twenty-fifth day of the third month of the year, the Day of St. Dysmas, the Penitent Thief. His own Portsmouth parish church, the Church of the Good Thief, was dedicated to St. Dysmas, the only edifice so named in the Christian world. Thieves and murderers had quarried the stone for the church, thieves and murderers had hauled it up the hill from the penitentiary stone shed. What could be more fitting than to dedicate it to them? Father McDonald believed with all his heart in the promise Christ made to the Good Thief; his mission was to bring these dismal convicts to believe it too.

Christ was crucified between two thieves, evil doers, convicted of crimes like yourselves. They were scourged, as many of you have been, by order of the court of that day. They were humiliated, fixed to crosses raised beside a public road, in a conspicuous place, where they could be scorned by all who passed by, their fate held up as an example to others who might be tempted to break the Roman laws. They were stripped naked and left to die in the sun under the watchful eye of the centurion, who stood guard to prevent the theft of their bodies.

Theirs was a slow, torturous death, one that could take three days or more, the pangs of starvation and thirst multiplying their suffering. But these men were not left on their crosses for long. They were crucified on Friday and since Sunday was a feast day, the legs of the thieves were broken to hasten their death. Not so our Lord, who with the blessing of his heavenly Father, died swiftly and mercifully. And before he breathed his last tortured breath, he promised to one thief eternal salvation.

And why do we call St. Dysmas the Good Thief? Not because

he was successful at his trade. A laugh rumbled through the chapel. Father McDonald paused and smiled.

No, he continued soberly, St. Dysmas was a Good Thief because he understood that he deserved his fate—and that Christ did not. *We receive the due reward of our deeds.* He admitted his sins. He welcomed his punishment. He accepted the justice of it. He did not, like the thief on the left hand of Christ, ask the Lord to save him. He simply asked, *Jesus, Lord, remember me when thou comest into thy kingdom.* Thy kingdom. He did not question whether the man at his side was truly the son of God. *Thy kingdom.* In that simple phrase he rendered unto Jesus Christ the respect and devotion that He deserves, that He demands from us.

And what was the Good Thief's reward? His reward for admitting his sins and recognizing the Lord Jesus in his midst? Everlasting life. Nothing less. *Today shalt thou be with me in Paradise.*

This is the lesson of the Good Thief, my friends. It does not matter what you have done that has brought you inside these stone walls. In one way or another, we are all sinners. *For all have sinned, and come short of the glory of God.* A sinner is guilty before God. The trial is over: he is condemned. *The wrath of God abideth upon him.* But he is not lost. *You* are not lost. Jesus Christ has seen to that. He is your Saviour. Your guide to Paradise. It is never too late. You have only to recognize him. *Remember me when thou comest into thy kingdom.* Recognize Christ, admit your sin, and you will be saved.

Credo in unum Deum. Patrem omnipotentcm, factoren caeli et terrae, visibilium omnium et invisibilium ... Dominus vobiscum. Et cum spiritu tuo. Oremus.

The prisoner bowed his head and closed his eyes. In the blackness he saw the thief on the cross, his legbones shattered, his head hanging limp. And at his side the guard who would cut down his body and that of his brother thief. And then what? he thought.

Two convicts had died inside Kingston Penitentiary that month. The quickest, surest way of getting out, the prisoner had thought. Death, at least, would take them home again. But it wasn't so. One convict had no next of kin: his body was sent to the medical school at Queen's. The other was shipped back to his family. But when the dead convict's mother opened the coffin, it was not her son she saw. Her boy's hair was red; this man's was black. She buried the unknown convict and pleaded with the penitentiary to send her son to her. But the man was in pieces, carved up by the scalpels of the university's medical men.

In the penitentiary at Portsmouth, thought the prisoner, even the dead didn't stand a chance.

• • •

Severing the connection with the convict should have brought Phyllis relief. It did not. She had written the letter telling the convict of her decision early Saturday morning while the sun still struggled to clear the penitentiary walls, but she had not been able to bring herself to hide it in the tool box under the Palace. She had carried it with her throughout the day, opening the pages and reading them again and again as she worked at her chores. The weather was glorious, the kind of spring day that made the spirit soar, yet the words she had written weighed her down. How could she abandon him after all they'd been through? With the firings and the mix-ups at the penitentiary, his situation could only get worse. Yet when she stood by the burning barrel and held her letter over the flames, she couldn't seem to drop it, though the heat seared the skin of her hand. Protecting herself and her family was surely the right thing to do. Or was it a cowardly, selfish act?

All day she avoided the quarry road. She stayed indoors at the hour when the gangs passed. If she saw him, she knew she'd be swayed. After the penitentiary bell sounded, when the convicts were safely in their cells, she climbed up to the attic and sat by the window staring at the willows, their black branches etched against the sky like hieroglyphs, characters from some dead language she could never hope to understand.

Darkness had all but settled when she heard her mother calling gently at the bottom of the stairs. She grabbed the letter from the sill and scribbled on the back of the envelope:

> *P.S. Daddy, I have thought the whole affair over and I have changed my mind about not writing. I will write twice a week. I will go to the box only on Saturday & Monday so that I won't be noticed by the neighbours too often.*

Even before the first sentence was finished she knew she had done the right thing.

> *Hasn't this been one grand summer's day?*
>
> *Peggy*

•••

On the second last day of March 1920, the Minister of Justice sat down to write a letter to William St. Pierre Hughes.

The Superintendent, the Minister had decided, needed to be reminded of his place. This Hughes was more refined than his brother in outward appearance, perhaps, but he was cut from the same cloth. A man of privilege, accustomed to having his way. Ever since his appointment, the Department had been barraged with urgent recommendations for one reform or another. Ministerial silence had not dissuaded him, though it had gone on for months. Nor had rebukes over his public relations campaign with the press.

The time had come to remind William St. Pierre Hughes who was in charge. The day before, the Minister had named a new Warden to Kingston Penitentiary. John C. Ponsford was no pantywaist reformer. He had ruled first Stony Mountain, then Alberta Penitentiary with an iron hand; he would whip Kingston into shape. The Minister had not consulted the Superintendent on the appointment: let it come as a surprise. As would this letter. The Minister was serving notice: he would not take orders from a bureaucrat, most particularly one named Hughes, not on appointments and not on penitentiary rules. He would take the matter out of Hughes's hands and give it to the politicians, who were as slow about their business as they were easy to control.

OTTAWA, 30th March, 1920.

Dear Mr. Hughes;

The draft revision of the Penitentiary Regulations which you submitted recently does not any more than those already in force give effect to the principles which I endeavoured to explain, and I think it desirable for purposes of proper consideration to have a draft prepared embodying my proposals. To this end I have asked Mr. O.M. Biggar to consider the whole subject and to prepare a complete revision upon the lines which I have suggested. He may find it desirable to visit one or two of the larger prisons, and if so you should instruct the Wardens to afford him all requisite information and assistance.

Yours sincerely,

Chas. J. Doherty.

•••

The Northern Lights lied. Or Phyllis's mother had read them wrong. At the close of the month, Kingston was the warmest spot in the Dominion. A Iamb had tiptoed in with March on its back and now the lamb gambolled out. The temperature rose to sixty-four degrees Fahrenheit overnight. The snow melted and the ice began to rot. Horses broke through the ice road to Wolfe Island and the postman switched to punts to make the trip. A heavy wind swept down the lake, caught up the massive shards of ice and pounded them into the narrow funnel of the St. Lawrence River. Within hours, the harbour was clear. Even before the whistle of the Wolfe Island Steamer sounded, everyone in the village and in the penitentiary knew: spring was here.

SPRING, 1920

Because a man commits one bad act,
we have no right to say he is a bad man,
any more than a man who does one good act
should be considered a good man.

———————

WILLIAM ST. PIERRE HUGHES

April

Under a pale morning sky, a convoy of twenty-five motorcars pulled away from the door of Alberta Penitentiary. The prison, erected inexplicably near the heart of the provincial capital, was only a few blocks from the train station, but a march of fifty convicts through city streets, even at such an early hour, was considered too dangerous a prospect for the citizens of Edmonton. And so the convicts had been escorted from their cells, two convicts and two guards to each waiting car, until the stone walls and steel bars confined nothing at all.

At the station, John C. Ponsford watched the orderly transfer of the convicts from the automobiles to the special train he had devised, the windows fitted with bars, the doors with reinforced locks. As a pre- caution, each convict was shackled, ankle to ankle and wrist to wrist.

Ponsford stood at the front of the locomotive, his hand resting flat against the machine's massive cylinders, as if he were afraid it might bolt at the approach of its cargo. Steam drifted through the half-light, obscuring the men, the clatter of their chains muffled in the engine's low hiss.

The Deputy Warden shook Ponsford's hand and climbed into a coach at the front of the train. Faces stared from behind the bars at every window, but except for the Warden, the platform was deserted. The pistons strained, the couplings flexed and the locomotive pulled smoothly out of the station, heading east across the prairie to Stony Mountain where Ponsford's penitentiary career had begun.

Ponsford watched the convict train until it was a smudge on the ruddy horizon. He did not lift his hand in farewell. He stood outside the station and waited in the chill, hardening light until his own train appeared, pulling into Edmonton from Vancouver, on its way to Toronto, Halifax and points between.

It was Ponsford's last day as Warden of Alberta Penitentiary, the little prison he had guided through its decommission, weighing the last bag of oats, the last ton of coal, toting up the columns in the register books, tidying up as he went out the door. Before the month was out, he would walk through the North Gate of Kingston Penitentiary, Warden to the nation's most desperate convicts. The thought was not daunting. Quite the contrary: it filled him with pride, stirred something in his loins like desire. After six years in the West, John C. Ponsford, the contractor's son, the tax collector, the army captain from St. Thomas, Ontario, and lately El Paso, Texas, was coming home.

• • •

William St. Pierre Hughes had not slept. When he closed his eyes, the face of the Minister hovered, bloated and incorporeal, above his bed.

The expression was hard to place. A slight upward curve of the lips, drained of pleasure or warmth, a mask of smug satisfaction, as if he had always wondered at the fate of flies whose wings were plucked and now he knew.

Hughes slipped out from the covers, put on his dressing gown and, careful not to waken his wife, went to the kitchen to heat some milk. It cleared his thoughts to have something to do.

The Minister had overstepped his bounds. Parliament had given the Superintendent of Penitentiaries responsibility for revising the Penitentiary Act. The Civil Service Commission was charged with hiring penitentiary staff. No Minister of Justice, not even the Prime Minister's personal friend, could take these matters into his own hands. Charles Doherty had no right to name John Ponsford Warden of Kingston Penitentiary. He had no right to appoint a politician like Biggar to decide how the prisons would be run. Hughes took inventory of these facts as he would a private arsenal. The question was: how to put them to use? He had already made one critical mistake. He had underestimated his opponent. Wars had been lost for less.

The Minister, William knew, held no affection for any Hughes. Self-righteous megalomaniacs, teetotalling Orangemen, paranoid power-mongers, aggrandizing mountebanks, loose cannons: Samuel had brought these epithets and more on the family name. All his life, William had floundered in the backwash of ill will generated by his unorthodox brother. The struggle had made him a restrained, methodical man, not without his own grand schemes, but content to keep to the shadows, preferring well-laid groundwork, privately prepared, to his brother's public *Sturm und Drang*.

Sam's shameless politicking had won William his Brigadier-General's insignia, but it had almost cost him the Superintendent's job. Such was the measure of how far his brother's star had fallen in the last years of the Great War. A national hero, he'd been knighted for rushing Canada to England's defence, then suddenly, overnight it seemed, Sam Hughes was a national disgrace, vilified for requisitioning the woefully inadequate Ross rifle, for barring alcohol from army canteens, for promoting family and friends through the ranks of his hastily assembled fighting force. Every defeat of the Great War, all the corpses, had been laid at Sam's feet and as he faltered under the weight, the men he'd bullied, ignored and shouldered aside to build his Militia turned on him—and his brother—with a vengeful eye.

William was quite certain that Doherty had lobbied hard against his appointment, though the petitions and endorsements sent by soldiers and friends had finally swayed the Civil Service Commission to his side. The Minister had barely spoken to him since. Hughes had interpreted the rebuff as an admission of defeat. Despite his personal displeasure, Doherty would uphold the law—or so Hughes had thought.

That was his mistake.

Hughes watched the surface of the milk for the first sign of rising steam, his hand on the stove switch, ready to turn down the gas at the critical instant before it boiled.

He had been forewarned, although he realized it only now. Late in the fall, Doherty had ordered Alberta Penitentiary closed. Just days before, Hughes had recommended that the number of prisons be increased so that inmates could be classified according to their offences, first-time lawbreakers and petty criminals housed apart from felons serving long sentences for serious crimes. Hughes assumed that his proposals had not reached Doherty's desk in time, that the decision had been taken months before. He was annoyed that as Superintendent he'd been neither consulted nor informed, but he'd forgiven the oversight: it would take everyone a while to get used to having him around. In Parliament, Doherty explained the closure as a move to reduce overhead costs in the face of a prison population that was growing by leaps and bounds, but now Hughes saw it for what it was: notice served by the Minister that no one named Hughes was going to tell Charles Doherty what to do.

Hughes stirred the milk carefully. His first reaction to the Minister's letter had been shock, a moment of paralyzing disbelief before a storm of outrage swept through him. Necessities had propelled him through the rest of the day, but the fury stayed with him, bending his thoughts. At one point, it crossed his mind that the letter might be a joke. It had arrived on April Fool's Day, after all. But Doherty was not a man of humour. His timing was ironic and cruel. He had waited until the anniversary of Hughes's appointment as Superintendent, had waited until Hughes had laboured a year at his revisions, until he had played his hand, shown the finished draft to the wardens and leaked it to the press so that naming someone else to revise the Penitentiary Act would not only demoralize him but humiliate him publicly and undermine his authority inside the prisons.

Almost too late, Hughes saw the bubbles at the edges of the pan. Holding back the skin of milk with the spoon, he poured the steaming liquid into a china mug. He opened the back door and stood on the kitchen stoop, blowing across the top of the cup, sending little clouds into the darkness. As he sipped his drink, the stars on the eastern horizon faded. The moon, all but full, paled as the day broke but refused to disappear in the brightening sky. It moved steadfastly on its own trajectory until it set behind the backdrop of barren tulip trees.

The last of Hughes's anger dissipated with the night. He had not wanted this confrontation, had not, to his everlasting sorrow and regret, anticipated it. Now he saw that it had been inevitable from the start.

The milk and the early hour soothed him. He was reminded of all the dawns he'd passed as a boy in the fragrant warmth of his father's barn, the smell of hot milk steaming into the buckets, the soft comfort of the heifer's flank against his cheek as he leaned into the chore. His life had been hard but simple then, and the steadfastness with which his father had carved the farm out of the rock of the Ontario shield had seemed more his birthright than a virtue to be honed.

He would hold firm. He would not back down. He had right on his side, if not Justice. He'd been named for his mother's grandfather, General St. Pierre, who had fallen defending Bonaparte at Waterloo. William, too, would fight to the end, a credit to both the family lines. He would rally the last of his brother's friends in Parliament. He would marshal his allies in the press.

The campaign, Hughes decided as he drained his cup, would take place on public ground. He would distance himself from the action and avoid the taint of self-interest that dogged the Hughes name. He would welcome Ponsford, while he lobbied the Civil Service Commission to investigate how the man had been hired. He would not respond to Doherty's letter. Instead, he would wait until the issue of appointing a politician to do the new Superintendent's job was raised in Parliament and the Minister was forced to resign for flouting the rules in his own Penitentiary Act.

My triumph will not be imminent, thought Hughes, but I will celebrate in the end.

Hughes rinsed his mug and set it upside down on the drain-board. The warm milk had done its work. He could rest the entire day if he wished: he had no engagements until the evening when his presence was required in the Hughes family pew for the Good Friday service at the Ottawa Methodist Church. Hughes climbed the stairs to the bedroom, his bearing erect and his conscience clear, only faintly aware of the bitter aftertaste of the barely scorched milk.

For two days every spring, the convicts in Kingston Penitentiary were one with Christ: wrongfully accused; innocent, though convicted; imprisoned in stone.

How had Christ passed His time inside? How exactly had He got out? The part of the story that nagged at the prisoner, the Bible skipped over as though of no account. Through the first hours of the long lock-up of Easter weekend, the prisoner read the accounts of Matthew, Mark, Luke and John. Their stories were identical, as if the apostles had spat in their palms and made a pact. The body laid in the sepulchre, the stone rolled in place, a guard posted to prevent the theft of His remains or the escape of the risen Christ. Then suddenly, on Sunday morning, when the two Marys arrived, the guard gone, the stone rolled back, Christ nowhere in sight.

Did He slowly stir, as if from a sleep, a segue from a dream? *Where am I? Oh, I remember. The cross.* Or did He startle awake, His eyes blinking open to the blackness, limbs tingling with yesterday's pain, an acrid taste on His lips, palms burning, an ache in His side? *This, then, is death.*

The angel of the Lord, they said, rolled back the stone. Did the winged apparition bend over Christ's body and rouse Him gently to the light, shaking His shoulder, whispering, *Wake up. It's time to rise.* Or had Jesus sat on the edge of His rock bier all day, the winding cloths unravelled at His feet, waiting, impatient for His liberation, eager to see His Father and start a new life, uncertain of what would happen next, cursing the dark, silent stone.

The prisoner paced the floor from the bars to the Judas slit and back again.

The window across the corridor framed a starless sky. How he longed to see the constellations spread out above him, the Pleiades, the Great Bear, Orion's Belt, Cassiopeia's Chair. To deny a man the sun blanched his body, but to deny him the stars parched his soul. The prisoner climbed on his bed and strained to see through the filter of bars and glass and accumulated dirt. Across the yard, the limestone edge of the Prison of Isolation glinted under what he thought must be a full moon. He grabbed the bars in his fists and hoisted himself a little higher. Cold steel striped his cheek. He searched his slab of sky, but the moon hung out of sight, suspended in someone else's heaven.

• • •

The congregation of Portsmouth United Church huddled on a knoll at the edge of the Rockwood Asylum lawns, their eyes fixed on the penitentiary sprawled at the other side of Hatter's Bay. They clutched their hymn books and shifted foot to foot, stamping bald patches in the fresh snow. The women pulled the woollen collars of their winter coats up around their throats. The pale messaline silk and georgette crêpe of their new spring dresses was insufficient for such a premature Easter Sunday.

The minister, mindful of the cold, kept the resurrection service brief. He had lingered in the church basement until twenty minutes before the exact time of sunrise as predicted by the almanac that protruded from the pocket of his overcoat. Phyllis and the older girls who were to serve breakfast after the service had busied themselves setting the long tables while the men carried in the chairs and the women warmed the teapots. As the little group set out from the chapel, the yeasty, cinnamon fragrance of hot cross buns warming in the oven trailed after them across the white expanse of lawn almost to the water's edge.

Now upon the first day of the week, very early in the morning, they came unto the sepulchre, bringing the spices which they had prepared.

The minister's words were but a whisper in the vast cathedral of God's creation. He cleared his throat and raised his voice.

And they found the stone rolled away from the sepulchre.

And they entered in, and found not the body of the Lord Jesus.

And it came to pass, as they were much perplexed thereabout, behold, two men stood by them in shining garments:

And as they were afraid, and bowed down their faces to the earth, they said unto them, Why seek ye the living among the dead?

The minister glanced over his shoulder, modulating his message to the glowing red globe pushing up from the stone. It was a challenge he set himself every year, to pace the reading of the Scripture to the rising of the sun so that at the very moment it cleared the penitentiary walls and balanced triumphantly on the southeast tower, he declared,

He is risen.

The Sun of Righteousness is risen today.

The minister paused and turned to face the light. The sun levitated beyond the limestone, reclaiming the sky. The minister turned back to the Bible spread open in his palms.

Thus it is written, and thus it behoved Christ to suffer, and to rise from the dead the third day:

And that repentance and remission of sins should be preached in his name among all nations, beginning at Jerusalem.

And ye are witnesses of these things. Let us pray.

Phyllis bowed her head. She had counted on this moment to fill her with fresh hope, as it always had, the sun's first rays christening her cheek like the hand of God, unexpected and warm. New Year's Day, her birthday, the first day of school, Easter: a whole calendar of new beginnings, days when she could wipe the slate clean and try once more to live a life free from sin.

The task would be easier if she knew what constituted a sin. In resuming her connection with the convict, was she putting her own soul in peril and jeopardizing her family for the sake of a criminal? Or was she earning a place in heaven?

It was not reason that kept her writing kites and buying goods for Daddy Long Legs. It was a decision of the heart. And because the heart held sway, though no commandment had explicitly been broken, she suspected that what she did was a sin just the same. Writing to Daddy Long Legs always brought her happiness. She'd allowed herself to think it was the joy of the righteous, a just reward for Christian charity. But perhaps the pleasure of those moments was the shallow delight of worldly things. Perhaps the convict was God's temptation, and the whole affair, a test of her soul.

No amount of thinking could sort it out. What Phyllis wanted, what she needed, was a sign. But though she stood and waited, head bowed, the minister's words worked no magic. The sun was just another star, and she shivered with cold. Fresh ice groaned against the shore. Overhead, grackles huddled on the bare branches of the trees like wizened replicas of the dark-coated men and women hunched in silent prayer on the asylum grounds.

Across the bay, the brilliance of the rising sun sharpened the penitentiary to a black paper-work silhouette. Between the two west towers lay the Dome, and beneath the Dome lay the convict, stirring awake to the day. At that thought, the warmth that until then had been denied her seeped sweetly into her heart.

The minister closed his Bible with a slap.

Turn your eyes upon the Lord Jesus and look full in His wonderful face and the things of this world will grow strangely dim in the light of His Glory and Grace.

• • •

Easter Sunday <u>P.M.</u>

Dear Friend Peggy:—

You have no idea of how much your kind & encouraging kite cheered me up. Honestly my little friend, its as good to read your Kites as for me to receive mail from any of my friends. Its always the very first thing I look for & its quite hard to keep from running down to the halfway house to read them immediately: for you must understand that I always wait for an hour or so. One of the men working on top of the hill has to be carefully watched, as he is a detective (stool-pigeon) or commonly known in prison slang as a <u>Rat</u>, one who tells every-thing he sees or hears to the Authorities in order to gain their friendship, etc.

This Hair-pin must belong to you, does it? I found it near the Box. Hum-Bug-Kid said when he seen me pick it up—Good luck Joe, put it in your shoe & your wish will come true, so this I done. If this does not belong to you then there must be more than Peggy visits the Quarry.

Now that I am writing on this most interesting subject, <u>Hair</u>, I was up to see the Acting Warden, & I explained to him how slow my hair grows & that I had it on since last December & it was only commencing to be long enough to part, & that it was very thin; so he had a look at it & he is quite a kidder, for he says, well, you can't have hair & brains both. I told him it was "H" when one didn't have either. He asked me how long more

*I had to do & many more questions and ended up asking me if
I was ever in any trouble. This I told him, for I knew he only
had to look up my record & see for himself. If a lie would save
my hair from being cut, why I would tell a hundred. However, I
told him when I first came in I was found disobeying the rules by
talking & once for Smoking, & once for being caught with Tob
& money. Oh, oh, says he, well that's much different, says he.
You cannot expect to have any privileges if you have disobeyed
the rules & regulations. I said to him, Sir, I don't consider any
of these crimes as serious, especially smoking & talking. Well
says he, its the rules, & its up to me to see that they are kept. If
I was punished for smoking every-time I smoke, I would not live
long enough to finish my punishment. Any-way he says, I'll see.
That's what they all say! He told me to come back next week
when the new Warden arrives, but to "H" with him. I'll get it off
& be done with it.*

*When you notice this blood on the paper, do not think I was
trying to commit suicide but rather I stuck the end of the pen-nib
in my thum & here I am writing & sucking my thum, ha, ha.*

*You say you are fond of Potery; well next summer or early in
the fall when I come on that promised visit, then I will recite for
you some real nice potery. I know one resestitation, very long &
some-thing that was said to be one of the most beautifulest pieces
ever written. Perhaps you have heard it or heard tell of same. The
title is—Dan the Actor. I would write it out for you but I believe
you would rather wait & hear (foolish me) recite.*

*Say, am I not having a wonderful time writing this Kite.
This is the 2nd terrible disaster all within a few minutes: I
knocked over the ink well.*

I am wondering what you will be thinking when you go to the

Box to-night & find no mitts. I was up on top of the Hill until the very last moment, watching you & that other little girl swinging, with the result that I forgot until too late to leave them, that is, without Knowledge Box seeing me.

Peggy, if it would be just as easy for you to put every-thing in the hole in the glass in the Palace, I believe it would be much safer. I'll tell you why. We have working in the Quarry one of your Kingston Boys, & his Bro comes out & leaves him things. But I know he is going to get caught. This A.M. his Bro passed in an Auto when we were going in & shouts out so all can hear him, Did you get that ok? Why a blind man or a child could get wise to him. I told him he better be a little more careful, but he did not like to be told anything. What can one do? So if it makes no difference to you, drop the "Stuff" (except Kites) in the hole. Hum-Bug always gets the Key & opens the Palace B/4 any one else gets up.

Hum-Bug is the <u>only</u> one who knows any-thing concerning our connections. He has been tried on different occasions & proven loyal & true: they at one time put him in the Dungeon & kept him there for six days trying to make him tell some-thing, but all they got out of him was: I don't know what you are talking about. It was all over a $10 bill. A stool-pigeon seen him with it & threw him up. They tore all his clothes trying to find it but he had it under his false teeth. He has never told me, but I've heard from different sources that he should never of come down here, that it was his Bro he was punished for. I was not surprised to hear that, for he is just the one who would take some-one else's punishment!

I was just having a smoke & thinking of how I would like to be able to get my Bro's Auto to come on that promised visit. I sure would love to take you & your Mother out for a lovely long ride.

To me, this is one of the real pleasures worth living for. You can bet if I have my health & every-thing goes as I expect & hope it does, I'll own one of my own the following summer, if not B/4. Gosh, I wish July would hurry up & come so I could get out & see what the world holds.

I see the lake is brocken. Now I'm looking to see the leaves sprout out on the trees, then it will not be long.

Well little Pall, I best close up for the time, hoping to hear that your Head-Ache has long left you, & may God bless you with all the blessings of excellent good health, also, all who you are interested in,

so <u>Bye Bye</u>

Friend, DaDy Long Legs

<u>N.B.</u>

Please excuse all the blots, also scribling and many of the other mistakes

(Trust me)

●●●

Her headache had not left her. Neither had the pain that skirted her lungs. For the week of Easter holidays Phyllis lay in bed, contemplating the snow that obliterated the tiny thumbnails of narcissus and daffodil that had pushed up through the ground. What was ever to become of her?

Portsmouth held little promise. The village was but an extension of her own house. She could walk the streets blindfolded, name the members of every family and recite their ages, describe the set of their eyes, tell the stories of their pasts. She knew where to find the sweetest honeysuckle in May, where the yellow warblers raised their young; she knew where the wild grapes grew and when the orange pippins ripened in the abandoned orchard by the marsh. The village was studded with the markers of her past: the low stone wall where she fell and chipped her tooth, the tree she climbed on a dare and clung to in terror till her father eased her down, the corner of the schoolyard where the boys had taunted her, naming the spot of blood on the back of her dress. The pavilion at Lake Ontario Park where she'd felt the Holy Spirit descend on her brow as the evangelist prayed; the clump of grass where she'd first spied the convict's kite.

Yet when Phyllis imagined her future, it was set in Portsmouth village despite herself. Phyllis Halliday, the doctor's wife, pouring orange pekoe tea and passing cream cakes in the afternoon, the housekeeper tidying the kitchen, a nanny tending the children, her health fragile but preserved.

Or Phyllis Halliday, chatelaine of French House, bequeathed to her by Uncle Jim, the Reeve who never married nor had children of his own. Delicately pruning the purple clematis that twined up the stone walls, receiving the children of her girlhood friends for music lessons on Saturday afternoons. An elegant spinster, as refined as Aunt Annie, with pure-bred spaniels for company and Siamese cats stretching lazily on silk pillows in the parlour.

Or perhaps, Phyllis Halliday, the daughter who sacrificed a life of her own, and the love of a good man, to care for her ailing mother and father. Remaining in the family home long after her brothers and sisters moved on, reluctant to leave the task to her yet relieved to have it off their hands. A hard life, this one, as the paint chipped off the picket fence and the lace curtains grew threadbare, and the arthritis ached in her joints as she emptied the chamber pots. But a noble life, and pure.

Praised to her face, whispered of in wonder behind her back: a sacrificial lamb, a saint.

The life she truly wished for, Phyllis dared not imagine. Given form prematurely, it would surely be stillborn. So she lay on her bed and drifted in wordless dreams, lulled by the heavy beat of the crusher that had been moved into the quarry, a deep, steady rhythm that prevailed upon her heart.

• • •

5:15 Tuesday, <u>AM</u>

Kind friend Peggy:—

Indeed I'm much obliged to you for the quick delivery of that letter. Its contents some-what discouraged me, as Sis is again sick, not seriously, so no doubt she is well by this time. She sent me a little more money, which was enclosed in same.

Well Peggy have you stopped going to school. I do hope not: & how did you make out in your exams?

The sun is now shining in through my window promising a beautiful day. Always up early on these nice mornings. I can tell the evening B/4 if its going to be a fine day: I was operated on for appendicis & if the Scar is bright & shining, its as a rule nice, & vice versa.

I can get up on the Top of the hill more often now, mainly on account of the machinery being in operation, for you see Peggy, the Big Fellow has to stop down below & Knowledge-Box is not so quick to see things. When any-one starts talking to him, he then forgets every-thing around him, & that's the time I generally take to slip up & have a look at you.

Well Peggy my little friend, the guard on night duty will

soon be around on his rounds so for this time I must ever again
conclude, with pleasant & happy days to you & your friends:

Faithful friend

DaDy Long Legs

(Trust me)

• • •

The bird swooped up and down the range. It wheeled through the corridor, banked sharply at the barred gates to the Dome, climbed swiftly to the rafters above the fourth tier and dropped abruptly back into sight, scribing arabesques in the air. At first the men cheered it on, delighted by the acrobatics. The bird plunged and soared, flicking its tail at the men, disdainful of gravity, unmindful of the walls that hemmed them in.

The prisoner continued to watch long after the others lost interest and, as if the bird knew as much, it came to rest on the railing of the catwalk in front of the prisoner's cell. He crouched at the bars, face to face with the bird. Never had he seen such an elegant creature of nature so close. Pigeons were no strangers to the range, of course. They murmured sympathetically on the window ledges, gathered in flocks on the roofs of the cell blocks and wheeled in shifting formations around the Dome, their wings rapping a hollow applause so vigorous it could be heard deep within the tiers. At night they entered by the dozens to perch on the rafters: in the morning, the catwalks and corridor were slippery with droppings. The convicts in the upper cells amused themselves by carving bows and arrows to shoot at the birds. Their accomplices in the cells below reeled in the plump booty and smuggled the birds into the officers' kitchen where, for a price, they were roasted alongside the staff dinner for a surreptitious feast.

But this bird was too small to be worthwhile prey. Sensing this perhaps made her bold, brought her swooping within inches of the bars.

The bird preened the rosy feathers of her breast with elaborate strokes of her beak, cocking her head now and then to look the prisoner in the eye, then she turned her back on him, flaring the elegant split fan of her tail. The prisoner made clicking noises with his tongue, whistled lightly through his lips. She did not respond, but swooped across the corridor to the window sill where she strutted up and down, poking her beak into the corners and darting at the cluster flies crawling up the glass. She looked up at the prisoner, still crouched at the bars. She tilted her head as if considering him seriously for a moment, then opened her wings, the colour of deep southern seas, and lifted off.

The prisoner jumped to his feet and craned his neck to stare through the bars, but she'd slipped between the rafters and was gone.

Reluctantly, he returned to the task that had absorbed most of this Sunday afternoon: determining the date of his release. He'd been working it out in his head all week, calculating the remission that was his due, but he'd arrived at a different figure every time. Today he was determined to get it right. On the wall beside his bunk he'd scratched twenty-four grids, one for each month of his sentence, his time in the penitentiary at Portsmouth squared off, day by day.

He knew the rules by heart. No remission for the first six months. He scratched a zero under the grids from October 1918 to April 1919. Six days a month, maximum, for the next year. He added up the row of sixes. As of this month, he'd have seventy-two. After that, his monthly allotment increased to ten: he scratched "10" under the grids for May and June 1920. By the first of July, his remission days would number ninety-two. He put his finger on the last grid and carefully counted backwards from October 9, the day his sentence was due to expire. If he earned his maximum remission, he'd be released on the tenth of

July. And if they gave him three days off for working a third of that month, on July 7 he'd be free.

The prisoner etched a circle around the seventh day of the twenty-second grid. This was the best he could expect. He drew another around October 9. If he'd earned no time off for diligence and good conduct, this was the maximum length of time he'd have to survive inside.

Ninety-two days' remission. An extra three months of liberty, every second of it dependent on the guards and the little passbooks they carried in the breast pockets of their coats, removing them at the end of every shift to make the fateful marks.

Every day the prisoner laboured, he could earn three industry marks. None on Sunday, of course, or on holidays, or on a day like the first of March when the convicts had been locked up so the guards could attend the Chief Keeper's funeral. And he'd earned no industry marks when he'd been sick, although even in the hospital those who rarely complained could earn good conduct marks. Only in the Hole had he earned no marks at all from one sound of the bell to the next.

Three marks for industry, three for conduct: six marks, maximum, per day. Exactly how many the prisoner earned was up to the officer in charge. Some gave full marks to every convict as a matter of course, others made sure their friends walked the streets before those who'd made their jobs hard. Some awarded marks on the basis of merit. One, two, three: poor, fair, good. Others sprinkled them at random across the page, trusting to Fate to divvy up the windfall.

At the end of the month, the Chief Keeper transferred the marks from the passbooks to the remission register where each convict had his own page. At the top left-hand corner, under the convict's name and number, was his sentence written in years, the currency of the courts. Underneath, his sentence in days, the hard coin of the penitentiary.

Joseph David Cleroux. Two years plus a day. Seven hundred and thirty-one days.

The page was divided into columns. Under "Actual Days Served" the Chief Keeper entered the number of days in the month— twenty-nine, thirty or thirty-one. The next column was "Remission Days Earned." If a convict had earned the maximum of six check-marks a day every day, the Chief Keeper wrote "6" in the column: six days to be subtracted from his sentence. If a convict earned less than half the maximum number of marks that month, the Chief Keeper wrote "o." Between all and nothing, it was up to the Chief Keeper to decide. If the prisoner earned three-quarters of the maximum check-marks, he might get five days' remission or three or one. Or if his score were too far from perfect, he'd find himself in Warden's Court. The Warden provided the numbers for the last column: "Remission Days Forfeited." Whole days could be docked as punishment, up to thirty days at a time. Five months' worth of hard work and gritted teeth lost in one stroke of the pen. Three days forfeited for smoking, or ten, or two for failing to earn full conduct and industry marks. Punishment on punishment. And if the forfeits brought the total remission days earned down below seventy-two, the ten-day maximum a month was reduced to six again.

Like a thick-headed schoolboy, the prisoner added up the days he knew he'd served and the remission days he thought he'd earned, subtracted the days he knew he'd forfeited and those he suspected he'd lost. The whims of the guards, the Chief Keeper and the old Deputy Warden, he took them all into account. Beaupré, who liked him; O'Leary, who did not. And all those months when the top jobs at the penitentiary were vacant and the books may not have been kept at all. He counted and recounted, worked the numbered squares this way and that, adding them up and taking away and adding them up again, though he knew that only when the guard appeared at his bars, discharge papers in hand, would he know for certain whether his sums had come out right.

Say he'd earned half, no, three-quarters of his conduct marks, lost sixty marks for industry when he was sick, and say they took ten days off for smoking . . .

A fluttering at the bars drew the prisoner's eyes from his figures. The bird was back, bobbing for balance on the railing. Or was it the same one? Another swooped through the range, brushing so close that the feathers of the first rippled in the wake of the other. The first bird took off and the other followed, swooping and diving, showing off to each other, matching arc for arc. When one landed on the railing, the other perched at its side. Together they preened, smoothing first their own feathers, then the other's, rubbing their necks softly together like horses in a meadow, sliding their beaks back and forth.

The prisoner put his slate on the shelf, lowered his table and laid down on his bunk. The numbers didn't matter. He just wanted out.

• • •

Sunday, Evening

Good friend P:

Well Peggy I got the Hair cut off. But I fooled them at that, for I gave the barber some Tob and he only took it off light. I have about one month's growth on.

One of the boys in the Quarry is going home in the morning. He has been in here 30 months. He sure is a happy one. He is going out on parole, he has about 15 months to do yet, for he was sentenced to 5 yrs.

This Sunday has not went so bad. I started to read a story last night & it got very interesting, & so I finished it this after-noon, it was a love story.

But I'm very fond of good love stories. Are you, P? Say, P, that "C" was delicious, so much so OK & I eat it all as soon as we got it. Are we not pigs? I'm a great eater, not a heavy meat eater, but eggs, fruit, preserves, oh I sure can devour my portion. I never remember ordering a meat meal in my life & I've been eating at restraunts & hotels for years. Some-times when I'm home I may eat a veal-cutlet but that's the limit. I've eaten more meat in here than in all my life past or future. Say P, have you got your garden in yet? I expect, if all goes well, to be down on that promised visit about the time your Garden will be at its best.

I've been thinking about asking you a few questions for a long time. I know I can trust you, so please P tell me the size of your Mother's shoe & waist. I would think about 38 or 40. Also, if "Dady" smokes a straight or crooked stem pipe. The size of your finger will have to be sent to me but these others I can always remember. For this reason do I want to know them. You see, I'm all over in a week & opportunities come to me from travellers who carry <u>nothing</u> but first-class sample material, & the best is none too good for such people as you.

This is all the paper I brought in with me, so trusting you & I are the only ones to know our secerets, I remain

True friend DaDy

(Trust me)

• • •

The barn swallows were back, for that was the name Beaupré had given to the birds when the prisoner pointed to them swooping over the quarry. Disbelief must have played on the prisoner's face because the quarry instructor had been sharp. I should know, he said curtly. His brother, after all, had a collection of bird nests, eggs and skins that was the envy of even the Royal Ontario Museum.

It was not disbelief but disappointment Beaupré had seen. The prisoner could hardly believe that these exotic birds with their rosy waists and indigo suits were the swallows he'd known all his life, random black specks scattering on the wind. He'd always admired their daring, marvelled at the chances they took, pulling out of a plummet at the last possible moment to soar straight back up into the clouds, flicking their wings in the face of God. They flew as he imagined the pilots of the Great War must have flown: swift, bold and sure. But he'd known these birds only in the plural and at a distance. He'd never seen one so close, never known its particular beauty.

The swallow appeared on his railing in the morning, the evening and sometimes at midday too, bits of straw or wool or paper in her beak. She would sit clutching the iron railing as if awaiting his approval, then hop down to the sill to shove her gleanings into the pile of debris accumulating in the corner of the glass.

What a place to choose for a home. The prisoner had a mind to shoo her off, throw out a line to disrupt her start at a nest. For her own good. But each time she flew back to the railing, her breast was so rosy, her eye so sure and bright, that he couldn't bring himself to make her go away.

●●●

April 11th/20

Dear friend Peggy:
The Hum-Bug-Kid did not like me having my hair cut. He's
cursing the Authorities yet. Him & I are almost one, he is

*continualy saying to me, "J" I wish I was going out the same
time as you. But, say Peggy, I'm going to send him a piece
of money via you. Will that be alright? Or it may be a parcel.
Will you mind me sending it? for he does not go out until next
Feburary & then he has lost about 50 or 60 days remission.*

*I would love to come up to the top of the Hill & have a peep
over in your direction more frequently. But one never knows who
is looking. I mean the men I'm working with. Gosh—it must be
lovely to be able to go & do what one pleases. I've been under this
discipline for such a long time I almost believe I'll not know how
to act, once I do get back to the world . . .*

• • •

Phyllis walked to school in the morning through a mist that rose up
from the lake and held the season in suspension. Each drumlin of dis-
solving snow, each emerging shoot seemed isolated against the matte
white backdrop, as if arranged for an artist's still life: jade crocus
shafts thrusting up through the leaf mat; forsythia buds exploding like
golden fireworks in the tangled hedge; and disappearing into the haze,
maple branches studded with tiny scarlet-black bouquets.

Walking home from school at the end of the day, Phyllis half
expected the mist to be there still, hanging over Portsmouth like a veil
that no one had thought to lift. But, of course, it was gone, disinte-
grated to an icy drizzle that pricked holes in the snow, prodding the
frost out of the ground.

Inside her coat, protected from the dampness, Phyllis held her
report card to her chest. Hesitating beside her desk, Miss Irving had
handed the paper to her with reluctance. You've missed so much, she'd
said sadly, apologetically, as if the failure were hers.

Phyllis longed for the enveloping obscurity of the morning's fog. Although that wasn't it exactly, she thought. Rather, she wished that certain parts of her life could be excised. Bits and pieces removed here and there like cutwork, snippets of linen on the floor, taking nothing substantial away from the fabric yet giving it a pattern more interesting, more beautiful than the bolt of cloth laid out whole. Miss Irving. Snip. Snip. Kingston Collegiate Institute. Snip. Snip. The hateful Winnie. Snip. Snip. Snip. The awful ache in her chest.

By the time Phyllis reached the house, the pain had crept up from her gut and wrapped itself firmly around her heart and lungs and started to squeeze, though it was her brain and her limbs that felt drained, not the organs within her ribs. She shook her head at her mother's offer of tea and went straight upstairs to her bed. The report card, the admonitions, the promises and recriminations, it all could wait.

• • •

10:45 A.M.
Say Peggy will you get me 1 lbs. cheese & remainder in Bull. OK
& I are hungry, ha. ha.

DaDy

• • •

From the moment John C. Ponsford's name appeared in the Kingston *Daily British Whig,* his presence was felt inside the walls of the penitentiary, like a strange lake breeze billowing through the cell blocks, down the catwalks, across the yard. Nothing anyone could put a finger on, but there he was, just the same. An inkling, hardly worth mentioning, except the heart skipped a beat and everything changed.

The prisoner no longer knew what to expect. The guard who always slept through his night shift was making forty-minute rounds. And the guard who searched the gang coming in from the quarry was grim-faced, his hands probing, no longer brushing over the surface of the cloth as if feeling for dust. There were rumours of connections broken. Tobacco, suddenly, was in short supply.

The officers had been on edge since the medical examiners appeared in February; now they acted like fresh recruits their first day on the job. They scrabbled among the lint in their pockets and at the back of desk drawers for the buttons they'd lost. They rubbed at the scuffs on their boots. They yelled at the convicts to clean up their cells, to stop their infernal racket, to get on with their work. As if the rules had changed. As if in a week or two they could rein in years of slack.

Rumours about the new Warden flashed through the work gangs like sheet lightning through gathering clouds. A monster, a brute, a pushover. Tough but fair. Eagle-eyed, a pantywaist, a simpleton, a second Solomon. Strong as an ox, cat-o'-nine-tails in one hand, a paddle in the other. A bleeding heart, a pussycat. Jack Canuck. Salt of the earth.

• • •

Sunday, April 18th

My good friend Peggy: —

I was just thinking: its a good thing I never had to depend on this party who said he would send me some writing material. I would of had a long wait, wouldn't I? Its very hard for me to make connections now on account of that Druggist fellow whom I was telling you about, he has gone out, went out last week Thursday.

I may go to work for my former "Company" at Hamilton.

If so, then I would be down around this part every other month or so. I honestly don't know my own mind yet. My Bro wants me to come back with him. I know Peggy what I would do if I had about ten thousand. I would go into the Automobile Business, that is, in Garage, storage, repairs, etc. But, who can tell the future, eh Peggy.

I received a letter from Sis last P.M. & she is much better & back home with her husband in Detroit. Sis was never like this B/4. She's a woman of sound constitution but this last six months or so she has been complaining regularly. I often wonder if I'm the cause, for I know it hurts her more to know I'm here than if it was her that was undergoing the punishment. As soon as she was informed of my trouble, why, the train couldn't bring her fast enough, & she came rushing into where I was, all panting & out of wind. Down to Ottawa she has been, & oh so much she has done, & I know that she would throw herself on her knees B/4 the Minister of Justice. He must be a <u>Hard</u>-hearted old devil. He told her once that on account of me not belonging to <u>Canada</u> he could not grant me Ticket of Leave (Parole) and that she must see the deportation officers. But that was only to get rid of her. At least they might of given her a decisive answer & saved her all the unnecessary labour. But no, they would (seemingly) rather have her suffering also. That's the way I figured it out! If one in a family makes an err & falls, the whole family is compelled to suffer.

Revenge—Revenge—Revenge. But revenge is too dearly purchased at the aughtful price of liberty.

Oh don't mind me writing thus—that cheese has gone to my head, ha ha.

I had to smile when reading your kite of yesterday when you mentioned that teacher would get a <u>Surprise</u> if he struck you

*again. I don't doubt your word in the least. By all means stick
up for your own convictions, & give it to him good. He put me in
mind of this new Chief Keeper. He sure is showing his Authority.
He has given orders to take all post-cards, photos, letters, etc out
of our cell. I've taken all my little personal belongings, & gave
them to the Hum-Bug-Kid & I'll have him send them to me after
I leave here.*

*Yes indeed Peggy, it will be the happiest day of my life, the
morning I go out: 72 days more, that is, short time. I'll know the
exact day I'm going out, for I have a friend who will look over
the books & inform me. But I will not know until some-time in
the latter part of May or early in June.*

*Peggy will you once again allow me to bother you: 3 chewing
& remainder smoking, both McDonlands.*

*The other day we saw a man discharged from this inistua-
tion. We were up close to him & noticed the clothes that were the
issue: <u>disgraceful</u> & an old checked cap. I'm greatful to know I
have my own clothes, & you can bet that I will lose that Guard
Old Kennedy, as soon as I reach Kingston & Pembroke Station,
for every-one must know that some discharged convict must be
with him, & any-thing I love is to have strangers yaping at me.
I'll drop you word on my arrival home, perhaps only a post-card
with the promise of a letter following in a few days or so.*

*Say Peggy, would you mind giving me the evening paper
after you are all done reading it, for I'm anxious to learn of what
is going on in Europe & U.S.A., I used to get one or two a week,
but the new change in day & night shift for the officers threw me
out of that connection.*

*Well my little friend, my hand is commencing to ache after
doing so much scribling & grouching & complaining. But, I know*

you will overlook all my mistakes & blunders, leave it to my
unfortunate circumstances.

 So hoping you are going to keep at school & continue
studying hard. But by all means <u>don't allow them to boss you!</u>

I am Peggy
Your Trustworthy Friend
<u>*DaDy Long Legs*</u>

 <u>*P.S.*</u>
Now I'll go to bed & think-think-think,
B/4 I fall to sleep: of the future,
especially of the day of my release
(Josie)
(Trust me)

• • •

PISGAH: <u>P</u>ray <u>I</u>n the <u>S</u>pirit that <u>G</u>od will <u>A</u>lways <u>H</u>elp

 Phyllis had abandoned her Lenten vows. Although she followed the family to church and bowed her head with the others, she did not pray with her heart. The words of the pastor, picked from the dry parchment of the Testaments, fell about her like husks. The regimen of Bible readings and daily devotions that had sustained her in the winter seemed pointless exercises now. She had not abandoned God, but these things, she felt certain, no longer pointed the way to Him.

 PISGAH: Devoted to the Material Welfare, Bodily Healing, Moral Uplift and Spiritual Life of the Stricken in Body, Victim of Drink, Dying, Outcast, Cripple, Hungry, Friendless and Whosoever is in Need of the Waters of Life.

 When Phyllis read of the good works of the California religious group, she'd sent a twenty-five-cent piece to the box number advertised in the newspaper. By return mail she'd received the *Pisgah Home Movement Journal*, a few closely typed, stapled pages filled with inspirational messages from Pisgah workers. Here, at last, was a church of deeds and not just prayers, men and women for whom Christ's teachings were not only wise words, but also a call to action.

Wrecked lives have been built up and established. Diseased and suffering bodies have been powerfully and gloriously healed. They have gone down before the mighty power of God. Jesus has proven himself a conqueror, mighty to save.

Phyllis did not read the journal: she drank it in, every story, every sentence, every word. The lesson from Sister Goodwin. *Faith and obedience come from the same Greek root, and mean nearly the same: you must obey God, and when you obey, the faith will come.* Brother Theo's "Thoughts on Prayer": *Very small things often put large power lines out of action. A bit of glass no larger than a dime, chancing to get between the contact points of the switch, will cut off the current. In like manner, a small amount of selfishness, envy, hate, avarice or other carnal impurities may find their way into our hearts, cut us off from God and stop our prayers at the very threshold of our hearts.*

Outside, the steady beat of the quarry crusher was background to a nearer, thicker pulse. The thwack of carpets being beaten in the yard below. The clang of a bucket on the stairs. The sharp smell of lye. Everyone except Phyllis was busy ridding the house of winter, scrubbing away the yellow glaze of woodsmoke on the walls, the speckled wake of flies on the window glass, the chamber-pot splatters on the bedroom floors.

Lying in her sickbed, exempt from the spring cleaning ritual, Phyllis revelled in the testimonies of the healed. Eyesight restored. Tuberculosis banished. Asthma relieved, all of them by the miracle of PISGAH. *I have used your blest handkerchief and have been cured. Mrs.*

G.B. Sibley, Ohio. The Lord has blessed me with a job. Thank you for your prayers. R.F. Selma, Louisiana. My little girl I asked you to pray for is in excellent health. Mrs. W.E., Toronto. China; Oregon; Auburn, New York; Detroit, Michigan; Chatham, Canada: the power of PISGAH knew no bounds.

Here was the proof Phyllis was looking for. *Therefore if any man be in Christ, he is a new creature,* promised PISGAH. *Old things are passed away; behold, all things are become new.*

Enclosed in the *Journal* was a pamphlet, *12 symptoms of a Declining State.* The soul of Phyllis Halliday showed every sign of decline. And if she doubted that for a moment, her body offered further proof. The doctor's remedies had had no lasting effect because it was her spirit, not her heart, that was sick. If the ministers of PISGAH were right, the pain in her chest was just a symptom, as were her lies, the uneasy sorrow that weighed her down, her restless craving for some other life.

In her letter to PISGAH, Phyllis asked first for a healing handkerchief to pin next to her heart. And please say prayers for my friend who is in prison, she added, that he might find work when he is released and live a happy life.

She folded a dollar bill between the pages. There was no fee for the help that PISGAH offered, but they depended for their survival on offerings from those who believed. Sealing the envelope, Phyllis felt joined to the miracles she had read about, as if she had witnessed them herself, as if her own eyesight had been restored. It would be just as PISGAH promised:

They that wait upon the Lord shall renew their strength; they shall mount up with wings as eagles; they shall run, and not be weary; and they shall walk and not faint. Oh hallelujah!

•••

Sackets Harbour, New York

A mirage of the city of Kingston was plainly discernible shortly after noon on April 19. St. Mary's Church, Fort Henry and the light house tower were faintly outlined hovering 50 feet above the level of the lake. Other buildings near the waterfront were also noticeable. The condition of the air is held responsible for the spectacle.

DAILY BRITISH WHIG

April 20, 1920

• • •

Tuesday, <u>P.M.</u>

Dear friend Peggy: —

I received with pleasure beyond words to express, your kind encouraging Kite; as you know, its the long ones that I am always looking forward to. Many thanks for your sympthy in conection with my visit to the Warden, but as you say, I'll have enough in 60 days time.

Thousands thanks for this writing paper, also envolps. I told the Hum-Bug-Kid that I would be able to send him some few little things, Tob etc, after I leave here, & oh he feels so pleased to think you will be so kind. Not meaning to flatter you people, but he has said on different occasions, "Joe, "they <u>must be</u> exceptions to the human-race!

How did you make out in your examinations? I'm anxious to learn. I'm sure all the things you say about yourself are not true. Every knock conected to your Character with me is always a boost. So you see, I understand you, <u>don't I?</u>

This <u>PM</u> some gentleman dropped a fine cigar, & I'm sitting here writing & enjoying the smoke. Its a genuine Havanna.

Say Peggy would you have a little piece of blotter, for every time I scrible a page, I must sit & wait until it drys. I don't know if its on account of so much water being in the ink or if its the nib.

Water plays a wonderful part in our existence while incarcerated in here. Although lately our food has been put up much more palatable mainly on the account of having a new Chief and apparently he seems to be taking much interest in our meals, & how they should be served. But, after all, the whole world is changing so this "H" cannot be an exception.

So Peggy you say you have never been out to Kingston Mills. I was there one time in an Auto, went there for a friend of mine & saved him the expense of coming down when I done a little trick for him. You see Peggy its done like this: Supposing I was at the King Edward in Toronto this Sunday. There I would come in contact with several commercial Salesmen & we would make our plans; if I was coming east, I would do a "Trick" (for Trick is what it is known as) for perhaps two or three of them, in this way it would save them spending money on a ticket that week, & they will do the same for me. This we are under strick orders never to do, & it is as good as our position are we found out, but some months I've cleared as much as $100 in expense money.

Eight new men came in the prison to-day. All young men too. The oldest don't look to be any-more than 20 & their sentences, so I've been informed by a guard run from 8 to 15 years! My, but it hurts me to see that. And three of them are returned soldiers. Half the prison are returned men. One poor fellow in particular goes around on crutches. He has onely one leg, the other one was amputated above the knee. I give him Tobacco every other day or so, for he sure has my sympathy. Yes indeed Peggy, this is a place of sighs & tears.

> The sighs that echo through the nights
> Through every range of cells
> Speaks plainly of the misery felt
> And the _paying price_ it tells

Image what them poor boys must feel like with 8 & some 15 years in front of them. _God_ pity them.

Concerning this _Water Boy:_——He is an Italian, I've never spoken to him, but to what I hear, I would be safest to not even seek his company. None of the Boys speak to him. He is not in here for Stealing, & perhaps you are aware, but a thief considers himself a gentleman when he is slowed up with people who are in here for unnatural crimes. I'm sorry for writing this, but I am sure you will understand. Company is picked in here, even more so than out-side, for you must remember little one, there are _some real wicket people_ in here.

I'm right out of paper, & I feel like writing you a real long Kite. Well Peggy with the usual excuse of my scribling etc.

> Affectionate & Trustworth Friend
> _DaDy Long Legs_

_PS_

> On account of a few debts I owe for eatables if you please invest that $1.00 in McDonland Smoking & if you insist on paying postage, invest the remainder in Zig-Zag papers Many thanks, 'Joe"
> (Trust me)

• • •

The weather warmed. The quarry stirred. Where the sun touched the stone, water trickled down its face like sweat, gathering in pools on the quarry floor. March flies, silvery in the slant of morning sunlight, swarmed about the convicts' knees in clumsy, convoluted dances. Above the steady grind of the crusher, peepers no larger than a man's big toe complained to each other in single strident notes. Kildeer wriggled their rumps into the stone rubble and laid clutches of pear-shaped, pebbled eggs, screeching and flapping and dragging their wings through the mud when the prisoner strayed too near. Garter snakes slithered out from shady crevices to take the sun on tumbles of stone. Swallows with sawed-off tails poked their heads out from the mud-holes plastered to the rock cliffs, glided in long ellipses from wall to wall, sometimes dipping to skim the pools and wheeling back to their nests in heady roller-coaster climbs.

The prisoner crouched by a puddle as if to tie his shoe. A few weeks before, the water had been snow; a few weeks more and the hollow in the stone would cradle dust. But for now it was a sea of possibility, an aquatic universe to the Jesus bugs that skittered among the island stones. In the shallow, stained water he could see a dimple of shadow around each slender foot, a depression in the liquid, as if the insects rested on a pillow of coloured glass. Every so often, one would lift its front leg and beat a tattoo on the still surface of the pool, tapping the water into wavelets, sounding an alarm, he supposed, or a mating call.

The prisoner bent to scoop a water strider and missed. Propelled on the oars of its long middle legs, it scooted out of reach, ruddering with the legs that dragged behind. The short front legs with which it held its mate close could just as easily deliver a death grip. The prisoner had watched once as a Jesus bug seized one of its own kind between its powerful front legs and squeezed until the victim was an empty husk.

The blue damsel flies or the delicate mosquito-eaters that hovered over the pools might have given him pause, but the prisoner had no qualms in trapping the Jesus bugs. Their world was like his own: provisional and ruthless, where one lived by one's wits, ate not to be eaten, and understood that whatever one perpetrated, one could expect to endure.

The prisoner scooped his hand across the water's surface and this time closed his fist around a strider. Careful not to crush the insect, he folded it inside his handkerchief. By the time the gang left the quarry for the midday break, he had five imprisoned in the cloth, three of them still faintly twitching.

Back in his cell, the prisoner waited until the swallow left her nest and perched on the railing, then he tossed one of the insects onto the catwalk. The bird fluttered at the sudden movement and edged away. He tossed another close to her beak.

The prisoner had worried about the bird for days. She hunkered on her nest, rarely moving, her eye glazed, as if she barely had the energy to hold up her head. Occasionally she flew up between the rafters, leaving the prisoner to watch nervously over the three speckled eggs until she returned, rolling them this way and that with her beak, then settling back, cupping them with her wings against her breast, leaning her beak on the lip of the debris, exhausted from her foray. He had offered her crumbs of bread from his tray, bits of grass and the leaves that sprouted between the quarry rocks but nothing caught her interest until now. She snatched the last Jesus bug out of the air and flew back to the sill with it.

Satisfied, the prisoner tore up the dandelion leaves he had smuggled in for himself and stirred them into the thin stew on his tray.

After almost two years on prison diet, his body was all knobbly bone lashed together with sinew, the skin drooping in folds at his elbows, at the backs of his knees. His face, when he caught a glimpse of it in a window glass, looked bruised from the permanent shadows that pooled in the hollows of his cheeks and eyes. The greens tasted bitter, but he ate every shred, swallowing them slowly, a tonic. He would not leave this place, he vowed, with the penitentiary etched like scrimshaw on his bones.

The way the prisoner saw it, a man condemned to prison had a choice. He could obey the rules, he could connive to break them, or he could scheme to get out. He knew convicts who toed the line like monks, accepted the hunger, the cold, the silence, the beatings, the rats as their due. They had broken the law: they deserved it all. He knew others who could not bear to be confined, who spent every waking moment plotting to get out, their eyes sharp for a break in routine, a preoccupied guard, a length of rope or wire left carelessly about. But the prisoner was neither of these. Unwilling to accept his lot and unwilling to risk escape, he obeyed the rules when he had to and broke them when he could, insulating himself against the barbs of prison life with bits of stolen clothing, pilfered food, smuggled tobacco and reading matter, staying out of authority's way, concocting his own ingenious balms and opiates to counteract its sting. Neither the devil nor the deep blue sea, but the shifting ground between where he and most of the others inside the penitentiary at Portsmouth dodged the jabs, danced around the snares, ran the gauntlet of steel and stone. Never imagining, even in their dreams, that the arsenal of ancillary weapons could be taken from the officers' hands, that the edge of privation could be blunted, that a prison sentence could mean loss of freedom and nothing more.

The prisoner mopped up the last of his stew. Whispers swirled through the range like early morning mist. Though he tried to ignore the words, they filtered through the bars and he heard, Ten of us to one of them . . . can't shoot you for standing still . . . refuse to work . . . not enough solitary cells . . . the press.

The prisoner listened, his eye fixed on the bird. Bolshevik plots. A handful of men, Russians and Finns, convicted for possession of treasonable documents and unlawful literature in the mining towns of the north, had brought their preaching inside with them. Toivar, Pelto, Grishick. Dark-haired foreigners with funny accents and dangerous thoughts. He pushed away his plate and pulled down his blanket, damp with the change of season. He was as keen to have a little comfort as the next man. But he was on his way out. He wrapped the blanket around him and hunkered on his bunk within sight of his still, little friend. He could wait.

· · ·

Friday <u>P.M.</u>

Dear friend Peggy:

Sunday the long lonesome day will soon be here again. In here only, for on the outside, they are the pleasantest of all days. Only 8 more, & then they will be too short to suit me. I suppose, now that it is nice weather, you plan a lovely long walk for Sunday. I know that's what I would be doing about this time of the year if I was enjoying liberty. Its lovely to have a nice car & a few good friends to go out after church, & bring a lunch & stop out all the day. Do you like that kind of sport?

I noticed old Davis with a kite tied around a piece of stone & watching his opportunity to throw same over towards you. I do *hope he does not make a blunder & allow any-one to notice the transaction. I cannot say anything to him as he is <u>very</u> jelious & would do any-thing to knock anyone. I would not say he was a stool-pigeon, but he has been around here so long & often that he has an idea no-one but himself should know or do any-thing. Along with that he is a little simple. Poor old fellow, I hardly blame him! but, as I say, he must be watched. He is very sus-picious if he sees any-one with Tob & he does not know where it comes from. Of course, my good little friend Peggy, I do not mean to knock him, only I do hope there will be no one sees him throwing any-thing, because it certainly would hurt me more than you. I'm very much afraid it would mean more remmission lost, for I <u>know</u> that I could not restrain from punishing him. But oh it will never come to that, will it Peggy?*

I got a parcel this A.M. also Kite. Good idea in wrapping Kite with the parcel. If you noticed, the Box has been shifted around some this past few days. Do you notice my Auto (wheel-barrow)? Well P that is where the Hum-Bug-Kid & I are working or rather putting in the time. So you see I'm climbing nearer to the top all the time, that's what I tell Knowledge-Box. Also, that nobody can keep good men down, ha, ha. I tell Knowledge Box that I must get my dainty little hands in perfect order B/4 I leave & also, that any one with short time should be allowed to rest up the last couple of months. He only laughs. One fine thing about him, he is not a slave driver, at least he never bothers me or Hum-Bug.

Say I've had a little hard luck this week, a fellow borrowed some money of me & went out on parole the following day. I sent him $5.00 & he has gone, & of course so has the five. He may *write to me & send it. But I firmly believe he gave it to some one to give to me & the "some-one" is holding out.*

Well my good little friend Peggy, I am going to close this dry uninteresting Kite, hoping you enjoy your Sunday.

I remain

Trustful Friend

DaDy Long Legs

PS Excuse scribling

Please!

(Trust me)

• • •

The city flickered past the corner of Ponsford's left eye like the frames of a moving picture, but he did not allow himself to be distracted. He held Hughes in conversation, their words a taut leash between them until the taxicab eased to a stop. He opened the door and unfolded himself into the cool spring breeze blowing in off the lake.

Before the stern grey face of the mother penitentiary, Ponsford was momentarily humbled. The structure was nothing like Alberta Penitentiary, which except for the barred windows could have been some austere millionaire's estate. The imposing bell tower, the spreading limestone flanks of the penitentiary at Portsmouth reminded him more of Stony Mountain. Approaching across the Manitoba prairie, Ponsford had always stiffened with pride at the sight of the prison, shimmering like a tiara on the horizon, growing awesome and grand as the gates drew near. But there was no such easing up to Kingston Penitentiary. One arrived at the North Gate as if parachuted to the foot of a massive monument: its height and breadth could not be taken in with a single glance. Walls older than the country itself held a third of the nation's criminals, and all of its most notorious. The stone seemed to surround him, and he felt dwarfed.

Hughes, joining Ponsford at his side, suspected none of this. The new Warden was built like his brother, Sam: staunch and beefy, bull-necked, barrel-chested and heavily jowled, though Ponsford's form, Hughes suspected, was shaped less by athletics than appetite. Still, the new Warden had a physique that drew others unconsciously to attention. He could do worse, Hughes thought, than have Ponsford at Kingston's helm. A Clydesdale of a man, hard-working and single-minded. Lacking in subtlety perhaps, but one who could be counted on to get the job done.

On the train from Ottawa, the two men had ranged across the field of penology, picking up this issue and that like rocks they stumbled upon, turning them over in their minds, offering theories to each other on how such impediments had come to pass, what they might mean, and what was to be done with such a pocked and littered terrain.

There was much they agreed upon. The increase in the prison population alarmed them both. Thirteen percent at Kingston in one year. Fifty percent in the two years since the end of the war. But when Hughes predicted that Prohibition would turn back the rising tide of crime, that the crest had reached its peak and would soon subside, Ponsford all but jumped out of his red plush seat.

Prohibition won't keep men out of penitentiary, he countered, because drink was never responsible for the great majority of them coming there in the first place. Ponsford thumped the arm of his chair, a gesture Hughes found coarse and distasteful. You can go through the whole cycle of crime, consider it from every angle and you come back to one thing—indolence—every time.

You don't find shoemakers and carpenters in prison, he continued, unaware of the hardening around Hughes's eyes. Those who come to penitentiary are drifters, men without a trade, men who never learned to work. They've got to have money, and so they turn their hand to crime.

Work and more work, that was Ponsford's idea of reform.

The doors at the centre of the North Gate swung open. A double row of convicts dribbled through. Carts rumbled across the cobblestones. The men in the brown and purple striped uniforms elbowed each other, nodded their heads and stared at the men in the neat black suits waiting outside the gate. An officer on horse-back trailed after them into the street, reining tightly as he passed the motorcars that paused to let the parade of convicts through. At the last moment, he turned towards the men in civilian dress and raised his hand in awkward salute.

Poor breeding, not indolence, that's what Hughes saw in the faces of these men. Boys indulged or too often whipped, men as different in their backgrounds—and their souls—as in the colour of their hair. Where Ponsford saw a uniform filled up with muscles to put to work, Hughes saw the face lean with hunger, eyes clouded with old, musty hurt, a mind warped by drink, bent out of shape by fast cars and jazz.

Nothing much could be brought out of a man but what had been put in. The challenge for the penitentiary, as Hughes saw it, was to discover the peculiarities of each inmate and determine how they had come to be. Discover the social conditions under which a convicted man was reared, how he had lived before he came to this place. Only when they knew the reason for a man's wrongdoing could they make it worth his while not to repeat the crime. Were he a betting man, Hughes would wager his salary from now to the day he retired that if he could dig to the roots of the crime of every inmate, he would not find a single source that fed them all. If Prohibition was not a cure-all, then neither was indolence the sole cause. But Hughes had kept these thoughts to himself.

It was evening by the time the Superintendent and the Warden finished touring the penitentiary. Together they had gone over the books and registers, walked through the workshops and the barns, stood at the edge of the quarry and watched the men cleave yet another burden of rock from the limestone face.

The sky, which had not lightened from a dull grey all day, tarnished to a deeper hue as they waited on the steps of the Warden's residence for the taxicab to arrive. Hughes sucked on his cigar. They waited in silence, advice and assurances long since exchanged.

Below the steps, across the loop of macadam in front of the Warden's house, down the stone stairway that cut through the slope of lawn, across Front Street, up in the tower that topped the North Gate, the bell tolled, rippling the tinplate sky. A black car pulled up to the steps.

Good luck, said Hughes, extending his hand. He meant the words for himself as much as for Ponsford. This afternoon he'd announced to the penitentiary staff the resignations of Deputy Warden O'Leary and Hospital Overseer Wilson. A significant victory, though as fast as he dispatched old adversaries, it seemed, new ones appeared.

By the time the car turned out of sight up Palace Road, the sound of the bell had stopped. Ponsford gazed down at his penitentiary, the roofs of the cell blocks a silver rime above the walls. He let his gaze slide down the street, miraculously empty now, as if the ringing of the bell had swept the traffic from the tarmac, sent the last of the day's loiterers scuttling home. He took in the bay, the jumble of shipbuilding sheds and squat stone shops, the straight rooflines and budding treetops of the village that curled against the slope of the Warden's lawns like a cat against a warm flank. The sweep of his vision settled back against the prison walls, grey in the fading light, the mortar lines erased, stone eased back to clay, waiting to be refashioned by his strong and steady hand.

• • •

April 28, 1920

Dear Friends: —

I feel quite safe in addressing you as such after receiving your very kind letter.

I am so glad you have recognized the real good in my brother. I can never find words to express my gratitude. I am sure he will never forget you after he has left that terrible place.

You can feel sure your secret will be kept in regards to what you have done. I realize the great chance you are taking for him & to think you are only strangers too.

Thanking you again,

I am yours
Sincerely
<u>Ruth</u>

May

Ponsford's first official order: Search the penitentiary. A surprise attack, three-pronged. The Warden, the Chief Keeper and Chief Watchman, men he'd brought with him from the West, officers he could trust. Every one else, convict and guard, even the Deputy, was suspect.

Out of the Warden's office at the sound of the morning bell. The inspection neatly mapped, shops to kitchens and stores. Moving swiftly ahead of the gangs and behind, clipping the lines of communication that spread convict news. A show of cunning, more vital than strength.

Instructors startled, keys jamming in the locks. Bags of wood shavings upended; bolts of cloth unfurled like bunting. Fists plunged inside half-made boots. The beams of their flashlights plying crevices and cracks. Cupboards wrenched open; crowbars groaning against oak floorboards.

At the end of it, a heap on Ponsford's desk: bottles, flasks, muslin bags, tin-foil packets, sheets of newsprint folded small. Three officers, the assistant overseer of the hospital, the hospital guard and Paynter, instructor of the shoemaking shop, clearing out their lockers in the room below.

Rules are made to be kept, murmured Ponsford, his voice flinty under the purl of words. With a brush of his arm, he swept the contraband into a pasteboard box on the floor.

• • •

This is how the prisoner heard it during choir practice:

The shoemaker's gang filed up the sweep of flagstone stairs, into the workshop dome, innocent and unprepared. The cobbler's shop was capsized; Paynter, not in his place. Stunned, they spread their legs, lifted their arms for the morning search, darting glances to secret caches, comprehension rippling through the vaulted room like earthquake aftershocks.

Okay. Now get to work.

Hey, where's Paynter?

Get to work. Clean up this mess.

The guard prodded with his stick. The convicts jostled but stayed where they were. Then someone spoke.

No. Not till you tell us what's going on. We have a right . . .

You. You're on report. The rest of you, move.

They stood transfixed.

The pause lengthened and swelled. Other gangs tramped through the silence, along the gangway that circled the dome, past the cobbler's shop door. One guard made a move towards the small window covered in mesh but thought better of turning his back on the men.

I said, get moving. Menacing now.

A disjointed chorus, low and rumbling, like distant thunder. No ... No ... A syncopated roll call of dissent. No ... Unshackled by a syllable, a shake of the head. Destiny warming in their fists.

We'll work when you tell us where Paynter's at.

Get to work. Or it's back to your cells. And Warden's Court.

The men stood still, the wary pleasure of the moment almost too much to bear.

If that's the way you want it.

The guard unlocked the door. The convicts filed out. The old lifer shuffling his mop down the flagstones of the range looked up in surprise. The convicts grinned foolishly as they passed, schoolboys on a spree.

• • •

Bread and water diet. All of them, thundered Ponsford. Whether they go back to work or not.

• • •

News seeped cell to cell through the midday meal. McCauley, Dowsley, Paynter: dismissed. Connections unravelled. Deals undone. Hard-won stashes rooted out, gone. The quarry gang, moving back to work across the yard and into the street, buzzed and hummed like disconcerted bees. Second from the front, the prisoner murmured steadily, spreading the word, his voice pitched with excitement, his heart calm for all the hubbub, knowing his own source was secure.

Nothing happened all at once. No plan had been laid. That afternoon, in the mailbag department, the sewing machines clattered to a stop, first one, then another, until the long hall fell silent, convicts standing lank-armed by their cloth. In the stone shed, a hammer laid down, a second, a decrescendo of tapping stone.

The gangs that refused to work were led back to their cells. The guards uncertain, sympathetic, too, indignant at what the Warden had done. The convicts, dazed to discover a muscle never flexed before.

Working in the quarry, the prisoner knew none of this. But while the sun was still high, Beaupré gave the signal and the men trailed down the ladders from the stone ledges and formed a line by the Palace in front of the row of extra guards with rifles who waited to escort them back inside the prison walls.

They marched straight to the Dome, up the stairs to the second tier. Though it was barely midafternoon, there was a man in most every cell. Not lounging on their bunks or hunched over trays, but standing slit-eyed at the bars, or pacing stiffly back and forth.

When his gate was pulled to, the prisoner moved to the back of his cell, eased the loose brick from behind the toilet, removed his stash and returned the brick to its place. The rolled cigarettes he flushed down the toilet. Then he dismantled the works and buried the parts separately and deeply in the mattress ticking. With one of Peggy's ribbons, he tied up all but two of the tobacco plugs and pushed the parcel through the Judas slit. The end of the ribbon he fastened to the grate, his fingers fumbling in his haste to blacken the exposed bit of fabric with mud from his boot. It was a bold hiding place, but he counted on the guards being too busy searching cells to sneak down the secret passageway. The last two plugs he worked in his palm as he surveyed his cell for evidence, then he spread his legs and squatted, burying the last of his stash deep inside himself.

The penitentiary's first mutiny gathered force like a storm seeded far out at sea. A murmuring mutter, a low howl, a caterwauling groan. From the bottom tier to the upturned bowl of the Dome, a rising ululation. Metal mugs clamoured on the iron grates; boots, spoons and marrow-bones. Cacophony, spawned in fits and starts, multiplied, a syncopated rhythm rising, caroming off the stones, clawing at the vaulted Dome. Bedlam begot, catching unwitting, unwilling convicts in its sinews, tangling them up with the righteous and the restless till all the men in the penitentiary at Portsmouth bellowed with one great open maw.

The prisoner sat gripping the edge of his bunk, his back pressed to the bricks, against the grids he'd etched with such care. In the throbbing pandemonium, he heard his calculations come undone. The swallow swooped in terror through the corridor, dodging the paraphernalia hurled through the bars. Chaos swirled around the prisoner, inside him, too. He hung on to his bunk as to a ship sinking in roiling seas, watching for the moment to jump, that instant when he judged his voice could no longer be identified by authorities but its absence would be noted by his friends.

He grabbed his tin cup off the shelf, gripped it in both his hands and swayed before his bars, clangouring back and forth, a demented ringer of otherworldly bells, thrilling to the convict chorus.

•••

We are all for one and one for all, the convict witnesses declared. But Ponsford ferreted out the leaders and brought them, one by one, from their dungeon cells to the Keeper's Hall.

The Deputy took the convict's shirt, ordered him to stand at one end of the strapping bench, built solid and narrow with a padded leather cover stained hospital green. A converted surgeon's table, where boils had been lanced, festering tumours cut out, shattered bones set, eyes pressed closed with coppers when all efforts failed.

Unbutton your trousers.

The convict bent over the table, arms outstretched past his head, a sag of brown and purple denim trussing his feet. The Deputy buckled the convict's wrists in leather cuffs, fitted his ankles in the small wooden pillory, secured with an iron strap and padlocked. Around the convict's waist he cinched a wide leather strap and fitted leather goggles over his eyes. Manacled, fettered, blinded, bound.

Ponsford slid his hand restlessly over the broad surface of the paddle, a swath of stiff harness leather, twenty-six inches long and three inches wide, soaked in water to a deep russet brown. Nine small holes perforated the leather, four rows of two, one at the rounded tip. Ponsford held no sympathy for the man laid out before him. A convict knew the rules. And he knew the consequence of breaking them. The law put the paddle in a Warden's hand to hold over the convicts' heads, to subjugate those disposed to run the place. The rioters brought the paddle down on their own bared backs.

Ponsford and the Deputy stood by as the Surgeon examined the convict to confirm that he was fit for what the Warden prescribed. Every rule of the law, meticulously satisfied.

The paddle was not the crudest form of punishment the penitentiary had known. The hose, the tub, the thirty-five-pound yoke. A windowless coffin called the Box. The lash, a long tapered whip with nine thinly braided strands, a cat-o'-nine-tails. Five hundred strokes could kill a man; three hundred, flay him alive. The law in 1920 allowed only ten, administered at the beginning of a sentence and again at the end and only by order of the court for crimes committed against the person: robbery with violence, assault and rape. All other forms of corporal punishment had been taken away, leaving a Warden with only the paddle, a heavy leather strap not unlike the ones that lay in teachers' desks and fathers' bureau drawers. No more than ten strokes at a time. No more than once a month. But a Warden could still make a convict bleed.

Such punishments had once been public, to reinforce their moral effect. But Ponsford did not need an audience: word of what was about to happen was certain to spread. The convicts' hearts would harden against him, but they would learn to obey. And his officers would know that he meant what he said.

On his first morning at Kingston Penitentiary, Ponsford had lectured his ragtag staff:

Henceforth, nothing loose. Nothing slipshod. Nothing slack.

Guards and convicts would salute as they passed, stand straight as soldiers, march smartly on patrol.

Many a man comes in contact with discipline here for the first time in his life. We teach obedience first of all. They must comply.

Ponsford handed the paddle to the Deputy, who moved into position behind the convict, his back already glistening with sweat despite the chill in the Keeper's Hall. The Deputy raised his arm, leaned back, brought the paddle against the man's bared white buttocks. The convict jerked forward, wrists straining against the straps. The Deputy stepped back, raised his arm, struck again. The convict let out a deep, lowing sound. Nubbins of flesh bulged through the perforations in the paddle. The Deputy struck again. Beads of blood swelled and trickled into the furred crevice at the top of the convict's legs.

Give it all you've got, man. That's the law! Ponsford was breathing hard.

The hand raised. The sharp, sucking thwap. A moan. The paddle slick and black. Seven. Eight. Groans sharpened to cries, then silence. Nine. Blood streamed down the convict's thighs, pooling in the tendon cups of his buckled knees. Ten.

The Surgeon loosened the straps, took the convict under the arms. The Deputy unshackled his ankles and lifted his legs. Together they lugged the convict, unconscious, to his cell.

We've warmed his ass, called Ponsford as they moved into the hall, past the others waiting their turns behind padlocked wooden doors. That's only the beginning! You'd have been justified in killing him.

On his way back to his office, Ponsford paused in the lavatory to sponge dark flecks from the front of his shirt. He held a damp towel against his eyes to calm the wild, surging rhythm at his temples.

According to the Penitentiary Act, corporal discipline had to be reported. On the train, Hughes had made his position clear. *Society cannot order a man's mind by regulating his body, through either the rule of silence or the lash.*

Regulation 26 might also apply. *The Warden shall report immediately by telegraph, and by first mail in writing, anything of an extraordinary or serious nature that may occur.*

Ponsford regarded himself in the mirror above the sink. He looked calm enough. The insurrection, surely, was a minor event. *The convicts' clumsy scheme to show their resentment that the source of contraband supplies had been cut off.* That is how he would characterize it in his report. *A bravado expedition that the convicts thought they would be smart to pull off.* Nothing to bother the Superintendent about.

He had doubled the guards on the towers and the North Gate. The convicts were locked in their cells. He'd keep them there until they settled down. They could do no harm, except to themselves. The penitentiary at Portsmouth was secure.

Ponsford adjusted his tie. He would not be cowed. The cell searches would continue. The firing of the officers would stand. He had everything under control.

•••

The prisoner lay on his bunk and stared at the white ceiling, willing himself into the void. Beyond the scratchings and squeaks of the rats revelling in the mouldering bread pitched onto the catwalk through the night; beyond the footfalls of the guards as they moved cell to cell. The whiteness sucked at him and he rose sweetly off the cot, his fetal shape preserved in denim down below and him above, slipping towards oblivion, up, up. Away from the rip of ticking, the splatter of books on a floor, the thud of flesh against stone.

Move to the back. Spread your arms.

The Chief Keeper opened the gate. A guard passed inside. Bedding tumbled on the floor, hands roughly palming where he slept, where he ate, his books, his walls, his cup. The smell of their sweat and his. His gut churning against the wad insinuated deep inside his bowel.

To the wall.

The new Chief Keeper fixed him there. The guard knelt by the toilet, traced his fingers over the mortar joints and pried at the brick, but found nothing behind.

Take it down.

The Chief pointed with his stick to the tiny photograph of his mother he'd pasted with porridge to the wall above his table, barely visible between the utensil board and the Convict Rules. Everything else he'd given to OK, but he hadn't had the heart to part with this.

It's my mother.

I don't care if it's the Queen of England. Warden says nothing on the walls. Take it down.

What are you going to do with it?

None of your business. Take it down.

The prisoner picked at the corners of the photograph, prying it from the brick. He paused, holding it in both hands. He looked from his mother's face to the Chief Keeper's, then back again.

The first rip split her in two. The second cleaved her head. The Keeper grabbed his arm, too late. She drifted in shreds to the flagstones, scraps of sepia-toned paper sticking like shards to his boots.

Take it then. The prisoner kicked the fragments into the air. Take it if you want.

•••

Tuesday <u>PM</u>

Good little friend P: —
All your pleasant Kites was carefully read this A.M. I could plainly see you did not know of my trouble, & I'm sorry that I told you. This place is being turned upside down, searching all the cells & every where. This last few days there has been not less than 35 or 40 reported smoking, talking & all such trifles. Gosh, I'm glad I'll soon be released, but oh how I do feel for these poor fellows. I am going to say this P & you mark my words, just as sure as we are alive, there is going to be a riot & murder in this place. Its aughtful what there doing, & all on account of the new Chief & his staff.

You know P, there certainly are some bad people inside of these walls. It takes alot to get them stirred, but when they do, well, I hope I ain't around. But seemly they are not interfering with the Quarry. I received every-thing all ok, Tob, newspapers, etc. <u>Many many thanks</u>.

Say P would you believe it, but I'm the only one in the Pen that has Tob. I was offered $1.00 for two plugs, but I would not

*give it to him that way, rather I gave him six plugs, as I knew
I could get it any time. These guards are all so afraid, even
Knowledge Box refused to buy OK a few sticks of chewing gum:
we always used to get him to get us it. This place is more like
"Hell" than ever.*

*Now P, this Kite is written in a hurry, as these new guards
on night I do not know & they must be closely watched, so hoping
you excuse this scribling.*

I am P
Your Friend
to Death
DaDy Longlegs

PS

P, can I bother you for a few more matches
Bye Bye

(Trust me)

*N.B. Say P, do you reconize this piece of ribbon? It was on
the candies you sent me last, never to be forgotten Xmas. Dady*

•••

The parcel was from PISGAH. Phyllis tore open the wrapper. Inside
a thin cardboard box lay a white handkerchief, a square of neatly
hemmed linen, without adornment. She lifted the tiny veil gently by
its corners and held it before her. The cloth was blessed.

*There is POWER in prayer, united prayer. We gladly join with
you and send you the little handkerchief to slip in the pillow or pin to the
clothing of one needing freedom from a habit or a pain.*

Phyllis fixed the handkerchief on the inside of her nightdress so that it fell over her left breast. She laid her hand over the sacred cloth and pressed it to her skin.

There is one way, and only one, by which you can be well.

It is not by medicine, or the doctors would cure you and themselves, too; but they cannot do either. When they are able to give you any relief it is in all cases by the sanction of the Lord.

He cast out the spirits with His word, and healed all that were sick, Himself took our infirmities and bore our sickness. Matthew 8:16,17.

In Jesus' name, she whispered, make my heart strong.

Oh, to be whole when Daddy Long Legs was free.

Now about that trouble that is wrecking your life, destroying your peace and joy, standing like a great shadow between you and the face of God: no matter what the trial is, you can have it all your own way if you have sufficient faith.

For Jesus Himself says, All things are possible to him that believeth. Faith is the substance of things hoped for, the evidence of things not seen.

• • •

The spring that William St. Pierre Hughes reached manhood was baptized in blood. The season was marked for him thereafter. Where others saw wildflowers blooming, he saw shreds of home-spun on wasted bodies in prairie grass, orgies of insects feeding on vacant eyes. Bone rising like new growth from crusted flesh, whitening in the sun. The sweet stench of death.

Fish Creek. Batoche. Battleford. He'd been there, had seen it all. Watched the mutinous Riel surrender, his face blacken as he hanged.

Hughes noted the signs of spring with dread. He knew now, as he had not then, that more than the earth stirred in spring. Plodding towards Winnipeg through soggy snow to his hips, he'd heard the Balm of Gilead trees whisper. Their message had been lost to him, but he understood it now. Insurrection, was what they said. The wind of change that melts the snow sparks defiance in the souls of men.

Hughes might have disbelieved his own experience, but the books on his library shelves bore proof: the bloody history of nations takes root in the spring. It was April when shopkeepers and farmers trampled the new grass on Lexington Green, stuffing iron balls into the muzzles of their muskets as the British advanced. It was May when the commoners of the Third Estate sat resolute in the *salle des menus plaisirs du rot,* refusing to leave though rifles aimed through the door. It was in the spring that Europe rose against Metternich. In the spring, Lenin made for Russia and brought the reign of the Romanovs to an end. And in the spring just past, working men had stood together at the barricades in the Winnipeg general strike.

Perhaps, thought Hughes, he should have warned Warden Ponsford: Spring is not the time to lean on those who already squirm under your thumb. But Ponsford was not a man to take another's word. And the mutiny, which Hughes had had to read about in the newspaper, might work to his own advantage in the end. Discredit Ponsford inside the prison and out. Draw off the first hot flood of resistance from the inmates and guards. Leave the ground clear for the next Warden, a more enlightened man, a man the Superintendent of Penitentiaries would choose.

• • •

Monday May 10, 1920.

To Daddy,—Oh I forgot all about your tob to-day. I raced right back to school & I meant to get it after 4:30 but we had company &

they stayed for tea & I forgot all about it, Careless Peggy. I will get
it in the morning & leave it in your mitt Tuesday <u>noon</u>. (Senator
Smoking & Mc Chewing). The other tob I will leave for you to get
Wed. A. M. Would you like it left in the Palace or the mitts?

Try & let me know. If possible leave a little note at noon
explaining.

Friend Peggy

You can explain on the remainder of this sheet

Thick-head-Peggy

• • •

Wensday <u>noon</u>

Good friend P,
Please P, don't say such mean things about yourself "Thick-
head" etc. and please P, don't worry so over such mere trifles. I
would that you please me in using your own judgment. I'm never
in a hurry for Tob or any thing. Always take your time.

You see the change on top, also the Palace moved. I will
have to be very careful in looking over your direction, but I will
come up on deck & will speak to Knowledge-Box & there will as
usual doff my cap, which means every-thing is ok, & hello to you
& ever so much it means. You know what is in my mind at the
time, only my position stops me from putting it into words.

P, can I worry you for a envlope, some time, <u>no hurry</u>. Bye
By. P

Yours forever
DaDy

(Trust me)

*PS. Why I asked you for a couple of envlopes is because, if you
note carefully, these in here are made in a very much different way,
& there may be some mark. Its only a suspicion. As I've said B/4,
not for the world would I want any-thing to come in our way.*

Josie.

• • •

Captain John Ponsford was the tenth Warden to run the penitentiary
at Portsmouth. The Warden's mandate had not changed in eighty-five
years: confine a convict for as long as the court ordained, reform him
during captivity and return him to society a better man.

Neither had the means to those ends changed: the penitentiary had
always been ruled by fear.

After Ponsford reviewed the day's long list of entries in the
Punishments Book, he flipped backwards through the pages of sentences his predecessors had prescribed, driven by some vague notion,
perhaps, of justifying the punishments of the past several days or
proving that his measures, by comparison, were not extreme. He
moved beyond the Great War, into the century before, past the date
of his own birth, to the penitentiary's first years, the leather covers on
the Punishments Books becoming progressively darker, stained and
worn, the ink faded, the writing elaborate, the paper brittle with age.
Eighty-five years of insubordination, violation and defiance: would
the convicts never learn?

The first Warden, Henry Smith, flogged convicts for every
offence. No one was spared, it seemed. A ten-year-old named Peter
Charbonneau was lashed dozens of times in eight and a half months
for such crimes as staring, winking and laughing. The entries for one
insane convict, James Brown, amounted to several hundred at least;

Ponsford lost count. One boy was given a bread and water diet for "making a great noise in a cell by imitating the bark of a dog." And an eleven-year-old, Alec Lafleur, was lashed on Christmas Eve for speaking French, his mother tongue.

Ponsford had heard Henry Smith's name long before he took over his office at Kingston Penitentiary. Smith was legendary among Wardens, even those in the West. His excessive punishments had provoked the first public enquiry into penitentiaries when the Portsmouth prison was barely a dozen years old. Stories still circulated about Smith's son Frank, a keeper in the kitchen who'd amused himself by raping female convicts and standing men up as archery targets, blinding one with an arrow through the eye.

The Punishments Book showed just how cruel Smith had been, but Ponsford couldn't help wishing he'd been more discreetly retired. For over every Warden's head hung the Damoclean sword of Smith's undoing: one false move, or at least one made public, and an enquiry would ensue, a Warden's work laid bare to the scrutiny of a self-righteous public, unschooled in the brittle truths of punishment and reform. Wardens were still charged with the godly task of remaking men, but they had never been trusted since the days of Henry Smith.

The Warden who took Smith's place didn't limit himself to the lash. Pummelling with a fire hose at short range. Successive near drownings in a tub. Surrogate death inside the Box. Bread and water diet, confinement in a dark cell, shackling ankle and wrist, the ball and chain. One man had been shackled continuously for nine years! How humane prison management had become, thought Ponsford, flipping through the pages, and how reduced was his own arsenal for keeping the peace.

Convicts were, and always had been, a bad lot. Lechers, scoundrels and miscreants, rakes and ne'er-do-wells, deserters, seditionists,

vile sodomists and pimps, loafers, sneaks and drunkards, sly black-
guards and rogues, shiftless forgers, perfidious bigamists, the most
heinous, reprehensible murderers, scum of the earth. In their mutiny,
Ponsford saw only a cunning, vulgar mob. Their complaints were
trivial—hair too closely cropped, unpalatable food, too little contact
with their families, little to read, nothing to smoke, no exercise during
the weekend's forty-hour lock-up. The ruse was a novel one: a protest to improve conditions, they said. Sympathetic reformers with soft
hearts and brains might fall for the convicts' scheme, but Ponsford
had been a Warden too long. The mutiny was just another means of
eroding discipline, of easing the way to mass outbreak.

Ponsford closed the last of the Punishments Books and squared
the pile neatly at the centre of his desk. It was oddly satisfying to
hold between his large hands every attempt to control the penitentiary at Portsmouth throughout its long and illustrious history. The
resolute perseverance of his predecessors gave him strength. He too
would come down hard on convicts who questioned the rules. And
he would come down just as hard on the guards. But he would keep
strictly within the bounds of the Act. The spotlight that turned inevitably on the penitentiary at Portsmouth would illuminate him too, he
knew. Where others had drawn fire for their harshness, he would be
celebrated for the results that his strict discipline would achieve.

Ponsford turned out the light in his office and climbed the stairs to
the widow's walk of his grand, new house. From this height he could
take in his penitentiary at a glance. It was as if he could hold it in the
palm of his hand. The perspective helped him marshal his thoughts.

He would make this prison run like a well-oiled machine. At the
core of his staff would be Alberta men, personally trained: Chief
Keeper Tucker and Chief Watchman Clayton, already in place, his
Clerk due to arrive before long, instructors for the carpentry and tailor

shops promised for the fall. The corruption that was O'Leary's legacy would be driven out. Every action, henceforth, would be ordered. Every movement spied upon. Guard against convict, guard against guard, convict against convict, convict against guard. The faintest whispers of intrigue circling back to him. Each infraction punished, however slight. No outcry in the village, no complaints in the press would save the perpetrators, stay the paddle or open the gates to corrupt officers again.

In the distance, Ponsford could make out the white gash of the quarry, the dark swath of the prison firm, the cluster of stone buildings that were Rockwood Asylum, and below him, the walled cell blocks and workshops pinched between the lake and the main road to Kingston. No fewer than five public thoroughfares cut through this patchwork of penitentiary lands. Village houses and stores pressed in on every side, civilized society insinuated dangerously, provocatively, between where the convicts worked and where they ate and slept.

An image of Stony Mountain came to him, a prison where convicts laboured in isolation, no glimpse of motorcars, shops or passersby to distract them from their punishment, no reminders of ordinary daily life to tempt them to discontent. The penitentiary at Portsmouth would have to be moved, he decided, and a brand new federal prison built, safely set apart, a model of order and work.

That legacy would take years to realize. In the meantime, there was much he could do. Enlarge the quarry to keep more convicts at hard labour. Strip and whitewash the cells. The convicts could stay in the old quarters for the insane while the tiers were renovated. A fresh, clean start: the slack, corrupt ways of the past banished with the filth. Ponsford pondered his plan, filled his mind with details until they muffled the memory of the convicts' puny riot like a rug flung over a sputtering fire.

•••

Friday P.M.

Good friend P:

Once again we have been moved, now we are bileted in the old asylum, but it's quite nice, all up to date, white wash basins, etc. But, oh, the beds. OK is going to sleep on the floor. Its only for this one night, but I wish it was morning!

From my window in font of my cell I look right out at Portsmouth, opposite the Boat Delivery with Gasoline marked on the doors. So all I do is look out & think! Now & again I walk up & down.

Two fellows came in from Toronto, one for life & the other 15 years, both for manslaughter. One is a returned man, was in the trenches 36 months. So this night guard tells me.

Here it is Sunday once more, time sure is flying. One week more & this month will look small. We will be locked up all next weekend, from Sat evening until Tuesday A.M. for I understand the 24th is a full Holiday. Queen Victoria's birthday or some queen.

Say P, I cannot for the world think of what's the trouble. I don't hear from Sis. I hope I hear from her tomorrow, to relieve my mind for this long coming Sunday.

Well, P trusting you keep well, & hoping I don't have to worry you much more.

I remain Always, Peggy
Your Esteem Friend
DaDY

P.S.

*Can I bother you for a little more writing paper. Always
wanting some-thing, eh?*

(Trust me)

• • •

At the close of school on Friday, May 14, the next to final report cards
were issued to the students at Kingston Collegiate. Phyllis rode the
trolley back to Portsmouth, choosing an outside seat where the breeze
moving through the open car fondled her hair and the scent of peo-
nies, heads dandling on new grass, washed over her sharp and sweet.

The square brick school building, the colour of dried blood in the
late afternoon light, receded behind her. She would not return, she
vowed. She would never go back. Final examinations were scheduled
for three weeks hence. Only half the class would pass, Miss Irving said.
Even three months, thought Phyllis, silently preparing her defence,
would not be enough to repair the damage of the year.

The truth was, school was no longer of interest to her. Her father
had always joked that one day she'd be working for him, a school
mistress hired by the Portsmouth Board of Education where he sat as
trustee. But she'd never imagined herself a teacher. She had no desire
to stand at the front of the room, on display, the butt of rude jokes
made by vulgar little brats. The virtual certainty of a job in Portsmouth
had long ago put the idea of teacher training out of her mind; though
she'd never said as much at home. Neither did she want to be a nurse:
her own ill health made her wary of the sick. And if she did not intend
to teach or nurse, then what was the point of staying in school, she
asked herself. She had no clear idea of what exactly she would do
instead, but she felt compelled to make herself free to choose.

That evening in the parlour, Phyllis told her mother and father she was quitting school. The decision, she declared, was her own, though in truth without the letter from PISGAH concealed in the Ovaltine tin under her bed, her resolve would have softened, if not under the bludgeon of her father's dire predictions, then in the shadow of her mother's fading hopes.

> *PISGAH Home Movement*
> *Los Angeles, California*

Phyllis Dear:

Enclosed is a little Bible study I have hastily written out. This will somewhat answer your question. Read the references.

God in no place puts a premium on ignorance, but neither does he put any premium on education. Christ prayed all night before choosing disciples, then chose them from the common people. Read first five chapters of Proverbs.

The foolishness of worldly wisdom and what the Bible teaches concerning it, or education:

God will destroy the wisdom of the wise and will bring to nothing the understanding of the prudent.

God hath made foolish the wisdom of this world.

The world by wisdom knows not God.

Not many wise, mighty or noble men called. (I Cor. 1:19-26)

Knowledge puffeth up. (I Cor 8:1)

All knowledge without love is nothing. (I Cor 13:2)

The fear of God is the beginning of wisdom.

Mouth of righteous speaketh wisdom. (Psa 37:30)

Stand your ground and hold your faith. Many preachers & others have so much head knowledge they are top-heavy and heart empty.

> *Keep pressing on*
> *Yours for the faith*
> *Sister Goodwin*

Phyllis held to PISGAH's revelations as to the linen at her breast.

• • •

Monday. P.M.

Good friend P —

*I sure was pleased to get that letter from Sis this A.M. but was
also a little dissappointed at not receiving any cash, for as a rule,
without asking, she usually sends a little. Perhaps she thinks
I'm not in need for awhile yet. I shouldn't be at that, only when I
have it I like everyone to have it too.*

*Say P, has not this been one grand day? Really the first
summer's day we have had. I see you was not at school to-day. I
see you & some friend in the Garden this A.M. You sure have one
lovely spot. When the leaves come out on that big tree, it surely
must be beautiful!*

*I've been looking out of my window watching a couple of
young fellows fishing. It makes one crave for liberty, rowing
out & around & my but the water is so clear & nice this P.M.
Gosh, I wish it was July! Well P my little pall, once more I must
conclude,*

> *So bye bye,*
> *DaDy*

(Trust me)

• • •

Hughes was losing ground. This was not Courcelette; it was Ypres. A blasted ruin of rotting flesh, mud and stone, a few square miles of cratered Flemish farmland desperately clung to in the spring of 1916 by the British and Colonial Command. Hughes had come close to court martial that spring. Reported to the British command for failing to hold the miserable mound that was his to defend, he'd been rescued by Sam. Instead of disgrace, he'd won promotion and a new command.

Hughes was a survivor. His star was somehow blessed. It may have been privilege that led him to the arenas where his life had played itself out, but it was by his own cunning and luck that he'd endured and prospered there. It had never occurred to him that this might not always be so.

In his hand, Hughes held a purloined draft of Bill 138. With a single piece of legislation, Charles Doherty was hoping to claim the high ground. In 1918, when the position of Superintendent was created, amendments to Section 15 of the Penitentiary Act had shifted the power to write the rules and regulations into the Superintendent's hands. Bill 138 would add a clause to the very beginning of the Act, to Section 3, wherein the Minister of Justice was granted jurisdiction over the penitentiaries. *And he shall have power to make rules and regulations for their due administration, management, discipline and police and for such other purposes as may be necessary or expedient.*

The purview of the Superintendent pre-empted. Hughes, cut off at the pass.

The Bill's second provision neatly dispatched Hughes's complaints to the Civil Service Commission about the manner of John Ponsford's appointment. Wardens and Deputy Wardens, the bill declared, should be considered appointed for the penitentiary service in general and, once hired, the Minister could move them from prison to prison as he saw fit.

Unless Hughes could marshal his forces against the passage of Bill 138, Doherty's friend Biggar would make the rules and John Ponsford would be at Kingston Penitentiary to stay.

• • •

Wensday, May 19/20

Good friend P —

Around 4:30 I was up on deck & you were away at the far end of the Garden, reading a book. I've noticed that you are very fond of green. So am I! But you're in season. Every-thing is getting green, for them leaves certaintly are coming out this last few days.

You did look so forsaken away down there by your lonesome. I was just thinking, What would you say if I was to walk in on you when you are reading & sneaked up to you, put my hand on your shoulder & said "Hello." Would it not be a surprise? Ha, ha. But no, you will know when I'm coming, at least you will have an idea! Every-time I go home after being away for awhile, the first thing Mother says is, Oh J, are you going to stay home? Why no, mam, I've only come to say Good-bye, & then she would laugh. I would get her to make some apple pies & oh how she can make pastry! Say P, you mark my word, some day you are going to know all my people, for if I have my health combined with a little luck, Sis & I will motor down here & take you back with us & keep you for a couple of weeks. Of course that would not be for perhaps a year. Gosh, how I do long for to be free once more. About 45 days yet. You know P its draging especially now that the weather is so lovely.

I certainly have a beautiful view out on the lake & this little bay. I often see girls & wonder if any of them are P! Say P if

*I do not get another letter from Sis B/4 Sat A.M. I'm going to
borrow, for I understand Monday is a holiday. But I'm hoping to
have some money B/4 then. A fellow in here owes me some but
has not made his connection as yet.*

*Always asking or begging for some-thing, Ain't I? I'll be
glad when it all ceases. One of the boys found ½ a plug of Tob
down in the old Quarry & a little note saying—Don't tell no one
& may call again. As luck would have it, a good boy found it.
Well must leave this, so bye, bye, P,*

DaDy

(Trust me)

•••

The space that school had taken up closed over like a wound. The
regimen of the classroom, the stale, breathless air, the cruelty of the
teachers quickly faded until the red brick building seemed as remote as
snow on a warm spring day.

How the world around her bloomed! Phyllis spent whole days
in the garden when the weather was fine, turning over the damp soil
with a spade, fingering the roots of quackgrass to their source, easing
them out, all of a piece. Squaring the boundary of the garden, feeling
her weight against the blunt tool as it sliced down through the turf,
shaking the earth from the tufts of grass that filled the bushel basket
like a mound of tiny scalps.

She worked side by side with the convict, the alders and black willows but a flimsy curtain between the quarry and her yard. She pat-
terned her day to his, waking with the sound of the bell, picking her
tools out of the back shed as he came up the road in the morning,
tidying up as he passed through the gate at the end of the day. She

chose a rock from the quarry's edge and as she used it to drive a stake at one side of the garden, then another at the opposite end of the row, the string taut between, she imagined her blows blending with his, stone to stone.

She knelt before the furrows and pressed the seeds into the ground. Long tracks of shrivelled grey peas, short rows of Cherry Belle radishes, spinach and lettuce, Grand Rapids and curly Black-Seeded Simpson. These would mature and grow bitter long before he arrived.

She took more care with the broad speckled beans, placing them exactly a hand's width apart. The cucumber and squash, parchment seeds so thin they hardly seemed able to harbour new life, she pressed five to a mound. The fine carrot seed she mixed with sand and funnelled slowly from her palm. The beans and cucumbers would be ready for harvest in early July. Baby carrots, too, sweet stubby fingers under feathered ferns. She saw herself move on weed-less paths between the burgeoning plants, the abundance in her basket a testament to her devotion and skill.

She imagined the dishes she would prepare for his visit: three-bean salad, glazed baby onions, thinly sliced cucumbers in a sauce of soured cream, a raspberry and red currant pie. She weeded the dandelion and wild parsley from the clumps of winter savory, chives and thyme at the front edge of the garden and filled the bald patches behind with sprinklings of fennel, chervil and dill. Chamomile and borage to settle the stomach, sage to soothe a cough, comfrey to clear the lungs, valerian for the fluttering of her heart.

She patted earth over the seeds and watered the rows, the spray from the copper spout freeing rainbows from the slant of morning light. In the time it would take the seeds to sprout and bear fruit, the convict would complete his sentence, the moment of their meeting not a season away.

She caught a glimpse of him at midday as she stood her tools in the shed. The grind of quarry carts on the gravel behind the house drew her back to the garden again. When the planting and weeding and pruning were done, she sat by the lilacs and read of adventure, *The Call of the Wild* and Zane Grey. Sometimes she sat motionless for long minutes at a time, a book splayed carelessly on her lap. So still, a dragonfly perched on her shoulder, a lacy jet brooch. As she listened, the rhythm of hammers, chisels and picks came to her like the music of a distant marching band, practising for a parade, and a small smile played on her lips.

• • •

Sunday. P.M.

Generous Friend:
After many hours of serious thinking & reflecting, also writing
out on paper, only to turn around & tear same into shreds, it has
taken all my self-respect, manhood & nerve, to ask what I am
about to ask you to do for me. Please <u>understand</u> that I am more
than <u>ashamed</u> to ask you this after all you have done for me, also
after once being told that you would not like to put yourself under
such obligations. But, as I've studied the affair, there <u>will</u> in <u>no</u>
<u>way whatsoever</u>, be any name, address, etc connected with this
place. Here in brief is all that would be necessary. I give you my
letter. You, after noting its contents if you should desire to do
so, would drop the address in same, & one week from that day,
you will receive $50.00 There will be no mail sent to you, that is,
in hand writing. You will only receive the money as if you were
receiving a regular Government Allowance & I am sure it would
not be noticed. Another & much easier way would be to have it

addressed to General Delivery, Kingston, Ontario. You will
not have to be uneasy about it not arriving in due & proper time.
After you had received same, hold it until you think it ample &
proper time, & then give me same. If for one moment I thought
you were in any way in a dangerous position in doing this, I
would never ask you. Rest assured <u>never never never</u> in any way
would you be allowed to suffer. There is no fear of any leakish, &
it will never happen again, only this once, & then I will be ok for
the remainder of my punishment here. So hoping & praying that
you will do this favor for me, & see it in the same light as I do, &
oh please forgive me for being so selfish & bold, but one placed as
I am will do almost anything for the little necessities . . .

Fifty dollars would buy a dark grey tweed suit for her father, a voile dress for her mother, new camisoles for her sisters and shoes for both her brothers. It would buy a water-powered washing machine and a wireless set. Food for the family for weeks.

Fifty dollars. Phyllis had never seen so much money at once. She could grasp it only in equivalents, not as numbers in a bank balance or a stack of bills in a purse. A professor's salary for a week. Her father's wages for two. When he was on strike, what he earned in seven weeks. Were Phyllis lucky enough to find a job as a house-maid, a seamstress or a clerk in an ice cream parlour, she would not bring home that much in a month.

Where would the convict get fifty dollars? And what did he need it for? For the first time since their correspondence began, it occurred to Phyllis that Daddy Long Legs, like his namesake, might be a wealthy man.

● ● ●

His cell was stripped, wiped utterly clean.

The prisoner set down his tray and passed his hands over the walls. The graffiti had been sanded smooth, painted over so thickly that the convicts who had gone before him, his companions through the long nights, seemed impossibly distant now. The calendars he had scratched where the bunk met the brick wall, staring at them as he fell asleep so his dreams would be of liberty: gone.

The walls had been as familiar as the body of a beloved, each dimple and flaw noted a thousand times over, the landmarks of intimacy. Wrinkles and flakes of paint, cracks in the mortar, each committed to memory as he explored the limits of his territory day after day, each pass of the eye making the surface of the four walls and the cube of air they contained a little more distinctly his own. Something to be counted on. A place to bury his head knowing in advance exactly what would be there when he opened his eyes again. Only in such static surroundings could one day bleed into the next, time passing unnoticed in an unbroken stream.

But the cell was changed and he was a foreigner. His first day in prison all over again.

With a start, he turned towards the corridor. He had been moved from the cell just as the fledgling swallows hatched, three bald pink creatures with bright orange beaks far too large for their slippery bodies.

The guards had been thorough. Even the sills had been wiped clean.

The prisoner poked at the congealed rice on his tray.

He lay down on his bed. The paint high on the walls had not yet dried. In the spring, the brick and stone harboured the cold long after the air had warmed. Often the prisoner had written messages in the glaze of condensation, his frustration and longing evaporating with the passing hours. The painters had not taken the dampness into account. Patches of grey mottled the pristine white, shapeless splotches that reminded him of mouldering plaster in cheap rented rooms.

He turned his face into the mattress. Outside the lake steamers bore through the fog. They bellowed to each other across black acoustic waves, lost souls in the night.

• • •

On the anniversary of his first month at Kingston Penitentiary, John C. Ponsford took his ivory-tipped cane in hand and went for a walk. He waited in the Keeper's Hall as Chief Keeper Tucker unlocked the barrier to the Dome, eyeing the convict tally above the door: 615. Rising steadily every day.

Down the corridors of the ranges he caught glimpses of khaki and striped denim. Convicts pushing mops, guards posted at the railings of the catwalks above.

Under the cupola of the Dome, a great gleaming stillness, hushed as a church.

What a change he had wrought in just four weeks. The floors glowed like polished marble under the soles of his high leather boots. The bars of the cell grates winked like chrome in the late afternoon light, a parade of thin, silver palings, receding in perfect precision. He turned ninety degrees, stopped and made another quarter turn, facing one range after another, the glinting grates, the polished floors, the pale apple green of the freshly painted walls, each of the four corridors radiating from the Dome identical to the one that came before and after. He felt the pride of a builder, though he'd never laid a stone.

The Warden paused to breathe in the prison air, redolent of carbolic, lye and whitewash. It refreshed him, as a tonic would. An elixir.

He walked to the centre of the rotunda, ivory staccato against flagstone. The double saucers of the brass gong, mounted like an inverted chalice on the round wooden radiator in the middle of the lofty room, shone. Everything he looked at gleamed and winked.

He lifted his cane and brought it down once, sharply, against the polished brass.

Figures instantly materialized. In the corridors, convicts stood at attention, eyes snapped front, mop handles upright at their sides. Guards, poised at every exit, tense, awaited his command.

The smile that passed his lips barely riffled his moustache. From a distance, no one would have noticed.

All right! he roared.

The Warden's words shot up into the Dome, ricocheted off the clerestory panes and reverberated down each range like well-aimed cannonballs.

Carry on!

June

On Queen Victoria's birthday, the weather suddenly warmed, as if the season took its cue from Portsmouth gardeners who on that day by unwavering tradition planted the last of their vegetable seeds. For a week the days were hot and clear, the nights balmy. When Phyllis strolled in the evenings to the quarry, letters and packets in hand, her bare arms glowed white in the moonlight.

By the first of June, gardeners were praying for rain. The tomato and sweet pepper plants, coddled in cold frames through spring frosts, looked dazed in the parched earth, drained pale by the heat. New sprouts trembled and drooped. Phyllis mounded soil around their stems, whispering words of encouragement as she pulled weeds from between the rows, ripping out the hardy so the tentative might survive.

She did not work for long. The air was close. It pressed on her chest painfully. She pulled the canvas chair to the edge of the shade from the big elm trees and leaned back to watch the sky. Puffed-up, flat-bottomed clouds moved across the heavens with stately speed, like dowagers in a rush. The wind whipped their bulk into marvellous shapes: a stout queen in a trailing gown metamorphosed into a spaniel balancing a ball; then a cooing, round-cheeked baby; and finally, the convict stooped over his barrow, his head turned to her with a smile.

She must have dozed watching the heavenly parade, for when next she looked up, the clouds had turned sullen, slowed their pace. They rammed into each other, their edges blackening as if bruised, blue sky brusquely shouldered aside. Phyllis wrapped her arms around herself and huddled deeper into the chair. Though it was still midafternoon, the light was shot with the sulphurous orange of an uneasy sunset. Abruptly, the wind died. Phyllis felt the breath drawn out of her into the space it left.

The first stroke of lightning lifted her from the chair, drew her to the open ground of the garden, between the rows of lettuce, silently counting, eight . . . nine . . . Thunder erupted deep inside the clouds, circled ominously from a distance. Raindrops, heavy as satchels, splattered around her. She stood rooted, drops skidding off her bare arms, down her cheeks.

The storm gathered force like an argument. The rain turned sharp, needling her skin. The branches of the elms and lilacs bent before the resurrected wind, leaves furled, tearing loose. Lightning crackled, jagged strands of spittle against the bruised sky. Each flash illuminated the garden, the house, the trees in eerie silhouette. Thunder blasted the clouds apart, caromed above her, Dome to quarry, quarry to Dome.

Phyllis lifted her arms to the rain, thrilling to the rush of wind that thrashed her skirts, whipped her hair. Lightning burst in sheets, ripping darkness from the battered sky, a single explosion of sound and light. The elm by the gate loosened its bark with a hiss. A butterfly tilted recklessly through the storm.

Something tugged at her arm. Phyllis did not resist. She longed to soar, to merge with the clouds, roll with the thunder, hold the lightning to her breast.

She turned in a daze and saw her father, his face slick with rain, his mouth contorted with words swallowed by the storm.

Alarmed, she shook off his hand.

His head bent close to hers. You'll come inside, young lady.

No! I want to stay! Her cries buffeted in the wind to a whisper.

Now!

She struggled as he pushed her before him, wild tears washed with rain, no words to say why she had to be out there, in the midst of it, her delirium constrained as her mother towelled her hair in the calm of the house, where it is true, she felt safer, but where she knew she would never be carried away.

• • •

This mutiny will not fade!

William St. Pierre Hughes spoke in a tone that did not invite response. The Warden sat before him silently bearing his reprimand. In his bullish attempt to take control of the prison, Ponsford had made a mess, though it was clear to Hughes that the Warden had no idea how the stain could spread, was spreading already, threatening to taint not only Ponsford and the penitentiary at Portsmouth but also the Office of the Superintendent and even the future of prison reform.

Hughes put both hands on the desk that separated the two men and leaned stiff-armed towards Ponsford, locking him in his gaze, letting the silence fill up with the Warden's discomfort. He took advantage of the pause to renew his own strength. The sun had not yet reached its azimuth and already this was Hughes's third meeting of the day. At first light, he'd stood in front of the veterans of the 21st Battalion, presenting the colours to the handful of men who'd survived of the thousand he'd mustered five years before. From the stone walls of the Kingston armouries to the penitentiary's stone walls, from wars won to battles not yet engaged. Another band of uniformed men had met him in the Keeper's Hall: the dismissed officers of the prison staff. They'd conscripted their own Brigadier-General, A.E. Ross, the Member of Provincial Parliament for Kingston, who'd stoked them with promises of public scandal and a commission of enquiry if they were not reinstated in their jobs. The three men had stood before the Superintendent, determined, cocky, ready for a fight.

It's not our fault, they'd said, explaining the contraband Ponsford had found.

Whose then, if not yours? It was found in your shops, was it not? Hughes's enquiries were polite. His Distinguished Service Order flashed at his chest.

For years there's been lax discipline, countered the spokesman. The others nodded their heads. There's been a steady turnover of Wardens: in eight years, six different men. We never knew what to expect or what was expected of us. We shouldn't take the blame, he insisted, concluding his arguments as rehearsed. We shouldn't be made to pay for the failure of the government to appoint competent superiors to oversee our work.

The fault, it seemed, was his.

Hughes had been firm. The firings would stand. The penitentiary officers knew their job: it was spelled out in the Act. There was no excuse for trucking with inmates, not under any circumstance. The lapses of their superiors in carrying out their duties was a separate matter, one that had already been resolved. Had not Chief Keeper Atkins, Deputy Warden O'Leary and Overseer Wilson already been dismissed? If the officers before him had valued their jobs, they should have watched more closely the inmates in their keep.

The men had left the room sullenly, unconvinced. Now Ponsford sat before him wearing a similar aspect.

The defiance of the officers and the inmates' mutiny, taken separately, were neither one a serious threat, but simultaneous attack on two fronts was a test of Hughes's skill. Of the two, it was the mutiny that concerned him most. The public would be sympathetic to the firings—penitentiary officers were considered not much better than the men they guarded—but no one would support a Superintendent who let the inmates slip out of control. When society felt threatened, it became at once foolish, blind and ruthless.

Hughes kept his eyes fixed on the Warden, taking a measure of the man. Was Ponsford an inept ally or a particularly shrewd adversary? His timing could not have been more damaging. The second reading of Bill 138 was only days away. The last thing Hughes needed as he fought to keep the right to make the rules was for his management of the federal prisons to be questioned. In his darker moments, Hughes wondered if this was all part of Doherty's master plan: hire Ponsford to push the convicts to a revolt that would discredit the Superintendent and shift the power over the penitentiaries firmly back into the Minister's hands.

You must announce an internal investigation at once, Hughes said, straightening. Take the press into your confidence. Share with them the difficulties facing a Warden dedicated to making a prison safe, secure *and* efficient. Get them on your side. At all costs, watch your tongue. Don't say too much. Assure them that the inmates are under control, that the dismissals are in the interests of law and order and that you are preparing a report for the Superintendent. Which you are. And have it on my desk without delay.

Ponsford appeared to take in his words, though his small, dark eyes were set so deep in his fleshy face that they gave little away.

Hughes turned his back on the Warden and strode to the door. The subject was closed. He had done what he could. He would not allow this skirmish to keep him from moving forward on other fronts.

Hughes motioned Ponsford into the corridor. Now show me the sample uniform you have produced.

The tailor shop was empty; the convicts were locked in their cells for the midday meal. The instructor, who had been just about to leave for his dinner, laid the pieces of new clothing before the Warden and Superintendent. The coat and trousers, the shirt and cap were perfect in every respect. A dignified, muted blue, well-cut.

You have turned out a beautiful suit of clothes, Warden. My congratulations.

Only a few bolts of red and grey checkered wool and brown and purple striped denim still lay on the shelves in the tailor shop. In October, Hughes had ordered all shipments of the garish fabrics stopped. It would take years before the old uniforms were worn out and all the inmates were fitted in plain winter blue and summer brown, but the day would come when the humiliation of such ludicrous issue would no longer drag a convicted man down. Hughes rubbed the fine wool between his fingers. If only the inmates had known what was at stake as they listened to the Bolshevists. But he would not let their ill-timed protest jeopardize his plans to improve their lot.

One further matter, he said.

Hughes pointed to the shirt front, to the bold white patch crudely stamped with large black numbers.

I want the identification patches made smaller and narrower. Get rid of the wooden stamps and order a set of brass numerals, not more than half an inch in length. The number will be reduced in size but it can be spaced so it is still easily read. Continue to sew the numbers on the front and back of the shirt and coat so inmates can be identified from a distance. But dispense with the number on the cap. It is unnecessary. Stamp the cap on the inside of the lining, not in plain view.

Though Ponsford nodded his assent, Hughes knew the Warden humoured him. Ponsford considered such refinements pandering to the sensibilities of convicted men. Fair enough, thought Hughes, call me a convict-lover if you will. Ponsford could impose military discipline. He would give them their self-respect. An inmate would need both if he was to leave the penitentiary a decent man.

• • •

Monday P.M.

Good friend P:

As yet every-thing is about as usual, no search or trouble, & it will soon be the middle of the month again. I was just noticing that my hair is commencing to get long again, & yes P, I believe I will have a pretty good crop by the time I go out. Gosh—I only wish the next month was over, then I could expect it any day. I had a friend who was going to tell me, he worked up in the front office, but he went out the other day. So I'm watching to learn who gets his position so I can find out the exact day.

This last few weeks I've been thinking very seriously over a proposition awaiting me at all times. I can see some-thing good in it, but its in Canada, & mostly in Montreal. If I should (which I may) take this up, then I may have the pleasure of calling to see you kind people often & perhaps wear out my welcome, for in this proposition it will call on me to pass through this city twice at least a month. Oh, but sure I don't know for a certainty what I may do yet. I'll have to be out, & look at every-thing, & do what I think best. Any way, I'm not out yet. _ha. ha_.

Say P, I have not read a story for several days, not even opened a book, but walk up & down & sit & look out of the window & _think think think_. Honestly P, this is a wonderful place to build castles & think of that bright & wonderful future, (sweet boon to man).

Oh I forgot to tell you. Sat. PM I got a letter from that party that went out some time ago & he mentioned that he paid my insurance to J.R. He means he gave the money I loaned him to this party, but I cannot make out who this can be. It's sure whoever it is, he has no intentions of returning same to me, or he would of done so long B/4 this: what would you think, P?

Oh well, perhaps he needs it more than me & no doubt he does. Money is easy to get, my trouble was always, _Hard to Keep_. This Pen has taught me a wonderful lesson, especially in people's idiosyncracies, & one that cannot be bought for Millions.

Well little friend: hoping I get by with this short uninteresting Kite, I beg to remain

Your troublesome Friend

DaDy Long Legs

(Trust me)

PS. I had a wonderful supper to-night.

• • •

Robert R. Tucker stood ramrod straight, framed by the door of the south cell block. He wasn't trying to impress anyone. Indeed, there wasn't a soul about. Ramrod was simply the posture of habit for Robert Tucker. In the penitentiary, in church, in his kitchen greeting the children at breakfast. No matter how he dressed, his comportment left no doubt: Robert R. Tucker was a military man. A major, one might surmise, since he lacked the swagger that identified the higher ranks. An adjutant, perhaps: he had that meticulous air about him. A man who could organize an entire battalion and do it in such a manner that smooth functioning would seem its God-given state.

The knock-off gong had sounded. The sentries had sauntered from their towers towards the middle of the wall where they leaned together chatting, elbows resting on the parapet, rifles slung on their backs. One appeared to be smoking, though Tucker could not be certain.

The Chief Keeper's brow creased slightly as he made a mental note of what he saw. He had an excellent memory and an alert mind, both of which were being exercised to their limits by the demands of his new job. As well as the usual responsibilities of Chief Keeper— maintaining the order and cleanliness of the convicts and the buildings, assisting the Deputy Warden in maintaining discipline and recording all entries in the Officer Defaults Book and the Prisoner Punishments Book—Ponsford had asked him to keep an eye on things, discreetly of course. And so Tucker observed and made notes and at the end of each day he met with Ponsford to discuss his findings. The failure, for instance, of a guard to report the convict who waved from the hospital window to a fellow working in the yard. Or the hesitation of an officer when Tucker had casually asked how many convicts were in his gang. An officer should be able to give the answer as quickly as his own name: anything less was neglect of duty.

Ponsford's request had added to an already backbreaking work-load, given the filth and disarray of the penitentiary when Tucker arrived. But it was his duty to perform whatever services his superior asked of him. And if the Chief Keeper thought in these terms, which he didn't, he would have admitted that he quite enjoyed the task, marching into the stone shed or the shoe shop or the quarry, his pocket watch in hand, counting the seconds that passed before he was noticed and acknowledged with a salute. If Tucker admitted any satisfaction to himself, it was in noting the results of such surreptitious tests and passing the information on to Warden Ponsford.

A door across the yard opened. Tucker flicked his gaze to certain windows in the workshop building that overlooked the yard. The guards were in place. He nodded to the officer in the doorway. A gang of twenty men walked briskly across the yard, evenly spaced, single file. The instant the last convict was out of sight, Tucker nodded again. Another gang appeared. Evenly spaced. Single file. Not a word was spoken, just the brisk tramp of boots on the gravel path. Tucker nodded again, this time towards the side of the yard where the quarry gang waited at attention.

In less than twenty minutes, six hundred and twenty-one men moved from their workplace to their cells. No convicts crossed paths. Each filed past the kitchen, picked up his tray, held it out for his ration of food, his cup of tea, took his bread without pausing and proceeded to the tiers, all in perfect order. Waves of sound rose and fell behind Tucker as each gang of convicts marched to their cells and slammed their gates in unison, the locking bars sliding into place.

Tucker flipped open the lid of the gold pocket watch that was never absent from his vest pocket. Nineteen minutes, twenty-four seconds.

The Chief Keeper ate his lunch quickly and returned to his desk. There was nothing to detain him. Ponsford ate in the Warden's residence on the hill; the Chief Watchman came on duty at night. The rest of the staff had been less than welcoming to the officers who had come from Alberta penitentiary.

Tucker didn't mind. He was anxious to get back to his project: a device that would track every convict every minute of every day. He unfurled the plans on his desk. The Check Board, as he called it, would be fashioned in wood, a long rectangle with rows of small holes drilled across it. The holes represented the convicts' cells, arranged in order by tiers, ranges and cell blocks, neatly labelled. A peg of a certain colour fitted in a hole meant that the convict assigned to that particular cell was in the hospital. A peg of another colour indicated he'd been removed to a punishment cell. An empty hole meant the cell was occupied. (An awkward irony, but one that Tucker had not yet overcome without the use of hundreds of pegs.) What absorbed him at the moment was a further refinement by which a coloured peg would indicate the particular work gang or shop the convict was assigned to. Once that was established, the whereabouts of every convicted man in the penitentiary could be known at a glance, a vast improvement over the scrabble through work record books, punishment registers and sick files needed to locate one convict, never mind the dozens of convicts that were wanted for one reason or another throughout the day.

Tucker leaned back in his chair and pulled out his pocket-watch. Fifteen minutes to one. As if on cue, the Keepers filed into his office with the cell counts. He noted the numbers on his paper prototype, double-checked that the figures tallied, then he rolled up the drawing on his desk.

Tucker arrived in the Dome at exactly ten minutes to one. He confirmed it on both his pocket watch and the overhead clock. He stood beside Acting Deputy Warden Corby, a slovenly, sly-faced man. Tucker had heard stories about Corby, stories of beastly crimes, and he'd seen indications that the gossip might be true. The Acting Deputy made visits to the Women's Compound on the flimsiest excuse; there was an intimate, conspiratorial air to his conversations with the Matron; and there was a curious pattern to the posting of the guards on the northwest tower, which looked directly down into the women's cells. Less specifically but more disturbing, Corby had a braggadocio, a knowing smile when he spoke of the women's compound that brought to Tucker's mind the worst he'd witnessed in army field camps during the North West Rebellion. But Tucker lacked evidence. Corby's manner was personally distasteful to him, but he would not make a report until he knew his charges could not be denied.

Tucker checked his pocket watch. Eight minutes to one. He was about to give Corby a stern glare when the Acting Deputy struck the gong. The guards and instructors lined up before them in the Dome. Tucker nodded and the officers filed out. His watch lay open in his palm: the countdown had begun.

Every station manned, he announced.

The Acting Deputy Warden struck the gong again. A rattling of keys, the groan of range barriers swinging open, the whirr of the windlass releasing the locking bar from the front of the grates.

Tucker nodded to Corby. The gong sounded again.

The bars of the first cell on each tier opened. The sound of boots slapping stone as a convict ran to the far end of each tier.

Tucker nodded and the gong sounded again. The tapper at the top of A Range sprinted down the catwalk, hitting the bolt protruding from each cell lock with the palm of his open hand. Tap. Tap. Tap. Tap. The bars swung open as one and the convicts fell into step along the catwalk, down the zig-zag stairs, through the Dome to the kitchen. As they passed the Chief Keeper and Acting Deputy Warden, they saluted, balancing their empty trays in their left hands. Corby held his hand loosely at his forehead as if shading his eyes against the sun. Tucker returned each salute smartly, as if his life depended on it. Which, in a sense, it did. Let respect vanish for a moment, he believed, and the back of the penitentiary system would be broken.

The convicts of A1 were barely out of sight when the gong sounded again and the tapper on A2 sprinted along his tier. The gong, the taps, the heavy tramp of boots, fresh waves of sound that surged and receded in perfect, predictable rhythm. Automatons, Tucker thought with pleasure. Human flesh disciplined to the precision of cogs and gears. A prison that functioned like clockwork: Tucker's goal matched Ponsford's like a mated glove.

When the Dome was empty and silent again, the Chief Keeper snapped shut the lid on his pocket watch and rubbed it briefly on the wool of his waistcoat, polishing his thumbprint from its plain, rounded surface. Eleven minutes, forty-three seconds. To evacuate six hundred and twenty-one men. There was still work to be done.

• • •

The early summer of Phyllis's eighteenth year was the happiest of her life. The days passed with a sweet rhythm that was so assured and true to heart that it could surely last a lifetime.

She spent every possible moment out of doors, and though she rarely spoke to the rest of the family, she did not neglect her work. She tended the gardens, she picked bouquets for the parlour, gathered strawberries by the bowlful, washed them under the pump and sat on the grass, flicking off the hulls with a paring knife as she listened to the sounds of the convicts at work next door. In the morning, at midday and again in the evening, she slipped into the quarry to make her deliveries and retrieve the convict's kites, which she added to the

Ovaltine tin, now full to overflowing. In the afternoons, she travelled by trolley into Kingston on Daddy Long Legs' errands. All the months of successful forays made her perfectly at ease buying tobacco by the plug or by the pound. She had long since learned to avoid such places as Routley's, where she had made her first terrified purchase, places where she was likely to be noticed and recognized. Instead, she'd devised a routine whereby she distributed her trade evenly and at discreet intervals among the smaller establishments in the city. She imagined herself a kind of Florence Nightingale, making her round of calls for the confined. She no longer prayed to be forgiven for what she did, for she no longer thought it a sin. Although she did pray, fervently and often, giving thanks for the growing strength of her heart, for bringing PISGAH into her life, for the convict's impending release, for the beauty that God breathed into all His creation.

Though the penitentiary was on everyone's lips, the news of the Warden's harsh measures failed to filter through the veil of happiness that shimmered about her, lustrous as an aureole. She had never looked so well. When the gardening was done and there were no more strawberries to preserve or tobacco to buy and when her letters to the convict were sealed and ready for delivery, she took Watch on long walks along Front Street, past the Methodist chapel and the Church of the Good Thief, past Lake Ontario Amusement Park, out into the countryside where the air was ripe with lilacs and hay ready for the first cut. As she walked, she dreamed of their first meeting; of waiting for him outside the North Gate on the designated day, wearing the green dress he'd admired; of taking his arm and walking down Front Street, home to the garden; of speeding over these very roads, sitting close beside him in the front seat of his new motorcar.

On Sunday afternoon, when the convict was locked inside, she slipped into the woods on the far side of the quarry and sat in the shady clearing that overlooked the rough-hewn hole, knowing her parcel was already planted in the little red and white Palace at the centre, a secret gift for the convict who would retrieve it as she worked in the garden the next day.

She sat back on the grass, her legs curled under her skirt. The dust of the week had settled and the air smelled not of limestone but of clover, sweet and slightly fruity, like strawberries drenched in honey. She brushed at the blossoms with her hand, releasing fresh waves of fragrance. Their leaves were perfect rounds of three, embossed with a whitish watermark.

Phyllis's fingers strayed among the leaves, separating each set of three, idly searching for a cluster of four. Odd, she thought, that a four-leafed clover should be considered good luck. Three was the magic number of fairy tales: Sleeping Beauty's three god-mothers, three little pigs, three blind mice. The natural world had three kingdoms: animal, vegetable, mineral. Three dimensions: length, breadth, thickness. Three cardinal colours: red, yellow, blue. Man was made of mind, body and spirit. Lived through birth, death and eternity. And three was the holy number. God, His Son and the Holy Spirit: The Holy Trinity. She searched among the trefoils, cataloguing the world by threes. Three Fates, three Furies, three Harpies, three Graces. Three Musketeers, three Wise Men. The three Marys who mourned by the cross. Three crows of the cock.

Three questions.

And three wishes.

For Phyllis Halliday, the third child.

She brushed stray petals and leaves from her skirt and stood up. The stems had left imprints on her ankles. She stooped to rub the skin, and then she saw it, pressed against the back of her leg. She peeled away the flattened leaves, disbelieving, thinking a broken leaf must have mixed among a natural grouping of three. But no: four leaves sprang from a single stem, a little crushed, but intact.

• • •

Thursday, <u>PM</u>

Dear friend Peggy: —
It looked quite nice & summer like to see you with a nice white blouse on. It certaintly has been one grand day. I seen for the first time a big steam freighter going out in the lake; it was cheerful to see it winding its way along: & such joy run through me, at the time: for once, I really had one real good look at you.

  I've written this letter to-night & also done another little piece of work for a friend of mine. So please excuse thus Hurried Kite.

  (Trust me)

  I am until to-morrow PM
  Friend DaDy

  <u>Received</u> all ok

• • •

Phyllis was on her way back from the Palace, imagining again the scene of her first face-to-face meeting with Daddy Long Legs, this time accompanying him to the train station and waving a tearful goodbye while he leaned from the window and called out his vow to return just as soon as he could—when she heard a motorcar pass the St. John's Church and continue along Cross Street to the quarry. The evening bell had sounded only moments before. Curious, she thought. Other than the convicts and the congregation on Sundays, Cross Street was seldom travelled, and no one but the convicts went as far as the quarry.

The car wheeled sharply at the quarry gate, spraying gravel into the ditch. A small dapper man jumped out of the driver's seat, pulled aside the chain that blocked the road, leapt back into the car and with a scrape of gears, disappeared among the rocks.

Phyllis slipped quickly back across the road and crouched among the willows where she could see down into the quarry without being seen.

The slam of the car doors ricocheted off the stone. The echo circling the quarry walls made it seem as if a dozen motorcars had followed the first, but only the black McLaughlin was parked askew between the Palace and the halfway house. Three men gathered in front of the car. A big man with a thick brush moustache that drew down his cheeks into jowls at either side of his face. The trim little driver. And another, a tall worried-looking fellow about her father's age. The big man wore a black suit. The others wore the unmistakable khaki of penitentiary officers.

The big man gesticulated sharply, sending the others scattering across the stones to the ledge where the convicts had been hammering all week. Then the man in the suit took a ring of keys from his belt and opened the Palace door.

Phyllis pressed one hand to her heart, the other to her mouth.

They won't get away with this, thundered Ponsford, shaking his fist at the other two scrambling among the shadows. He turned and squinted into the little room. As his eyes adjusted to the dim light from the shuttered windows, he made out a potbelly stove, a rough table with ledgers spread open on its surface, pickaxes leaning together in a stook, a magneto, a roll of fuse wire, a wooden case with rope handles, stamped "Explosives."

The letters inside Ponsford's breast pocket rankled like an unlanced boil. One was from the instructor of the mail bag depart-ment:

June 12, 1920

To the Warden:
I would like a private interview with you this evening on my way out the gate at close of prison.

Yours respectfully
George Sullivan

The other was the letter Sullivan had handed over without com-ment when they met inside the North Gate not half an hour before:

June 12, 1920

Sire:
To whom this may concern.
That I except no favours for giving this information. But if the plan is carried through as I have heard it. It will endanger Officers lives and much property distroyed. Being sent on a message to the Carpenter Shop I was let in on this plan through three men that work there. Brown, Jackson, McGraw. Also the Electrician known as Charlie who works in the Electric Light room. McGraw gave Charlie a fair size Bottle of Turpentine that day. The plan being to soak waste and shavings in Turps placing them in a small bag with lead fuze wire, shoving them under the Mail Bag Department floor which is soaked with oil from the old Binder twine. Turning on a heavy curnt would cause the Fusze to shoot sparks in the soaked bag witch would cause fire. There plan may be only a scare. But it would do no harm to investigate soon.

Further more I have never been near the New Gate. But if a small size bar is placed at the end roller where the stem comes down holding it in place. It will give way. The outside one much easily by tapping the cog witch draws it to and fro. Some men say this gate can be opened in less than 5 minutes. It is also getting known through out the prison that it is weak.

Ponsford and Sullivan had torn up the floor of the mail bag shop and sure enough, they'd found the fuse and the bag of soaked wood shavings. Now they were in the quarry, on the trail of the conspirators' outside contact.

Ponsford's rage as he squinted through the stone dust in the quarry shed was a barely contained beast. He stalked around the tiny room, hands and feet jerking in spasms, knocking tools to the floor, sending boxes sprawling. How dare they! A mutiny and now an attempted breakout, all in his first six weeks. He kicked at the table and chairs, upended them sharply and palmed the surfaces underneath. They wouldn't get away with it, not with John Ponsford, who had wiped the word escape from the lexicon of convicts at Alberta and Stony Mountain. He pawed through the pickaxes and hammers, scattering them at his feet. Would that he could heave them over his head one by one and smash the crude little shed to splinters.

Tucker and Sullivan moved along the fresh burden, through the slant of late afternoon light, kicking and poking at the amber rock ledge. The place was like a bank vault, thought Tucker. Each crevice could hide a motherlode of contraband. He wasn't certain that their search would yield the civilian clothes and firearms, the stake to make good the planned escape that Ponsford expected, but he was willing to look.

The Warden opened the door of the Palace. Phyllis let the air escape from her lungs with a long, low sigh. He paced around the shack, running his hands over the walls, the window sills. He paused for a moment. Then he was on his knees in the gravel, scanning between the joists that supported the Palace on the rocks. Phyllis held her breath. She shrank back among the leaves.

Hey, boys! I found something! Ponsford was on his feet, waving a thick envelope with one hand, brushing at his trousers with the other.

No. Please God, no. No. No.

Phyllis sat perfectly still, unmindful of the spider that prickled across her ankle, the branch that nudged the back of her neck. The men in the quarry gathered round the parcel, unfolded the white paper, fanned the sheaf of five ten-dollar bills, slapped each other on the back and placed the parcel carefully in the back seat of the motor-car. Then they returned to the rocks and the Palace and searched until their own shadows fused with those of the stones. Finally, they cranked the car, backed it around and drove up the path, reset the chain and headed back down Cross Street towards the penitentiary, leaving a curl of pink dust in front of the Anglican church.

Night fell, drawing down a starless black curtain of sky. By the time Phyllis stirred, her dress clung to her, thoroughly dampened by the drizzle that had begun to fall.

• • •

The prisoner was back in the stone shed where he'd started, knees pressed on either side by those of the other men who leaned over the limestone boulder, hacking it to bits. Crusts of dust sealed his nostrils, rubbed the membranes of his lungs and eyelids raw. The tapping of a hundred hammers reverberated in his skull. For twenty-one months he'd managed to hold himself up inside this place, but he felt himself disintegrating now, pummelled to bits with the stone.

He tried to bolster himself with the thought that the contraband in the quarry and the fuse in the Mail Bag Department had not yet been traced to him. He was grateful to the guardian angel that had stilled his pencil on Saturday afternoon and kept him from leaving a kite signed "Joe," but the thought would not leave him that it had been the angel's parting gift. That after all he'd been through, his luck had finally run out.

Out of the corner of his eye, the prisoner watched a convict pass something to the guard of the stone shed as he handed over the water bucket. Nothing would stop the trade, thought the prisoner. The Warden had only raised the stakes. Convicts would have their meagre pleasures and guards would supply the means, so long as there was profit to be made. When the supply was down, demand only went up and made the risk of trucking more worthwhile than ever. If the prisoner had ten years stretching before him, he'd be looking for another connection too.

But he was on short time. When word had reached him about the Warden's find in the quarry, he'd torn his last plugs of tobacco to shreds and flushed them down the toilet in a panic. He'd spoken to no one since, written nothing down, passed no messages, except for faint whispers to OK in the next cell. He kept his head bent over his hammer and chipped away at the stone. He did exactly as he was told. He tried to believe he had only a week or two more to serve. But here he was back on the stone pile. As if his time had just begun, as if his sentence was forever and he'd never be free.

• • •

For the first few mornings Phyllis had wakened to the sound of the bell and had started eagerly to dress before she remembered. Then her fingers would begin to tremble so, she could barely tie the ribbons of her camisole.

Saturday night she had not slept. She arrived at church the next morning, red-eyed and pale. She told her family she was unwell: they would know the truth soon enough. It was only a matter of time before the man in the black suit knocked at the door.

Hunched in the pew, Phyllis prayed as she'd never prayed before. She spoke to God as a dear and trusted friend. She begged him to spare the convict, asked that her own punishment be short, that no one else in her family suffer. In return, she offered herself. Not the puny vows and promises she'd made so often in the past. On this Sunday in June she took her soul in her hands, poor thing that it was, and held it out to Him.

In the order of service lay a small bookmark, bunches of spring violets framing a scroll. *Choose you this day whom ye will serve.* She wrote on the back with a hand that shook not from fear but from having touched her own quivering core. *I choose the Lord Jesus Christ.*

No convicts had come to the quarry on Monday or Tuesday or any day since. At first, Phyllis kept to her bed. She did not have to bend the truth: the pain in her chest was a constant weight. But as the week wore on and no official appeared at the door, she grew impatient with her self-imposed exile and returned to the garden, where she could slip across the road and into the willows to see if the guard that had been posted on Sunday was still there. He was.

Phyllis racked her mind to recall what she'd said in the letter she'd watched them open. But all the words she'd written to the convict over the past ten months ran together like ink on a page left out in the rain. She could not reconstruct a single sentence. She remembered the thoughts she'd left unsaid more clearly than those she'd put into words.

At the beginning of the second week, with the quarry still closed and the guard still on duty, slouched against the stones, Phyllis ventured into the village. She lingered over the sausages in McGuire's butcher shop, considered the breads and oat cakes in Pound's bakery, paused for long moments contemplating the tins of biscuits and cocoa powder in Shortt's grocery store. She even dawdled at Baiden Brothers, absorbed in the leftover onion sets and seed potatoes that were on sale for half price.

The prison was on everyone's lips, and though she heard much, little of it added to what she already knew. The concern in the village was not for the convicts—the mutiny had been quelled and the leaders punished as they deserved. No, it was the men who worked inside the walls who held the villagers' interest. The women clicked their tongues sympathetically.

After all those years of faithful service, it isn't decent treating a man like that. They don't have any proof, you know ... Just because they found it in a place, doesn't mean it belongs to him. Or even that he knew it was there ...

The old men gathered outside the post office, leaning on their canes and passing the time in nostalgic argument. We ran a tighter ship up there in my day ... Oh, go on, Alex, there's always been brisk traffic ...

Every conversation ended in the quarry. The women, by and large, were thankful for the peace and quiet. The sound of hammers on stone had suddenly stopped, like a clock that someone forgot to rewind. They hadn't realized how persistent and pervasive the noise had been until it was gone. No more sudden blasts to disturb the baby's nap. No grind of the crusher to set the teeth on edge and send old women to bed with cold compresses on their foreheads. And the dust! When Warden Ponsford closed the quarry, he cut the workload of Portsmouth housekeepers in half. Every day was like Sunday, or a holiday. No more limestone grit on the window sills or in the soup.

And the wash could be hung out to dry without first checking which way the wind blew.

The talk of the men ended with Beaupré. The quarry, they agreed, was a hard posting, one of the hardest in the penitentiary at Portsmouth. Such a spread-out space, so much going on, only four, sometimes three officers, to watch the convicts, teach them a trade and get the work done, too. And the convicts, each one with a tool in his hand that made a handy weapon, a pickaxe, a hammer, dynamite within reach. It was a credit to Beaupré, they said, that there hadn't been trouble there for years. Compared to the escapes and murders the village had known, a little contraband didn't seem so bad. Not bad enough, at least, to cost a man his job.

No one, not the women nor the men, paid any attention to the short homely girl who was always within earshot of Portsmouth shop-keepers and customers during the last weeks of June. They spoke their minds, gossiping at leisure, sharing with anyone who would listen their opinions on the penitentiary, on the convicts, the officers and contraband. But Phyllis, loitering like a pale spectre on the fringes of Front Street, learned nothing new.

● ● ●

On the longest day of the year, the sun never shone. In the morning, a solitary black crow swooped so low over the stone pile gang as it marched briskly across the yard that the prisoner could hear the dry rattle of its wings. And at the end of the work day it was still there, perched like a gargoyle on the bell tower of the North Gate, its beady eye trained on him. He took it as a sign.

He'd counted on these last weeks to put meat on his bones, to ease the lines of prison from his face and from his body, so the women he dreamed of constantly now would not be disgusted at the sight of his laddered ribs and hollow chest when he pulled off his clothes. But he was too afraid now to negotiate a trade for extra rations. And he had no money anyway.

The prisoner pulled out the piece of mirror Peggy had given him and squinted at his face, wondering what another month, another year might do. The stone dust had turned his stubble grey, his skin ashen. The lines that framed his mouth were etched deeply with dark paste, like an actor made up for a play. His eyes were red-rimmed and rheumy as an old man's. Only the fine brown hairs leaning tentatively towards his forehead stirred in him something like hope. When he'd entered the prison, he'd added four years to his age. Turning the joke back on him, the place had added ten more.

What had he not lied about? His life was putty in his hands, to be reshaped as the moment demanded or allowed. He couldn't remember now why he'd moved his mother with her labour pains to Detroit for the girl's sake, or why he'd answered "Renfrew" when O'Leary barked "Place of birth." The genteel, small-town ring of it, perhaps, less worldly than Toronto or Montreal. A wayward lad, the name implied, not a hardened criminal. It was in Renfrew, Ontario, that he'd first stood before a judge, who sentenced him to the St. John Industrial School to punish him for his thefts, and when he'd proved too much for St. John's, he'd been sent on to the penitentiary at Portsmouth, three weeks before he turned seventeen.

Sometimes he lied with forethought, a twist on the truth to help himself out, at no cost to anyone else. On that first admission, he'd called himself a spinner, because he liked the sound of the trade as much as anything else. This time, he'd claimed to be a baker in the hopes of being assigned to the kitchen where he could pilfer food. For if St. John's, Burwash and his first stint in Kingston Penitentiary had taught him anything, it was that a man without something to trade can be used by all.

That particular falsehood hadn't gained him much. He'd been caught in the first week dishing out large portions to certain men, and was reassigned to the stone pile. He'd turned that to his advantage, too, securing the contacts that were the core of his trade once he moved out to the quarry. Now all that had collapsed. His trade was at an end, and the remission he'd earned would probably be lost. He might not be released until fall.

The prisoner squinted through the window, across the yard, to the row of pigeons crouched on the peak of the workshop roof in the silvery rain. He couldn't figure it out. He made friends at the drop of a hat, he only had to speak to be believed, he had a good head for enterprise. But no matter how carefully he set his plans in place, nothing good ever seemed to last.

• • •

William St. Pierre Hughes could not disguise himself. The Superintendent of Penitentiaries was a striking man, handsome in a polished, protected way, like a piece of very good, old furniture, finely crafted with lines of such fundamental, enduring design that it seemed modern in any age. But more than his distinctive good looks, it was his family, his rank and position in the government service that indelibly marked him. Among the anonymous visitors and aides sitting in the gallery of Parliament, the presence of William St. Pierre Hughes was unmistakable to those who took their seats in the House of Commons below.

Whether they understood what was at stake as they voted is impossible to know. Perhaps only Hughes and Doherty were privy to the contest being decided that day.

Everything that could go wrong for Hughes had. Knowing that Doherty would do nothing to quiet Ross and his strident calls for a royal commission, Hughes had written directly to the Prime Minister, urging caution and trust, assuring him in the moments of calm before Ross's whirlwind struck that the penitentiaries were under control ... *the complaints are one hundred percent exaggeration.* As one man in public life to another, Hughes appealed to him: the accusations were political, best to be ignored.

How Ross had got hold of his letter to the Prime Minister he could only imagine.

If Sir Robert Borden does not make a thorough investigation into these cases, I will appeal to the public and show up the system under which the penitentiary is being conducted, Ross had fumed on the front page of the *Daily British Whig. The facts brought to light by the dismissal of these officials show the utter lack of a system of reformation ...*

What utter claptrap, thought Hughes. Ross was just another politician making noise so his name would be heard. But the newspapers were short on scandal in the quiet summer of 1920. The Bolshevists that had not been deported or jailed had gone underground. The strikes had stopped. The great ship of industry had made its slow, grudging turn from wartime to peace and the men were back at work. With little else to occupy them, the newspapers played the penitentiary story to the hilt. They recalled the Royal Commission of 1913-14 and laid the failure of its implementation at the Superintendent's feet. They neglected to mention that the charges that launched the Royal Commission had come from William St. Pierre Hughes himself. But seven years after the fact, history was easily rewritten in printer's lead type, and suddenly Hughes was cast as the villain who thwarted the recommendations of the Commissioners, "three able and humane men."

Officials of the old school, of which the present superintendent is a strong representative, frowned down any suggestion to ameliorate the lot of the inmates ...

Inmates! They would still be calling them convicts were it not for him!

There seems to be no excuse, and can only be explained by the callousness of those in authority, and failure to appreciate the importance of placing prison management upon a scientific basis.

Ponsford had been no help. In his dealings with the press, he had hidden behind the Superintendent, letting Hughes take the flak that now flew fast and furious from the hacks' pens. *Warden Ponsford is only carrying out the directions of his superiors with regard to the policy in force and if there exists anything in the system calling for censure or criticism, the onus does not rest upon him but upon those who dictate his actions at all times.*

Thus were the simple acts of honourable men transformed. The just and overdue termination of a corrupt officer's career had metamorphosed into a callous firing by a scandalously reactionary administration bent on power, not reform.

Hughes would find time later to rail at the savagery done his personal reputation. What infuriated him now was that Doherty would have his way and paint himself a public saviour too, wresting the penitentiaries from the hands of his Machiavellian Superintendent.

The amendment to the Penitentiary Act was only one of many bills passed on that early summer's day. The members attended to their task briskly, anxious to be done with the business of Parliament and get home to their riding picnics and strawberry socials. Doherty's face was inscrutable as he registered his vote. No one would have guessed how much it meant to him to win back, after two years, what he had unwittingly let slip. Hughes barely stirred when the results were announced. He was remembering what Doherty had said to him as they'd passed in the corridor of the East Block earlier that day.

The mills of the gods grind slowly, Hughes, but they grind exceedingly fine.

• • •

Phyllis had stopped listening for the knock by the time it finally came. She opened the door without thinking, without first peering through the side pane, so that when she stood face to face with the Warden, she had not even a moment to collect herself.

Oh!

She recognized him immediately. The heavy brush moustache that dragged down the jowls, the little porcine eyes. He wore the same black suit although his hat, which had perched too small on his big head, now dangled from his wide, flat fingers like a round mouse from the jaws of a cat.

Good afternoon, miss. Would your father be at home?

The girl stared. She looked past him for the policemen with guns and handcuffs, klaxons and dogs.

Excuse me. I've startled you, he said, noting the anxiety and fear in her eyes, which pleased him in convicts and officers but not in young village girls. My name is John Ponsford. I'm the new Warden at the penitentiary. This is the Halliday residence?

Yes. Her voice was barely audible, even to her.

And is Mr. Halliday at home then?

No. No one's at home. Phyllis fought the urge to slam the door shut in his face and run to hide under the covers of her bed. My parents should be back soon, she managed.

There was an awkward pause.

May I come in and wait?

Phyllis opened the door and stepped aside. For long minutes they stood trapped in the hallway before Phyllis thought to motion the way into the parlour. Somehow she thought he would know: the floor plan of the house, the map of her heart.

He sat down heavily in her father's chair. She stood before him, uncertain. This was not at all how she had imagined her capture. It was so civilized. Had he not been so large and his eyes so hard, she would have fallen on her knees and blurted her confession.

I suppose you've noticed we've closed the quarry?

Yes. I have.

We had no choice, you know.

No, she murmured.

We discovered illegal goods, certain convicts smuggling contraband into the prison.

The skin at the base of Phyllis's throat paled to a shade one remove from the soft lime-green collar she wore.

Would you like some tea?

As she busied herself in the kitchen, dusting off the good china teapot, filling the matching cream pitcher and sugar bowl, a calm settled over her. She boiled the water. She set out a glass dish of strawberry preserves and put buttered tea biscuits on an octagonal glass plate, taking care with the design. When the water was hot, she swished a little in the pot to warm it, then spooned in the tea from her mother's best tin, brought the water to a fresh boil and filled the pot to the top. This is the last time I shall make tea, she thought. This is the last time I'll touch this tea cosy. She fit it snugly over the pot. She was not afraid. She felt noble, relieved that at last she would bear the consequences for what she had done. She would do so with dignity and grace.

Phyllis had carried the tea things to the parlour table and was pouring the Warden's cup, her hand barely trembling at all, when the screen on the back door slammed. The Warden stood and greeted her mother, extended his hand to her father, speaking his name. There was a pause as the Warden coughed discreetly. Her father looked at her sharply. Her presence was not required.

Phyllis sat under the elms for the rest of the afternoon, strangely serene. The yard had never looked so beautiful. She looked on each leaf and flower and budding fruit as if for the last time.

When the Warden left, he tipped his hat to her mother and lifted his hand to her in a wave.

Had her parents begged for his mercy? Had they agreed to send her away? Why was everyone smiling so?

The penitentiary is expanding the quarry, her mother said as she entered the parlour. They want to buy our land.

SUMMER, 1920

I cannot see the Hand divine
which shapes my destiny,
the Heart of Love,
which daily cares for me;
But, blessed thought, I know He holds the key:
And I can trust.

FROM PHYLLIS HALLIDAY'S SCRIBBLER

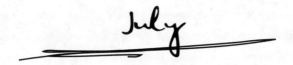

July

On the first of July, Phyllis joined the families lining the main street of Portsmouth village. Bunting billowed and flapped from every doorway and eave. In her family's parlour window, Phyllis had draped the huge Union Jack her great-grandfather had brought from England. Strings of red, white and blue pennants criss-crossed Front Street from the penitentiary's stone walls to the wrought-iron fence that enclosed the lawns of the Warden's residence. Under the snapping pennants, between hedges of flag-waving citizens, the Dominion Day parade moved in fits and starts, easing its way out of Kingston and through the village to Lake Ontario Park where there would be free donkey rides and merry-go-rounds all day long and fireworks launched from barges into the night.

Phyllis had taken up a position at the corner of Aberdeen Park closest to the penitentiary, apart from her family and concealed within the crowd. In the intervals between bagpipers and veterans, between Clydesdale mares with ribbons braided in their manes and merchant floats of the Fathers of Confederation, Loyalists and pioneers, she had a clear though sporadic view of the prison's North Gate.

If the convict's calculations were correct, he could be released today.

Phyllis kept her eyes fixed on the left of the three doors in the North Gate, the entrance for penitentiary officers and visitors, the final exit for convicted men. Had the Warden not closed the quarry, she would know the details of the convict's release. She would not have to stand on the street in a crush of acquaintances and neighbours wondering what had become of Daddy Long Legs, when he would be free and when they would meet.

From her vantage point, if she craned her neck, Phyllis could see the Warden standing stout and black-suited on the veranda of his residence, looking down on the parade and the crowd like a king, she thought, on his subjects. And where was Daddy Long Legs? In the dungeon, his time inside extended a year or more for their crime? Or was he pulling on his discharge suit, walking towards the North Gate, towards the door that blinked in and out of sight as another band marched by?

The more she thought about it, the more unlikely it seemed to Phyllis that the Warden would release a convict on a holiday, but then again, she had no way to know for sure. Details that the convict would have long since settled were looming puzzles to her now. Would he walk out the North Gate, or be transported to the train station in a car? At what time of day would he be set free: right after breakfast so he could get a good start on his first day of liberty, or during the evening rush, when few would notice an ex-convict slipped back into their midst? Were certain days reserved for discharge or would she have to watch for him all day long, every day of the week from now until October when his full sentence would expire? And if she was lucky enough to see him leave, should she greet him as a friend or pretend she'd never before laid eyes on him?

Her uncle or her cousins who worked as prison guards might have shed light on some of these matters, but Phyllis didn't dare ask. Instead she pondered the possibilities, and in the passing of the clowns and patriots, she planned her vigil.

●●●

On the second day of July, the prisoner's worst fears seemed confirmed. An officer entered the stone shed, showed a paper to the guard, who turned to the prisoner and smirked.

G852. Warden wants to see you.

The prisoner put down his hammer and climbed off the bench, avoiding the eyes of the other men. As he followed the officer away from the stone pile, he steeled himself for the Hole.

The benches outside the Warden's office were empty. The prisoner bent to sit down but the officer motioned him through the door.

The Warden eyed him for a moment. The prisoner could make nothing of his expression, of his hands folded loosely on the file before him on the desk. In a formal tone, he directed questions to the prisoner. What did he intend to do after his release? Did he have a job to go to? A family member who would take him in?

The prisoner had been prepared to defend himself against a charge of smuggling contraband. This tactic took him by surprise. His sister lived in Windsor, he said. His brother-in-law promised him a job. He mentioned the wife he'd concocted to get himself on an outside gang. He said whatever came to mind. Truth or lies, it hardly mattered. He was too experienced a convict not to recognize the Warden's game. Lift a man's hopes so that when they were dashed he would suffer more exquisite pain. The prisoner played a card of his own. Given the Warden's interest in his future, perhaps he would allow an extra family visit so the prisoner could firm up his prospects?

That won't be necessary, said the Warden abruptly. As if suddenly bored by the interview, he signalled with an offhand wave for the officer to remove the prisoner.

They turned down the hall. The prisoner could hear the gangs coming in for the midday meal. The Warden's little entertainment would cost him his dinner, he thought bitterly. The men in the kitchen would steal or sell his food. He'd have nothing to look forward to but bread and molasses at the end of the day.

It was his last coherent thought. The officer prodded him through a door and pointed at racks of suits.

Take your pick.

What? He grasped for the sense of the officer's words, the significance of what lay before him.

You mean I'm released?

His first thought was: what about my things? But nothing in his cell belonged to him. Then he thought, it's a trick, part of the Warden's twisted game. If he played along, would it come true? Or would his heart, swollen with hope, only break with greater anguish when they laughed and slammed the door to the Hole?

You're a free man, soon as the paperwork gets done. Get dressed, unless you want to wear those stripes outside.

But my own clothes . . .

Long gone, fella. Long gone.

The prisoner stared at the suits. Blue, grey, brown, black. Tweed, serge, pinstripe. Shelves of shoes, arranged in order from a size fit for midgets to enormous clodhoppers. Stacks of shirts, white or coloured. Socks, braces, ties, a leaning tower of handkerchiefs. A complete haberdashery. His to choose. Whatever he wanted. Free of charge. How long since he'd been offered a choice! He hardly knew where to begin. He tore off the brown and purple denim, threw it in a heap on the floor.

Can I wash?

The officer pointed to a basin of water in the corner. The prisoner splashed himself and rubbed off what dirt he could, then slipped on a pair of cotton drawers that flapped against his legs and gaped immodestly at the crotch. He scrabbled through the suits and shirts, no longer certain of his size. He pulled on a pale blue shirt, hounds-tooth trousers. The cut of the jacket was twenty years out of date. It had been made for a man with more breadth and less length of arm than he. But he was too nervous and distraught to risk an exchange.

His thoughts slipped into high gear, speedy as a Keystone Kops chase, the world opening up before him, blooming like a rose in accelerated motion, a thousand, million possibilities, freedom, family, liberty, love ... events of the moment slowing around him till they moved at a tortuous pace.

The Chief Keeper dug in his waistcoat for his pocket watch, checked the time against the clock on the wall and noted it in the Convict Register. His moment of release.

A guard slapped a yellowed envelope on the desk. His possessions sprawled before him. A brown leather wallet, empty. A tie clip. The penknife he'd won at a sideshow fair in Smith's Falls. A ring of keys for long-forgotten locks. Letters bound in a wide rubber band, their words too sensitive for a convict's eyes, his now to read.

He filled his pockets with his treasures—trousers with pockets!—and realized with a start he was the only man in the room not wearing a uniform. Thoughts of OK, the Irish lad, Father McDonald tumbled in a kaleidoscope with his mother's face, a glass of beer on a polished bar, women laughing through the haze of a good cigar. No time for goodbyes: he was being plucked from the penitentiary as if God's own hand had him by the collar. It couldn't happen fast enough.

The Chief Keeper left the room. The guards lounged, chatting.

But I'm a free man! the prisoner wanted to shout. Let me out! Now!

A guard walked with him to the North Gate. Light blazed off the bell tower, polished silver in the sun. The sky was an impossible blue, pale and shimmering, iridescent as the inside of a pearl. The prisoner, mindful of Lot's wife, did not turn for one last look at the stone buildings. He kept his eyes on the door straight ahead. The future was as tentative as hope. One false move, and they could snatch it from him. This could still be an elaborate ruse.

The bolt on the door slid open. He was inside the North Gate, between the stone walls, in the purgatory where he'd stood two Octobers before.

What were they waiting for?

Through the small barred window of the outer door he saw people passing by, motorcars in the street. A wild thought crossed his mind: he could make a break for it. Stab the guard with his penknife (was it still sharp after two years?), grab the keys that dangled from the keepers belt, bolt for freedom, race up the hill into the city where he'd never be found. But the force of penitentiary custom and the insane hope that this might, at last, be real, held him back.

He couldn't bear to stand still. He tested his freedom, pacing up and down in the vaulted archway between the two locked doors. No one yelled at him to stop.

The guard left him for a few minutes and when he returned, he carried the familiar tin tray with a mound of fish stew, slabs of bread, a mug of tea. Your last prison meal, said the guard, setting the tray on the bench. Go on—eat.

The prisoner picked up the bread. His stomach assured him he was ravenous but he took only one bite. The dough was sawdust in his mouth.

The door from the prison yard opened again. It was the Warden they'd been waiting for.

Ponsford stalked into the passageway and held out his hand. The prisoner paused before he took it, expecting a joker's buzzer in the big, fleshy palm, a handcuff snapped to his wrist.

You're a free man now. The Warden neither bellowed nor stormed. He spoke to the prisoner as he would to any man, as if what had been lost in two years could be pulled out of the air and returned to him in a sentence, surprise!

You've paid the penalty for your crime, the Warden continued, his voice smooth. You are released on the expiration of your sentence less good time. I have granted you full remission. The prison is crowded; we need the space. He took a breath, hardened his tone. We're giving you your freedom. Don't abuse it. Remember the lessons of the penitentiary. Work hard. Be disciplined. We don't want to see your face in here again. The Warden held out a five-dollar bill, wafting it lightly in the air between them until the prisoner realized it was meant for him.

Then the door was locked behind him and his feet touched the macadam in the shoes of an ordinary man, a black felt hat on his head, no number on his chest or on his back. He looked up at the red, white and blue pennants that waved above his head, and for one marvellous moment he believed they waved for him.

An officer was still beside him. He held open the door of a motorcar. The prisoner slipped quickly inside, rolling down the window as far as it would go. (For weeks, he would throw open the doors and windows of the rooms he entered, like a man desperate for air. He would stay outside in every weather, wandering the streets at all hours, returning reluctantly to spaces defined by walls, ceilings and floors.)

He stared up the street towards Kingston. The hum and shudder of the automobile thrilled him to the bone. As the car drove into the city, he sucked in the passing sights, a parched man in an oasis: elegant mansions, sedate behind a riot of roses and purple clematis that clambered up the stones; the pillared courthouse, which he silently cursed on behalf of his friends still inside; shops of every description. Children playing ball in the park, eating ice cream from paper cones. Ice cream! Women gathered under parasols, their skirts hiked above their ankles. Blonde, brunette, redhead: each more beautiful than the last. He peered out the window, keeping to the shadows with his too-short hair and stubble of beard, his unfashionable collar and garish necktie. (Why had he not chosen more carefully!) The officer made attempts at conversation, drawing his attention to points of interest like a tourist guide. The martello towers built to repel American invaders; the city hall designed to house the nation's parliament. But the prisoner did not reply. He was struck dumb, sensation after sensation washing over him, each hard upon the last, wearing his nerve endings bare.

At the station, the officer took him to the wicket, bought him a second-class ticket to Windsor, waited to see him on the train. The prisoner turned his back, hoping others on the platform would think them strangers accidentally thrown together in this public place. As the prisoner prepared to climb aboard, the officer put his hand on the prisoner's shoulder.

If I were you, he said, I'd forget all about this.

The prisoner pushed through the cars to the back of the train. He chose an empty seat that looked not on the station but on the wasteland of tracks, unused railway cars and overgrown fields that stretched to a limestone ridge on the far horizon. Away from the city. Away from the penitentiary. Away from Portsmouth. He tossed his hat on the rack, pressed back against the seat and closed his eyes.

The train whistle sounded. The pistons moved. And the prisoner was gone.

•••

The first days when Daddy Long Legs might have been released passed. So, too, the first week. Phyllis was not discouraged. She had the patience of a mother waiting for her child to be born, knowing for a certainty that it will happen, though not exactly how or when.

It wasn't easy contriving excuses to bring her within sight of the North Gate. In the mornings, she did errands on Portsmouth's main street: picking up the mail, buying a loaf of bread or milk of magnesia for her mother's sick stomach. In the afternoons, instead of settling on the canvas chair in the garden, Phyllis took her book to Aberdeen Park. The weather was hot and the breeze off the lake was cool, though it smelled of the tannery and the fishing boats tied up to the wharf. She chose a bench in the lee of the town hall, one that faced the penitentiary, and there she pretended to read for hours, holding up the book before her so that any movement by the penitentiary gate would register in the corner of her eye. She saw the Warden and khaki-uniformed officers come and go, and occasionally a visitor was admitted through the door. But only rarely did anyone leave the penitentiary whom Phyllis had not first seen go in.

At first, Phyllis worried that she might not recognize the convict without his uniform and slouched cap, without the backdrop of stone. But when she finally saw released men leave the gate, she realized she would not be fooled, for even in the ill-fitting discharge suits, she could tell that none of these men was Daddy Long Legs. The convicts who stepped into the waiting motorcars were always too tall, too fat, too thin, too dark.

Weeks passed and Phyllis kept her vigil. Every moment out of sight of the North Gate was an agony. She feared she would miss him, or had missed him already. She had no place to fix him in her dreams. Whenever she was at home, she worried he was walking through the prison gate. And as she sat on the park bench, her eye on the penitentiary, she imagined him striding up the path to her house, a ring in his pocket and a smile on his face as he waited on the veranda, turning away at last when she failed to answer his knock at the door.

• • •

July 18/20

Good little Peggy: —

No doubt you will be thinking I've forgotten you. But such is not the case. Many, many times I've thought of you all, but the sensation of being free once more has taken up all my precious time in realizing if its really a fact!

This will not be but a few lines, as I'm leaving in a few minutes for Detroit, but will be back soon. If you receive this & answer to this address:

Mr. Joseph Reid
560 Caron Ave.
Windsor, Ont   Personal
I'll get it by next Sunday. Sis & all is fine. Will write you a
long letter as soon as I hear from you,

DaDy, Long, legs

(Trust me)

•••

Phyllis's reply was in the postmaster's hand before the sun had set. As soon as she delivered it, she thought of so many things she had forgotten to tell him, so much she'd forgotten to ask, that she sat down and wrote to him again. She felt as if some dangling wire had been reconnected and she was marvellously, tinglingly alive. She knew where he was at last. He was safe. He would be coming for her soon.

All through July and August she wrote to him. She wrote about the garden, about the extraordinary, unremitting heat and her sister's engagement to the wounded soldier in Mowat Hospital. She wrote to him about the walks she took past Lake Ontario Park, about Watch and the kittens that were born, were almost grown now, chasing birds in the bushes that bordered the quarry road, though they had caught none yet. She abandoned her diary and poured her heart out to him.

She wasn't bothered that he didn't reply. He had so much to do to make up for the time he'd lost. What line of work was he in? she asked. Did he have his Cadillac yet?

She dressed with particular care each morning, knowing that he might appear at any time, ambling up the path when she least expected him. She daubed scent between her breasts, the perfume Jack had brought from Paris, France, in a tiny handblown vial, *La Gourde du poete*. She squeezed the juice of a lemon into a dish of lotion and rubbed it on her arms, her face and neck to bleach out the freckles and whiten her skin. Every other day she baked a pie—rhubarb, strawberry, cherry, peach, then pear, marking the passage of the season by the fruits that appeared in the market, then disappeared again. On his birthday, the twenty-eighth of July, she baked a cake and bought candles, just in case.

As the weeks wore on, she revised the menu of the dishes she would prepare for their first meal. The yellow beans were harvested, then the green. The cucumbers were sliced in brine. The squash began to yellow. The tomatoes swelled and reddened, clustered like giant cherries under withering leaves. She made juice and chili sauce. She brushed soil from the swollen tops of the onion bulbs and bent their leaves flat. She pulled the faded, crumpled pea vines from their stakes, uprooted the chard that had grown bitter in the sun. She drove her spade into the soil and turned up the potatoes, spreading them on the bare earth to dry.

He had missed her garden at its best, but the shelves in the fruit cellar were lined with her harvest, neatly labelled and sealed: mustard pickle, green tomato relish, spiced crabapples, red currant jelly. She would take him there.

Late in the summer the quarry reopened. The sound of the hammers struck at her heart. But when she caught herself longing to see his face among the quarry gang, she chastised herself sternly. Not for anything would she wish him in that place again.

She often saw OK, and when one day he lifted his cap in her direction, she passed among the rocks as she had so many times before, quaking with a fear she'd all but forgotten, drawn by the hope that he might have heard from their friend. He had not. In his kite he asked her for tobacco, and though she hesitated for several days, when she saw the saying in the *Pisgah Journal*, *That which docs not serve, dies*, she complied.

• • •

Sept 6th/20

Mr. Jos Reid
560 Caron Ave.
Windsor, Ontario   _Personal_

Dear Peggy:
Once again I take a chance of trying to reach you. This is several
times I've attempted to get word to you.

Or would it be that for some reason you do not wish to answer
my mail? I'm anxious to carry out my promises, so please Peggy
do drop me a line & learn me of every thing,

Trusting to receive an answer to the above address,

Don't put J. Claro!

Yours as B/4
Dady Long, Legs,

(Trust me)

• • •

On September 17, 1920, the convicts on the stone pile staged a protest. Fifty men laid down their hammers and paraded in the yard. The
guards drew their rifles and returned the convicts to their cells. The
leaders, six or seven, were sentenced to thirty days' lost remission and
ten strokes of the paddle each.

Ten days later, Minister of Justice Charles Doherty announced
the appointment of a committee of enquiry into the penitentiaries. As
chairman he named O. M. Biggar, the same man he'd appointed to
review the rules and regulations of the Penitentiary Act.

When Hughes received Biggar's letter of October 12, requesting the particulars of each of the two thousand convicts in federal penitentiaries *(their respective ages, crimes, sentences, criminal records)*, it was the Superintendent's first official notice that his penitentiaries were under review.

Three days later, the inmates of the penitentiary at Portsmouth mutinied again. For several days they refused to work. Warden Ponsford ordered them locked in their cells, where they raged night and day.

Hughes noted these events with fury and bitter sorrow. He could no longer change the rules for the better; he'd be hard pressed to prevent them from changing for the worse.

● ● ●

Oct. 21st/20

Mr Jos Reid
560 Caron Ave
Windsor, Ontario

Dear Peggie:
I make haste to tell you that I got your telegram, in which I was overjoyed, as I thought you were dead, or had forsaken me. So you say you have written? That I believe, but I never received same. I'm positively certain that to this address I'm sure to receive all mail, as I know the mail-carrier personaly & he always informs me of my mail, so the trouble is not at this end. If you answer this short epistle immediately, I'll notify you as soon as it arrives.

Oh well, let's talk about ourselves. How is my Peggy? Are you keeping well? & how is Mother, also messenger & all. This *last few days I've not been feeling excellent good. I do hope <u>you</u> keep in good health.*

That promised visit of mine is long coming, but you can rest assured it will be carried through. Some day when you least expect it, I'll be dropping in. Yes, I will be pleased to see you.

I see by the papers that there having trouble in my place of education. Too bad, poor fellows. Do you ever see OK or any of the old boys?

Peggy, I'm not seriously sick, but I'm writing this in bed & my hand is getting very tired, so forgiveness for this pencil & scribling & hoping to have an early & rapid reply, I wish to remain now as always your one most esteemed friend

DaDy Long Legs
XX Josie

P.S.

> <u>*Regards to all*</u>
> *Ans soon, bye bye*

(Trust me)

•••

Hughes prepared a twenty-two-page memorandum for the committee of enquiry, outlining in detail his proposed revisions to the Penitentiary Act, which he still believed would bring order to the prisons and remove the miseries that had precipitated the inmates' mutiny. Had the committee members read his Superintendent's Reports, they would have noted identical words and phrases, but he knew better than to assume that they would.

When he was called to testify, he answered their questions precisely and patiently, though spectators to the proceedings might have noted how dispirited the Superintendent seemed. They might have credited his mood to the failing health of his brother Sam, but in truth, William's sorrows were grounded in the men he addressed: he felt like an aged professor called back to grammar school to explain two plus two. The three men on the committee had not an hour's penitentiary experience to share among them. They did not even know what questions to ask. And—this weighed on Hughes to an irrational degree—they persisted in referring to the men in penitentiary as convicts, though the Superintendent corrected them time and again with exaggerated care. They are inmates, he said, enunciating the syllables slowly so they could take his meaning in. Inmates. And when they leave the penitentiary they are not ex-convicts. They are ordinary men.

Men who had sabotaged his efforts to improve their lot, he thought despondently. And yet when he saw them again, bent over the limestone boulders in the stone shed of the penitentiary at Portsmouth, Hughes was moved once more to act. Ponsford, the politicians, even the inmates had turned against him, made him the scapegoat for all that was wrong with the prisons instead of standing by him as he cleared the way to reform. No matter. He still had the power to make some things right.

In the late fall, Hughes launched his own investigation into the autumn riots at the penitentiary at Portsmouth. He dismissed six officers, retired another six. He suggested the Matron and Deputy Matron of the female ward find employment elsewhere. He suspended Deputy Warden Corby, charging him with immoral conduct. When Corby protested his innocence publicly, the Minister of Justice appointed one of the committee members to investigate what the Superintendent had done.

In the battlefield that the penitentiaries had become, William St. Pierre Hughes was under siege.

• • •

The sky darkened, the days shortened and still Phyllis waited. All through the winter of 1920-21 she waited, growing plump and pale thinking of the convict as she sipped her cup of hot water at the start of each day.

Her health failed steadily, as if her body were a timepiece running down. Her mother's illness worsened and she took to her bed. Canadian Locomotive laid off their machinists: her father had no work. The Warden's proposition, which they had so confidently rebuffed in the summer, now seemed the only sure way to survive.

Phyllis held herself aloof from the sadness that settled in the house. She kept her hopes to herself, lest Daddy Long Legs' silence become too much to bear. Through the long, cold months she acquired certain habits, idiosyncrasies that were not determined by will or desire but that appeared on her personality much as damsel flies alight on one who holds very, very still.

Phyllis became a collector, a collector of words. Not words in the singular, but grouped together in phrases, sentences and paragraphs. Homilies, adages and aphorisms, words of wisdom, the word of God. *And all things, whatsoever ye shall ask in prayer, believing ye shall receive.* She filled the back pages of an old scribbler with advice copied from books she read, verses of hymns that moved her, pungent phrases from the pulpit, conversations she overheard. *Have thy tools ready; God will find thee work.* And *Spiritual dissatisfaction is the surest sign of spiritual life.*

In the morning, she spread the *Daily British Whig* flat on the oil-cloth, a tiny pair of embroidery scissors placed just so beside her cup of boiled water.

She clipped the wedding and birth announcements of former

classmates, the notable accomplishments of cousins, the obituaries of her mother's friends who'd fussed over her like maiden aunts, fixing her tea with milk, complimenting her on what she wore, enquiring ever more discreetly as to her future plans.

She clipped an endless stream of poems. *I have a rose bush in my yard, Which once with bloom was gay. Time was, its blossoms I'd regard, The loveliest of May. But now no buds return in spring, Though strong the stem appears. Do roses, I am wondering, Grow weary with the years?* She clipped the words of physicians, their prescriptions for a healthy heart, strong bronchial tubes, and more obliquely, the proper care of her womanly parts. She clipped the Daily Bible Thought, the Seven Sentence Sermons and the Saturday Sermonette: *Let the wise man ponder the way of God till he mounts on eagles' wings, And the poor man press to his simple heart the gospel of simple things.*

She did not paste the clippings in scrapbooks: the pleasure was in the thin snip of blades through paper, the act of removal sufficient to make the words her own.

She kept the clippings in tins, and when one became full, she scrounged another. Ovaltine. Peek Frean. McVitie & Price Rich Apeldorn Wafers. Blue Bird Marshmallows. British Superior Reading Biscuits. When the tins proved too awkward, teetering dangerously on shelves and under beds, she begged the grocer for his empty fifty-pound sugar bags and stuffed these full, padding the paper clippings with worn-out camisoles, the pink silk drawers she had bought last summer on a whim, the nightdress with the embroidered P for Peggy, threadbare and faded now. She tied each bag with a lisle stocking too worn to darn once more and scrawled *KEEP* on one side. She hauled bag after bag to the attic, pushing it ahead of her up the ladder, lining it up with the others under the peak of the roof, like an ancient terracotta army rising rumpled and dun-coloured through the dust, marching towards the window that overlooked the quarry edging across the road towards her house.

She saved her grocery lists. *Coal oil 15¢. Pisgah 50¢ Books 15¢. Ovaltine 90¢.* She saved receipts for the pills the doctor prescribed, and the leftover pills, too. She made lists of vegetables she grew and their contribution to her health. *Carrots—a splendid food. They enrich the blood. Cabbage—a fine skin purifier. Lettuce—for internal cleansing.* She saved the message she left for the coal delivery man. And pages from her inspirational calendar, one for each and every day, printed with a Bible verse on one side. *He that dwelleth in love dwelleth in God.* She didn't save them all, only those that signified a special day—a new batch of kittens, the arrival of the pear trees from the gardening supply—and those that touched her heart. *Oh ye of little faith, why are you sore afraid?*

She saved the letters that PISGAH sent to her all through the year. *Your spirit seems to be so sweet in your affliction that we are sure you must be very precious to God. Those who continue to love and trust and serve Him without any evidence that He hears them, are being fitted for some especially holy and important work.*

She saved everything she read about the penitentiary at Portsmouth.

And once, although she cut the edges jagged in her haste, she clipped a line of print that was neither advice nor admonition, neither celebratory announcement nor the word of God. *It is better to have loved and lost, than never to have loved at all.*

This flimsy ribbon of words did not join the others in a biscuit tin or sugar bag. She tucked it inside an envelope on which Daddy Long Legs had scrawled *Phyllis* in his uneven, loopy hand. She found the maple leaf she had pressed between the Old and New Testaments, the mauve tassel of ribbon that had tied his Christmas gift, the crumpled four-leaf clover she'd found in the spring. These four things she committed to the convict's envelope. Perhaps she intended to send the talismans to him one day. Or perhaps she thought that by bringing them together in one place, whatever power they might have had would be revived.

• • •

Easter Sunday 1921

Detroit Mich
~~*Joseph Cleroux*~~
37 Crawford Ave
Windsor, Ontario

Hello Peggy:
If you answer immediately to this above address I'll get it as I'll be stationary here for a couple of weeks. I only yesterday got your letter, & I cannot understand of how I never received your mail. You send short message from OK & I'll write immediately, & it will be a nice long Kite.

So excusing this Rush
DaDy long Legs

I'll answer immediately & explain everything!

Josie

• • •

The Lord had answered her prayers, and she rejoiced once more at His resurrection.

• • •

Sunday, April 3rd/21

Joseph Cleroux
37 Crawford Ave
Windsor, Ont. Canada

My Dear Friend Peggy:
At last we really are in communication with one another, & more than a pleasure I take this to be. I embrace the opportunity of Scribing you a few lines in answer to your most interesting & long looked for letter.

So you say you see OK every day. His time is overdue, long ere this. But, poor OK has got into quite alot of trouble, consequently he has lost alot of remmission. But, he might soon to be coming out now, as his short time expired in January.

In a letter the other day from a young fellow who got out a short time ago, he was telling me everything. You know the young fellow I'm referring to: the one I said I hit on the hand with a hammer. Well, he is living at home with his dear old Mother in Toronto, so I made all haste & answered his welcome letter. He was telling me of how hard it was down there & about who was in charge of the Quarry, etc.

By the way Peggy, your opinions of me must be very much different than the first impression. What must you think of me, in not coming down on that promised visit? Surely I'll be there some of these days, when you all least expect me.

About that ring. I promised you should get a ring with Peggy engraved on it. You can rest assured of same. Will you please send me the measurement of your ring finger, take a piece of string or thread, get it a little large, as you are growing!

Say Peggy I'm going to send you a photo some of these days. Would you like one of me?

Well Peggy my good little friend, as dinner is ready & I've been called, I must make this brief hoping this finds you enjoying good health, and hoping to hear from you again soon.

I remain always,
True friend Josie

DaDy Long Legs

PS.

"Peggy"
Please send me your name!

• • •

With the spring came the sun. Phyllis had waited almost a year, but her faith never faltered. As she planted another garden, she knew the convict would finally come.

Her days were a mirror of the year before. Mornings in the garden, afternoons in the city's tobacco shops, evening walks to the quarry. But the letters that meant the most to her were not the kites she left among the stones: they were the ones she posted, standing in line with the other villagers at the wicket in the rear of Shortt's grocery store.

In July, on the eve of the first anniversary of Daddy Long Legs' release, Phyllis brought down the Ovaltine tin from the attic. Like a pastor who invokes God's presence by reading His word, Phyllis reviewed the whole of their correspondence, stretching the ritual over as many days as she could. In no particular order, she drew out his letters from the tin and read each slowly from beginning to end. Then she put them in an envelope, one envelope for each day, and on the outside wrote in thick purple lead, *Read July 1. Read July 2. Read July 3.* She placed the envelopes in the hunter green strongbox she had retrieved from deep between the Palace beams. Then she locked the box and hung the key around her neck on the horsehair chain OK had made.

It took her five days to read all seventy-nine of the convict's kites. Still he did not come.

• • •

July 12th/21

OK & Joe

All is well.
  Will write you later!
  He & I surely are enjoying all the pleasures of life.
    Daddy long Legs

• • •

Four months passed before the postmaster handed Phyllis what she waited every day to receive. The return address was Detroit. But the letter was signed OK.

Peggy do you hear from dady, I have not saw him sense July . . .
I met him in Kingston the day I left and he came home with me
and then I took sick and was in the hospital. The last I heard of
him he was in Montreal . . . please peggy write and let me no if
you no of his where-abouts, I must see him without fail . . .

• • •

The postcard arrived on Christmas Eve, 1921, with the last mail delivery before the holiday. Phyllis was standing by the front door, fastening her galoshes, trying to ignore the pain in her chest that rarely gave her a moment's rest now. The doctor had urged her to go into hospital, but she was needed at home: her mother was too ill to leave her bed; Betty was still a child; Marion had married and moved to Toronto. It was left to Phyllis to keep house for her father, and though she hardly welcomed the responsibilities that fell to her, they filled her days and pressed them swiftly past.

Gordon handed her the postcard. This came for you.

The quaint cottage pictured on the front faintly resembled the Halliday house, nestled in drifts of snow.

Just to say I think of You,
In the old, old way.

Phyllis paused for a moment, trying to guess who might send such a greeting. She hardly dared hope.

She turned over the card. There was no return address. The postmark, however, was clearly legible. The card had been mailed on December 18. From Albany, New York.

Hello Peggy: —
I'm still in existence.

DaDy long legs

• • •

Epilogue

The stories of the characters in *The Convict Lover* are as faithful to real life as possible.

Phyllis Halliday lived in Portsmouth until 1928 when her father sold his property to Kingston Penitentiary. The house her grandfather had built was demolished and the land was annexed to the quarry, where it provided hard labour for another generation of convicts and the limestone that built the first federal Prison for Women. Two years before, Phyllis's mother Gussie had died of cancer. Phyllis moved with her father, her brother Gordon and her sister Betty to a house in Kingston where she lived for the next half century, subsisting on occasional Christmas work at the city post office and meagre inheritances following the deaths of her father, Gordon, Marion, Uncle James and

Aunt Annie. Betty taught piano, and the sisters occasionally took in boarders to supplement their income. Both women remained spinsters all their lives. Phyllis died in September 1986, the last surviving sibling despite a lifetime of ill health.

The story of Phyllis's friendship with Daddy Long Legs was pieced together from the letters, diaries, photographs, clothes and clippings stuffed in the tins, boxes and fifty-pound sugar sacks I discovered in the attic of her Kingston house on what would have been her eighty-fifth birthday, August 8,1987.

According to her niece Dorothy MacDonald, who looked after Phyllis in her last years, Phyllis would reminisce about tossing cigarettes over the fence to the men who worked in the penitentiary quarry though she never mentioned one special convict. In her early twenties, she bought herself a dime-store diamond ring to convince her friends that she was engaged, but when Dorothy asked her why she never married, Phyllis would say with a shy smile, "Because no one ever asked."

Details of the life of Joseph David Cleroux have proved more difficult to trace. Much of what he wrote in his letters was a lie. He said he was in Kingston Penitentiary for "speculating with other people's money." In fact, I found out much later that he had had quite a criminal career by the time he started writing to Phyllis. As a young adolescent, he spent two years in St. John's Industrial School, a provincial reformatory located in Toronto. At fifteen, he was arrested for a series of burglaries in the Ottawa Valley that he carried out with his uncle Joseph Cleroux senior and his uncle's brother-in-law Narcisse Gerard. When the three escaped from the local jail, Josie was caught almost immediately and sentenced to two years and a day in Kingston Penitentiary. As F617, he was incarcerated from July 1, 1913, until his parole on November 25, 1914. Three years later he was arrested for stealing a car, and in January 1918 he was sentenced to two years at Burwash Industrial

Farm near Sudbury, Ontario. Burwash was an experiment in criminal reform: opened in 1914, it was a prison without bars built so deep in the forests of northern Ontario, its designers hoped, that no inmates would risk escape. But they did, in droves. In September, Josie, too, escaped from Burwash but was arrested under the Ontario Temperance Act in St. Thomas, Ontario, within a few days. Although Josie had changed his name to Frank Clereaux, the warden of the county jail recognized his face on a wanted poster, and he was sentenced again to two years plus a day in Kingston Penitentiary. As G852, he served his time in KP from November 11, 1918, until he was released on parole July 2, 1920.

Josie told Phyllis he was born in Detroit, Michigan. On his first admission to Kingston Penitentiary he listed Ogdensburg, New York, as his birthplace. On his second admission, he claimed to be a son of Renfrew, Ontario.

Josie told Phyllis his birthday was July 28, 1895, making him twenty-four years old when she met him. Penitentiary records suggest he was actually three years older. A search of the census records and birth and death records before the book was published failed to verify any of these stories of his origins. In fact, no trace of him could be found on official municipal or parish lists.

Joseph David Cleroux used several pseudonyms: Josie Claro, Frank Clereaux, Josie Charron. On the last Labour Day weekend before this book's original publication, I placed advertisements in the newspapers of all the cities Josie mentions in his letters, using all four names. The ads elicited only one response: a Joseph Cleroux in Windsor, Ontario, called to say that he thought his father, also named Joseph Cleroux, might have been a prisoner in Kingston Penitentiary in the 1920s. I had already noticed this other Joseph Cleroux in the penitentiary records: he was a decade older than Josie, and he was from Carleton Place, Ontario, where he worked in the Woolen Mill as a spinner. By coincidence—or to prevent a reunion—Joseph was released five days before Josie was admitted in 1918.

The similarity of the names was curious. I told the caller everything I knew about this older Joseph Cleroux, and he began to search their family roots. A year after the first hardcover edition of *The Convict Lover* was published, he telephoned to say he had found Josie. The Joseph David Cleroux who signed his name "Dady Long Legs" was his first cousin.

The truth is that Josie was born in Renfrew, Ontario, on June 27, 1895. He was the second of seven children born to Adélard and Mary Cleroux. Adélard's brother was Joseph Cleroux senior. The two Josephs, uncle and nephew, teamed up to terrorize the Ottawa Valley with petty crimes, including stealing ice cream off the parson's back porch and breaking into a local general store to steal cravats. The Josephs served time together in Kingston Penitentiary in 1913–14.

Five months after young Joseph's release, he enlisted in the 59th Battalion of the Canadian Overseas Expeditionary Force in Ottawa. Two weeks before the 59th shipped out for France, he was transferred to the 38th Battalion, and shortly before that battalion was sent to the trenches, he was discharged, the details of his discharge blacked out on his file. Less than two years later, Josie was once more in Kingston Penitentiary.

After his release from prison in 1920, Josie does not appear again in the KP convict register. It seems he moved to the United States, although he returned at least twice. He is mentioned (together with a wife) in the newspaper account of his sister Cecilia's wedding as among the out-of-town guests, having travelled from Providence, Rhode Island. And he is also listed in his father's death notice in 1945 as a surviving son, living in Philadelphia, Pennsylvania. When his mother died in 1952, her obituary does not name him among either the survivors or the predeceased. He simply disappears from the family record.

The Windsor and Detroit addresses Josie gave Phyllis after his release from Kingston Penitentiary were located in the tumbledown shanty-towns between the railway tracks and the Detroit River, a rum-runners' haven during Prohibition. One was an abandoned shed. All the street numbers and most of the streets have since disappeared in the upheaval of urban renewal. Street directories contain no record of his residence in 1920s Detroit, Michigan; Windsor, Ontario; Montreal, Quebec; or Albany, New York.

One curious detail has emerged since the book was first published: Josie had a sister Cecilia, but no sister Ruth. Frank Gallagher, Ruth's purported spouse, does appear in the 1920 Detroit Street Directory, but it now seems possible that he was a "business associate," not a brother-in-law. Josie likely listed Ruth as a sister so he could receive mail from her in prison, with news of his sidekick. Ruth's reference to Josie's mother's visit to Mrs. O.J. Hill is likewise suspicious as there is no record of a Mrs. Hill in Essex, Ontario, or in any of the surrounding communities. Whatever information she might have been conveying in code has been lost.

Most of what I know of Joseph Cleroux's character I learned from his own hand, from the letters he wrote to "Peggy." The pages as I found them were mostly loose and undated: it took me two years to arrange them in complete letters by matching handwriting and the contents of individual sheets of paper. In the same way, I tried to reproduce the original chronology, corroborating weather references and current events with reports in the Kingston daily newspapers from October 1919 to July 1920.

A news clipping among Phyllis's things completed the story of OK, whose real name was Dominick (Don) Waters. Sentenced to Kingston

Penitentiary for theft, he served his time as H5 from January 1919 to July 11, 1921. He was re-admitted to Kingston Penitentiary on April 4, 1929, after being convicted of burglary in Chatham, Ontario. Three weeks later, he died in the prison hospital. An inquest cited the cause of death of 1239 as acute Bright's disease. He also suffered from syphilis.

John Ponsford remained warden of Kingston Penitentiary until January 1932. His draconian approach to convict management is documented in a series of articles on Kingston Penitentiary published in the *Toronto Star Weekly* in the spring of 1923; in *Shackling the Transgressor,* the prison memoirs of Oswald Withrow, a doctor incarcerated in the penitentiary at Portsmouth in 1928; and in the memoirs of the Communist Party leader Tim Buck and the notorious bank robber Red Ryan, whose career in Kingston Penitentiary spanned 1912 to 1935. (The only two years during this time that Ryan was not in prison were the years of Cleroux's correspondence with Phyllis Halliday, though Josie would likely have met Ryan during his first incarceration in 1913–14.) In February 1921, Ponsford removed Peter Beaupré as head of the quarry gang, though "Knowledge Box" continued as instructor until he retired from Kingston Penitentiary in 1930 at the age of seventy.

Ponsford retired as warden nine months before the massive convict demonstrations of 1932, during which more than three hundred men in Kingston Penitentiary violently protested the lack of newspapers, recreation and cigarette papers. The report of the superintendent who investigated the uprising, D. M. Ormond, blamed the riot on a decade of mismanagement at the prison.

After thirty-nine years of service to Canadian prisons, William St. Pierre Hughes retired as Superintendent of Penitentiaries in January 1932, outlasting Ponsford by eleven days. He was in office long enough to see construction begin on a separate women's prison just a block away from Kingston Penitentiary and on the Collins Bay Reformatory Prison for "preferred" inmates. In 1929, Hughes arranged and planned the Canadian component of the only congress of the American Prison Association held in this country. According to Canada's foremost prison reformer, John Kidman, Hughes "took a deep and more than merely official interest in the penitentiaries" and was "the first Justice Department official to recognize organized prison welfare." In his book *The Canadian Prison*, Kidman notes that Hughes anticipated the reforms suggested by two subsequent commissions of enquiry and continued to reiterate them "until some internal pressure was used to silence him."

Less than half a dozen of Hughes's fifteen reforms were instituted during his lifetime. As a result of the riots of 1932-34, another royal commission into the penitentiaries was convened in 1935 and culminated in the Archambault Report, published in 1938, which again urged many of Hughes's proposed reforms, including the classification and segregation of offenders, training for penitentiary officers, abolition of corporal punishment and improved living conditions for inmates. The Second World War intervened and nothing was done until 1947, a few years after Hughes's death. Over the next two decades, new regulations gradually came into effect: inmates were allowed recreational time, the rule of silence was finally lifted and educational studies were allowed. After the riot of 1971, in which fourteen inmates were brutalized by their fellow inmates and two died, a full classification system was established. In 1972, corporal punishment for offenders was finally removed from the Criminal Code.

The report of the Biggar, Nickle, Draper Commission of Enquiry into Canadian Penitentiaries was handed to Minister of Justice Charles Doherty in the early summer of 1921. Hughes, in a letter to John Kidman, refers to it as a "foolish report" compiled by an incompetent committee: "No one of the three of them ever had an hour's experience in prison work. I might better be sent today to run your newspaper than for them to be sent to a prison to attempt to reform it." The press saw the report before Hughes did, and although much ink was spilled over it and a bill laid before Parliament, nothing came of it. Doherty fell victim to a cabinet shuffle in September 1921 in an attempt by Arthur Meighen to shore up the unpopular government he had inherited from Borden. The new Minister of Justice was R.B. Bennett, but his role was short-lived. In December 1921, two weeks before Daddy Long Legs's last postcard arrived in Portsmouth, the Tories suffered a stunning electoral defeat and Charles Doherty was removed from political power.

Today, Kingston Penitentiary is empty of prisoners, silent except for the footsteps of tourists who peer into the cells and workshops, trying to imagine themselves within those stone walls, stripped of freedom and, too often, basic human dignity. Through a series of coincidences—letters written and received at great risk, hoarded and hidden for the better part of a century—Josie Cleroux and Phyllis Halliday have left a record of what it was really like to call that prison home.

Author's Note

The details of prison life at the time of Joseph Cleroux's incarceration are drawn from daily newspaper accounts of the time; from the archives of the Correctional Service of Canada Museum in Kingston, Ontario; from National Archives in Ottawa; and from the testimony and reports of the 1914 Royal Commission and the 1921 committee of enquiry into conditions at Kingston Penitentiary.

Several books were useful in understanding the history and experience of Canadian penitentiaries, notably *Shackling the Transgressor* by Oswald Withrow (Toronto: Thomas Nelson *&c* Sons, Limited, 1933); *The Canadian Prison: The Story of a Tragedy* by John Kidman (Toronto: The Ryerson Press, 1947); *A Just Measure of Pain: The Penitentiary in the Industrial Revolution 1750-1850* by Michael Ignatieff

(Toronto: Penguin Books, 1978); and *Kingston Penitentiary: The First Hundred and Fifty Years* by Dennis Curtis, Andrew Graham, Lou Kelly and Anthony Patterson (Ottawa: The Correctional Service of Canada, 1985). Contemporary prison memoirs and analyses also helped put this story in context, especially Andreas Schroeder's *Shaking It Rough* (Toronto: Doubleday Canada Limited, 1976); *Cruel and Unusual* by Gerard McNeil with Sharon Vance (Toronto: Dencau and Greenberg, 1978); *Inmate* by George D. Scott with Bill Trent (Toronto: Optimum Publishing International Inc., 1982); *Call Me a Good Thief* by Donald Pollock (Transformation Information Centre, 1973); and, of course, Roger Caron's classic Kingston Penitentiary memoir, *Go Boy* (Toronto: Methuen, 1978).

The correspondence between Josie Cleroux and Phyllis Halliday now rests at Queen's University Archives in Kingston, Ontario. The letters as reproduced here have been edited for clarity and length. All of the italicized parts of the text are quotes and are reprinted with the kind permission of the Canadian Department of Justice, the *Kingston Whig Standard* (formerly the *Daily British Whig)* and the *Ottawa Citizen*. The quote from *In the Belly of the Beast* by Jack Henry Abbott (New York: Random House, 1981) © Jack Henry Abbott, is used with the kind permission of the publisher. The photographs on pages 3, 4, 5 and 8 of the photo section are reproduced courtesy of the Correctional Service of Canada Museum; the photograph on page 6, courtesy of National Archives of Canada, Ottawa. The Halliday family photographs on pages 1, 2 and 7, as well as the letters from Phyllis Halliday, are reprinted with permission from Dorothy MacDonald (nee Halliday) of Kingston, Ontario. Every attempt has been made to contact Joseph Cleroux: anyone with information of his whereabouts after December 1921 should contact the author in care of the publisher.

Although the names of some of the minor players in the story have been changed, all the events and characters in the book existed in life. Every effort has been made to represent them faithfully. The thoughts, feelings and conversations of the persons involved, of course, are the author's speculation.

Acknowledgements

Of the many people who gave unstintingly of their time and expertise during the research and writing of this book, I owe a particular measure of gratitude to:

David St. Onge, curator of the Correctional Service of Canada Museum in Kingston for his generosity, his curiosity and his dedication in keeping alive a past that many would prefer to see buried—there are thousands of stories in the penitentiary at Portsmouth, and this is just one;

Dorothy MacDonald for her enthusiastic reception to my project and her help in filling in the final details of Phyllis's life;

Jim Whalen, former penitentiary archivist at National Archives of Canada, for inspiring me early in my research, and Paul Banfield of Queen's University Archives for supporting me in the final stages;

Donald Swainson, professor of history at Queen's University, for helping me to understand what it was I had found, and for encouraging me to look beyond the small story;

Jennifer McKendry and Margaret Angus, for sharing their insights into Portsmouth's past;

Laura Elston and Julianne McCaffrey for their research assistance;

Marian Hebb, for her advice on delicate issues of copyright, and Wendy Thomas for her copy editor's eagle eye;

Jan Walter, Gary Ross and John Macfarlane for having faith when that's all I had, too, and especially to Jan Walter, my editor, for her deep understanding and sensitivity to the story;

Tom Carpenter, Matt Cohen, Brian Fawcett, Douglas Glover, Genni Gunn, Steve Heighton, Cynthia Holz, David Homel, Diane Schoemperlen, Andreas Schroeder, Ellen Stafford, Merrily Weisbord and Sharon Wright for conversations and erudite readings along the way;

Carolyn Smart, for Tuesdays and for her precious forbearance with early drafts;

Erik, who coughed with me in the stifling attic and lugged down what we found; and Karl, who read excerpts along the way;

and especially to Wayne, who never flinched for seven long years, even on those days when I thought the Great War had just been won.

I would also like to thank the Ontario Arts Council and the Canada Council, both the Explorations Programme and the Literature Office, for grants that sustained me through this work.

Finally, thank you to ECW Press, especially Susan Renouf, David Caron, designer Troy Cunningham, Rachel Ironstone, and the entire team for giving *The Convict Lover* new life.

MERILYN SIMONDS is the author of 17 books, and her work is anthologized and published internationally. Simonds's most recent fiction is *The Paradise Project*, a collection of flash stories hand-printed on an antique press with endpapers made in part from plants in her garden. The experience of producing the collection in both a digital and book-arts edition is the subject of her latest nonfiction work, *Gutenberg's Fingerprint: Paper, Pixels, and the Lasting Impression of Books*. She lives in Kingston, Ontario.